THE BEAT
VISION

THE
BEAT
VISION
A PRIMARY
SOURCEBOOK

EDITED BY **ARTHUR AND KIT KNIGHT**

PARAGON HOUSE PUBLISHERS
NEW YORK

Published in the United States by

Paragon House Publishers
90 Fifth Avenue
New York, NY 10011

Designed by Paul Chevannes

10   9   8   7   6   5   4

Library of Congress Cataloging-in-Publication Data

Knight, Arthur Winfield, 1937–
    The Beat Vision.

    1. American literature—20th century—History
and criticism.   2. Bohemianism—United States—
History—Sources.   3. Bohemianism in literature.
4. Authors, American—20th century—Interviews.
5. Authors, American—20th century—Correspondence.
I. Knight, Kit. II. Title.
PS228.B6K55   1986   810'.9'0054   86-22518
ISBN 0-913729-40-X
ISBN 0-913729-41-8 (pbk.)

To John and Nelda Scudder,
for being so supportive

CONTENTS

I N T R O D U C T I O N

By the beginning of 1974, we had lost more than $2,000 and believed we were about to lose $5,000 more publishing an issue devoted to the Beats that no one other than ourselves would want to read. In addition, my wife, Glee, was dying. We'd been publishing *the unspeakable visions of the individual* for three years, doing it as a tri-annual with a Beat emphasis, and while we were reasonably pleased with what we'd done, our Beat contributors spoke to us with an urgency that others didn't. Also, putting together a book that would have close to 75,000 words and more than 100 photographs had additional appeal: Glee had hardly left the house during the last year, increasingly crippled by rheumatoid arthritis, which she'd had since she was 2½ years old. A project with this scope, conceived and executed from the bedroom and kitchen of our small rented house in Appalachia, was something we could do together. *The Beat Book* became the last thing we shared.

We planned to publish 2,000 copies—more than double our average earlier runs—and if they ended up unread under our bed, well, other people spent as much on new cars that rusted away within a few years. We told ourselves each person should, at least once, try to realize a dream, and that even if we had fewer dollars for awhile, we had no place to go to have "fun" anyway given Glee's condition.

I'd wanted to publish a magazine since 1963, when I'd been the Associate Editor of *The Redwood Rancher*, a farm-oriented regional publication from the Napa Valley in California. The idea for a magazine emphasizing Beat writing came later, when I discovered the work of Jack Kerouac during the winter of 1967; Glee was hospitalized in Michigan, where she'd been raised, and I was left on my own for more than a month. Listening to a student of mine talk enthusiastically (and almost endlessly) about Kerouac, I decided to read him. I'd read *On the Road* as a student at San Francisco State College, but it had seemed, then, excessively romantic. I was to change my mind.

Reading everything I was able to find by Kerouac (primarily used paperbacks since most of his books were out of print), I was moved to write to him after reading *Vanity of Duluoz* early in 1969. In it he'd asked,

"Does it matter to five thousand sneering college writing instructors that I wrote seventeen novels after a youth of solitary practice amounting to over two million words . . . ?" In my letter, I told him that what he'd done *did* matter; if nothing else, I wanted him to know how deeply I'd been moved by his work, believing he'd done more for language than any writer this country had produced. Since I didn't try to elicit a response, I was surprised when I received one: Kerouac thanked me.

When Glee and I began to seriously discuss publishing a magazine during the summer of 1970, we had no idea what we ought to call it, though I knew, somehow, the title had to come from Kerouac. "The unspeakable visions of the individual" is both a refrain from *Visions of Cody* and an "essential" for writing modern prose from a list of thirty rules compiled by Kerouac.

The first issue ("in memory of Jack Kerouac, brother in eternity") was published in February 1971, and there were no Beat contributors. (Contributors did include Irving Shulman, H.L. Van Brunt and Dr. Wagner.) One hundred ninety-nine copies were mimeographed at the college one Saturday, and the next day Glee and I collated them with the help of friends; seven of us sat around the large kitchen table.

The second issue, published in July 1971, was done on multilith stencils, and contributors included Kerouac, with a reprint of "Rimbaud," and Ginsberg, with a reprint of "Friday the Thirteenth." Other contributors included Sidney Bernard and Elliot Fried. About 300 copies were published.

Our second year saw us switch to offset printing; the magazine took on a more professional look, though I still prepared the camera-ready copy on an electric typewriter borrowed from the college. Our most notable production probably came at the end of that year when we produced an issue, number six, dedicated to Henry Miller on his 81st birthday. (During college, I'd done a series of photographs of Miller, four of which appear in the issue.) If the issue lacked substance—and it did—it was, at least, visually striking.

By 1973 we were fascinated enough with the Beats to dedicate a "double" issue to Herbert Huncke. It included an interview with Huncke by John Tytell, a previously unpublished Kerouac poem (issued anonymously at the request of Marshall Clements, who supplied us with it), Ginsberg's preface to Huncke's *The Evening Sun Turned Crimson* (unpublished at that time), and two brief letters to the editors from John Clellon Holmes. The issue, like the one devoted to Miller, was a disappointment to us—about half of it actually dealt with Huncke and the Beats—and since we were tired of doing less than we believed we were capable of, we decided to produce a volume that would, we hoped, help define the Beat achievement.

Critical of this country on the one hand, the Beats were at the same time its strongest advocates, wanting us to recognize our strengths and failings so that we could function as humanly (and humanely) as possible in a society that had become increasingly desensitized, one in which the areas of consciousness had increasingly narrowed down.

Allen Ginsberg says, "The first perceptions that we were having, the first perceptions that we were separate from the official vision of history and reality, began around '45, '46, '47. We realized that there was a difference between the way we talked . . . and what we heard on the radio if any president or congressman or even literary person began talking 'officialese.'" While Ginsberg, Kerouac and Burroughs talked "heart to heart," as Ginsberg put it, people around them seemed to be "talking like some kind of strange lunar robots in business suits."

The Beats were part of a society that lived on the border of perpetual fright, one which would, before long, give way to the Cold War, McCarthyism and Eisenhower as President. This fear, with its concomitant conformity, surfaced by the mid-1950s (bomb shelters were built in many backyards), and it resulted in a society where the people, according to Ginsberg, were conditioned to "Ionescoesque hallucinations of language," regarding spontaneous, real speech as suspicious. This was something the Beats helped to change.

In the process of editing *The Beat Book*, Glee and I decided to publish material primarily designed to illuminate the source of the Beats' creative work. We emphasized interviews, letters, diary entries and other source materials that would help readers to understand both the physical journeys and the psychic undertakings the Beats had made. We wanted to show them participating in the "raw" experiences that became their "art."

Contributors to *The Beat Book* included Jack Kerouac, Allen Ginsberg, William S. Burroughs, Carolyn Cassady, John Clellon Holmes, Paul Bowles, Gary Snyder, Michael McClure, Diane di Prima, Neal Cassady, Carl Solomon, Lawrence Ferlinghetti, Herbert Huncke and Philip Whalen. For the first time, Glee and I had come close to achieving what we'd hoped. Doris Grumbach, writing in *The New Republic*, said we had produced "an indispensable compendium of writings on, about and for the beat generation," while Robert Kirsch, in the *Los Angeles Times*, devoted a full (and favorable) column to the book, giving our address.

It should have been a good time. By the summer of 1975, however, Glee was unable to walk. Since I needed help (and moral support) that I didn't have where we lived, we went to Michigan, where Glee was in and out of three hospitals. She not only couldn't walk, she had internal damage from taking cortisone for almost 25 years. When I returned to Pennsylvania to teach that September, Glee stayed behind. In October she lapsed into a coma and I flew back to see her; the doctors hoped my presence would bring her out of it, but she looked at me, as she looked at both her mother and sister, as if I weren't there—no change in her expression—and by the end of the month she was gone, officially dead from a heart attack. She was 27.

Early in November, I received a sympathy note from a young woman who had been a student of mine. Kit had never met Glee but, hearing me talk about her, she'd felt I was the only professor she'd had who actually seemed to like his wife. Others either referred to their wives disparagingly or acted as if they didn't have wives. With Kit's own marriage failing, a relationship slowly developed between us.

By the summer of the following year, we had decided to get married once Kit's divorce was final, and we were talking, too, about publishing a new collection of Beat work. For the first time I felt it was fortunate that I had never met any of our contributors—Kit and I could meet them together; it was something we'd share. Before the summer had ended, making a Bicentennial car trip across America, we'd met John and Shirley Holmes, Herbert Huncke, Carl Solomon, Allen Ginsberg, William Burroughs, Jr., Carolyn Cassady, Michael and Joanna McClure, and Harold Norse.

By late August we were married, and by the end of April 1977, our daughter, Tiffany, was born and we'd published *The Beat Diary*. While it had the same basic contributors as the earlier book, the material was generally more vigorous, more historically significant, and the reviews were gratifying. David Lenson, reviewing the book in *The Chronicle of Higher Education*, said it was "essential for anyone interested in modern literature," while Gary L. Fisketjon reviewed it favorably in *The Village Voice*.

Kit and I typed the camera-ready copy for *The Beat Diary* on an IBM Executive typewriter I'd purchased during the summer of 1974, when it no longer seemed feasible to produce the kind of work I wanted to do on a borrowed typewriter, and we've continued this practice, producing four additional Beat anthologies in the last seven years.

Early on, I was often asked why I published the Beats, since there was almost no interest in them in 1971. I responded—as Kit and I still do—by saying they've given us the only serious literary movement indigenous to this country and, on a more personal level, I like the fact that they write out of their own experiences, forging a collective consciousness from their individual identities.

We are also asked how we came to be in California, Pennsylvania and why we stay. The university has provided us with a base salary and the time to do our work, and no other institution has, as yet, offered us a raise significant enough for us to want to go elswhere. (Any offers?) Simply, living in a small community requires less energy than living in a city, so I have more energy to do those things I find important. I also believe Jorge Luis Borges is right: "Everyday places,/ little by little,/ become holy."

The Beat Vision—A Primary Sourcebook contains what we believe to be the "best" work published by us in the last decade and a half; we have also included some previously unpublished photographs.

This retrospective volume seems particularly timely in 1986 because the complacency and the totalitarian atmosphere that characterized much of the 1950s is again with us. The written word is currently under attack; the American Heritage dictionary was banned in Texas, and there is pressure to remove many classics from library shelves across this country. Twenty-five years ago, the rights of free speech seemed secure with decisions involving *Howl*, *Naked Lunch* and Henry Miller's *Tropic*, but those same rights are now endangered. Bills designed to repress the human spirit are proposed almost daily, and it is foolish to think all of them will fail.

However, the Beat writers who are with us today still maintain their vision of a free world. Through their dogged commitment to truth and through their continual championing of individual and collective liberty, they sing for those of us who would be free.

We trust you will hear their voices, as resonant as ever, in these pages.

ARTHUR WINFIELD KNIGHT
California, Pennsylvania
MAY DAY 1986

CHAPTER 1

Moving the World a Millionth of an Inch

Like the interview with Gregory Corso, the following conversation is one of a series of such interviews with the Beats, from the 1974 University of North Dakota Writers Conference. This one took place in Conference Chairman John Little's apartment, Tuesday, March 19, immediately following the first of four two-hour open microphone rap sessions between the assembled Beats and a steadily increasing crowd of students, faculty, and visitors to the campus. The atmosphere was loose, the wine plentiful, as interviewer McKenzie, joined by Little and colleague Maggie Leventer, talked with Snyder.

James McKenzie

Gary Snyder, Grand Forks, ND, March 1974. PHOTO BY DENNIS SORENSON

JAMES MCKENZIE: *I wanted to ask you if it's meaningful at all for you to think of the Beats as a cohesive group still, or if they have any continuing literary or cultural effects.*

GARY SNYDER: Well, I never did know exactly what was meant by the term "The Beats," but let's say that that original meeting, association, comradeship of Allen, myself, Michael, Lawrence, Philip Whalen, who's not here, Lew Welch, who's dead, Gregory, for me, to a somewhat lesser extent (I never knew Gregory as well as the others) did embody a criticism and a vision which we shared in various ways, and then we went our own ways for many years. At least I did. I was out of the country for ten years.

JM: *When it really became big,* Time *magazine and everybody making it The Beats . . .*

Gregory Corso and Gary Snyder, Grand Forks, ND, March 1974. PHOTO BY
DENNIS SORENSON

GS: Yeah, I was gone all during that time, although I maintained
constant correspondence with Allen and with Philip in particular, and less
correspondence with Jack, less correspondence with Lawrence. Where we
began to come really close together again, in the late 60s, and gradually
working toward this point, it seems to me, was when Allen began to take a
deep interest in Oriental thought and then in Buddhism which added
another dimension to our levels of agreement; and later through Allen's
influence, Lawrence began to draw toward that; and from another angle,
Michael and I after a lapse of some years of contact, found our heads very
much in the same place, and it's very curious and interesting now; and
Lawrence went off in a very political direction for awhile, which none of
us had any objection with, except that wasn't my main focus. It's very
interesting that we find ourselves so much on the same ground again, after
having explored divergent paths; and find ourselves united on this position

of powerful environmental concern, critique of the future of the industrial state, and an essentially shared poetics, and only half-stated but in the background very powerfully there, a basic agreement on some Buddhist type psychological views of human nature and human possibilities. I was surprised today even by the way Lawrence was speaking, and Michael, to see how much unity we've arrived at without any effort really to arrive at it.

JM: *You mean this wasn't planned? (laughing)*

GS: No, it wasn't planned.

JM: *Yeah, I know. I'm interested in a remark you dropped along the way there; you said that you still have a shared poetics. One of the things that's interested me about your poetry is that although you were all lumped together when I first experienced you, reading you as the Beats, I find that with very few exceptions, you all seem to have quite different voices. And I suppose just in your own case, if I had to pick (of the poets that I know) the person that you seem to be maybe closest to in some ways, I would say Rexroth, who you haven't mentioned. But I think of you as having in many ways quite different poetics. Ginsberg's being the very personal statements, whereas you retreat so much, avoiding the pronoun "I," leaving out those kinds of connections.*

GS: It depends on what poems you read. (Pause) I should've mentioned Kenneth; Kenneth is such a catalytic figure for all of us—his presence in San Francisco; his house, literally, was the place that we met, and Kenneth provided for some of us a very valuable bridge between floundering in Stalinism/anti-Stalinism at a time when the *Partisan Review* was talking about the failure of intellectual America. I don't know if you know all this literary history—early 50s?

JM: *I know some of it, yeah.*

GS: At any rate San Francisco, as a place with a cultural background, with an ethnic background, and Rexroth as a person in that place at a certain time, was a very valuable aid and bridge and teacher in helping me, and I think some others, retain our radical vision and radical

Kenneth and Marthe Rexroth, San Francisco, CA, 1957. PHOTO BY ARTHUR WINFIELD KNIGHT

perspective without falling into the either/or of American capitalism or Stalinism.

JM: *Would you say in political terms that that translates as his teaching you anarchism, perhaps, or getting out of those* Partisan Review *type fights?*

GS: Yeah, anarchism as a credible and viable position was one of Rexroth's greatest contributions for us, intellectually. Also, linking that to Kenneth's sense of biology and nature, his belief in poetry as song which he states clearly in the introduction to *The Signature of All Things* in the original edition of it, his interest in American Indian song, his interest in Chinese and Japanese poetry, which I started studying before I met Kenneth. But it was beautifully reinforcing to meet Kenneth and get the sense that here was an American poet of an older generation who saw value in that. Because you know, like, when I started doing things I was doing, I didn't know Allen, I didn't know Kenneth, I didn't know anybody. It was simply my own blind courage in the dark, so to speak. And it gave me, it gave others a lot of reinforcement to begin to realize that we weren't, you know, entirely crazy; that there were some other people who saw things the way we did.

JM: *Yeah, there's that nice statement that Jack Kerouac quotes from you in* Dharma Bums *that you thought there were only three people, or something like that, who thought as you before the reading of* Howl *in Six Gallery.*

GS: Yeah, it's very accurate. Now to go back to the poetics—I guess I meant that in the very broadest sense of the word, because I know what you mean: our poetics are different in other ways.

JM: *Yeah, you really all have different voices, I think.*

GS: Right. So when I said 'shared poetics,' I suppose I meant it in almost a Blakean sense of shared visionary poetics. You know, you can also say colloquial language, visionary, use of vernacular—all of that kind of thing. I don't know. I've never done analytics on my poetics.

MAGGIE LEVENTER: *I've just been trying to think about what's happened since the late 50s till now because seeing you all on stage gave me a different sense of things than what I had previously thought. I mean most of us tend to think that so much of what we've wanted has gone down the drain, been smashed, that the things you were saying, like in the* Oracle *interview, have not come through. How do you see the kinds of things you wanted, let's say, in the early 60s right now? What do you feel has been accomplished? Because so much of what you were all talking about has become part of the counterculture and has moved in.*

GS: That's why we're not talking about it now. Those are battles you don't have to fight. And maybe some of the students that came to that talk today were expecting us to talk about those things.

ML: *That's what I mean, and Corso seemed to stand for them, in a way, when he was saying get off your intellectual stuff, you know.*

GS: You know what Allen whispered to me? "The last of the Beatniks."

JM: *He kept referring to "daddies," which is a term you associate with the language of the 50s.*

GS: Well, I mean, Gregory really probably *is* the last of the Beatniks in that sense in that he's manifesting the same style that he manifested in the 50s. It's a matter of style.

JM: *Can I ask you a question that goes back to that original reading and to something that Kerouac says in* Dharma Bums? *Everyone always talks about* Howl *being read at that reading, and Kerouac talks about your reading some delightful coyote poems and I'm not sure what he refers to. There are a few in* Myths and Texts *that fit that description, but I wonder if there are some others that he's referring to that have never been in print?*

GS: You know what he's referring to specifically is "A Berry Feast" which was published in *The Back Country* finally. That was the poem I read there, the major poem I read there. I also read some things that later came out in *Myths and Texts*, but "A Berry Feast" was written before *Myths and Texts*, and I didn't have a place to publish it; I didn't have a cycle of poems that I thought it belonged with until I put together *The Back Country*.

JM: *You were talking in class today earlier about your own development as a poet and your writing nature poems, you said, and poems about yourself when you were very young; and I think David Kherdian talks about your having been influenced by your mother reading poetry to you. And somewhere else, someone reports you as saying at the time when you were at the University of Indiana taking anthropology for that one semester, something happened and you knew that you were going to abandon that at least professionally and that you were a poet. And then you mentioned earlier burning all your poems at some point. Can you comment on what it was that happened?*

GS: Let's see if I can remember what that was. I had set myself to the idea of becoming a linguistic anthropologist, and in graduate school with that intention, with the intention of doing it for the Ph.D. and so forth. It wasn't until I got into the graduate work that I began to really reflect on some of the things that I guess had happened to me the previous year. And what the reflections involved, as I recall, were first of all, I had come on my first Zen Buddhist literature which gave me reason to seriously question the usual occidental way of using the intellectual mind. I was really thinking about that. The second influence in that decision was the previous summer I had spent working in a logging camp with Indians, on the Warm Springs Indian Reservation and followed that by a long trip into the Olympic Mountains, backpacking. The Olympics had really soaked into me. And then something that Allen mentioned today at the talk which was something that he remembers (I'm surprised he remembered it)—I told him how I had this flash, you know, it happened to be during this summer, that everything was alive—you know, really had a gut level animistic perception which was shamanistic and animistic and maybe now when I look at it, ecological, but I didn't have those words for it then.

JM: *This was on that backpacking trip in the Olympic Mountains?*

GS: Well, actually it was in the spring before that even. So what I saw was that it was a matter of distributing one's energy properly. I realized that you can't do everything, and that if you want to do something well you have to limit your choices. And so I said there's some bridges you got to burn and there's some choices you have to make. And the work and the use of the mind and the energy, the nature of the energy required to get a Ph.D. would distract me too much, and so I'll go this other route. So that's what I did. But it was a very chancy feeling at the time, you know, like I had the kind of question that I was asking myself, the very prosaic question of like how am I going to make my living. So my answer to that was, I'll be a working man. So I worked for several years after that, logging, and I worked on the docks in San Francisco; I did just all kinds of things for a few years.

JM: *But you were also a poet.*

GS: Well yeah, sure. Yeah, that was part of it. That kind of choice, that was my own personal, and sort of scary at that time; although looking back at it now it doesn't seem like it was a scary choice at all, of course, but

Gary Snyder, 1973. PHOTO BY LAVERNE H. CLARKE

it seemed scary then. And America was much poorer then than it is now and there wasn't any welfare. (Chuckling) That kind of choice really is what lies behind the Beat generation as a literary movement. We weren't high school dropouts. We were graduate school dropouts—all of us. And we all arrived at that choice which was at that time a real existential choice in that . . . Like I remember talking with Allen when he was considering dropping out of graduate school at Berkeley, and Allen said, "Well, gee, I don't know if I should do it. How will I make my living?" And I said, "Allen, I used to worry about that but I don't worry about it anymore. Last summer I worked on a trail crew up in the Yosemite Park with a guy who was 60 years old and he could still handle a pick and shovel, and he could still handle dynamite. Now, if he can do it, we can. We can be working men till we're 60." I was serious at that time. We were serious at that time. We had an Eisenhower-McCarthy 1950s America . . . like there wasn't anything in our minds of any level of literary success. As far as we were concerned, it *was* a choice of remaining laborers for the rest of our lives to be able to be poets.

JM: *Was there also something that happened in your poetry that changed, too—that made you know you should take that risk. The reason I ask that is what you said earlier today about burning the old stuff. Did something change, or was it related to that experience of knowing that everything was alive; or how did you know that the old stuff was no good, but now you were going to write this other stuff?*

GS: Well, I burned the old stuff because I believed in the new criticism for awhile. (Laughter) Which I've never regretted actually because I had no desire to carry baggage around with me anyway. Leave no trace, ultimately. There's no reason to save things. I'm not a collector.

Now I'd like to go back to what Maggie's question was, which was how much do we think has been accomplished or changed in the meantime. You must remember that we never really articulated what we wanted except like what I recall articulating in several conversations with Allen and Jack and possibly with Phil was a critique of the national state as an unworkable entity, for one thing, and a critique of industrial civilization as being self-destructive because of its lack of understanding of the nature of biological systems. I remember working that out in the 50s. But there's another thing that has to be looked at in this, and since we're laying out a historical perspective, '56-'57 is one point in time that started a chain of events. The next point in time (I've said this before), the next key point was Castro taking over Cuba. The apolitical quality of Beat thought changed with that. It sparked quite a discussion and quite a dialogue; many people had been basic pacifists with considerable disillusion with Marxian revolutionary rhetoric. At the time of Castro's victory, it had to be rethought again. Here was a revolution that had used violence and that was apparently a good thing. Many people abandoned the pacifist position at that time or at least began to give more thought to it. In any case, many people began to look to politics again as having possibilities. From that follows, at least on some levels, the beginnings of civil rights activism, which leads through one whole chain of events: the Movement. And all of us and the younger people whom we influenced in the 50s who are now not so young, I think, went through these processes. Like there are some interviews prior to Castro's takeover of Cuba in which the essential line was "drop out," except we didn't use the term. It was just detachment from the existing society.

JM: *The cool 50s.*

GS: Yeah. Our point of view at that time was you can't do anything about it, but you don't have to participate in it—sort of Thoreauvian, really. But we had little confidence of transforming; that's why I say when we said we were going to be working for the rest of our lives, we believed it. We had little confidence in our power to make any long range or significant changes. That *was* the 50s, you see. It seemed that bleak. So that our choices seemed entirely personal existential lifetime choices that there was no guarantee that we would have any audience, or anybody would listen to us; but it was a moral decision, a moral poetic decision. Then Castro changed things, then Martin Luther King changed things, and then the '65 on psychedelic scene brings us to the point where Allen, myself, Watts, and Leary find ourselves speaking in that *Oracle* interview. In some ways, daddies, you know, and accepted or actually called on as such by the editors of the San Francisco *Oracle* who called on us and said, "Come talk to us," because they were in that in-between generation that in high school had heard about the Beatniks.

JM: *Yeah, that's us pretty much, I think.*

GS: So that is the link; and so there's a double link there, the hippie generation, kids who feel like that in high school, are now *again* talking to us. In essence, that's what I think Corso meant when he said "Daddies."

JM: *You seem to have gone, in some ways, to a less political stance again. I'm thinking of the poem, "Revolution within Revolution within Revolution," and "Spel Against Demons" in* The Fudo Trilogy *which talks about the revolution in terms of the back country of the mind. Have you turned to less political things? And the other thing I guess I'm interested in is the links between the political and the irrational or sacred such as you suggest in those poems and in some of those essays in* Earth House Hold.

GS: Well, *Earth House Hold* is the summation for me of what I thought had happened between 1955 and 1969. And personally it was clearly that, and also it was an attempt to clarify and locate it up to '69.

ML: *I think I have my question a little clearer; I mean, what we've really been talking about is the relationship between let's say the private world, the political world and perhaps also the ecological world. Well, what I'm wondering is whether you feel that the sense of powerlessness and/or disillusionment which the Vietnam War seems to have left behind influenced you and the other poets in any way. Has it left you free in certain ways for other things?*

GS: You see now, it's interesting that you say that because I don't think any of us feel a sense of powerlessness or disillusionment because of that. We've gone through that before. The difference between the people of the 60s and us is that perhaps they expected things to happen more easily and more quickly, whereas we were more seasoned, really. But our commitment to a vision of a different America is older and like it's deeply rooted, and we're willing to see that it won't happen tomorrow. The whole dope thing—like dope is, like it's "speed," you know. It speeds everything up and one of the drawbacks of LSD is perhaps that it's messianic and it makes you think that things are going to be accomplished right away. In some sense things are accomplished right away. But there was an overblown optimism quite clearly, like Timothy's messianism.

ML: *Right. I'm thinking of your corrections of him in that interview. He seemed to think that the personal individual revolution or transforming one individual or a few will transform the country or the world.*

GS: Well, I'd feel very happy if I could just make some changes in our local school board. (Laughter) On one level we talk in pretty vast terms, and in very visionary terms, but what Allen and I and the rest of us can say realistically, with absolute surety and with great pride, is we have moved the world a millionth of an inch. But it's a real millionth of an inch. That much happened. Not nearly as much as people think, perhaps, or would like to ascribe to it, but what it was, was real, and so, like, that much is possible, and the fact that that much was possible is what gives us a certain amount of confidence. If you can move it a millionth of an inch, you've got a chance. (chuckle)

ML: *When you said you were seasoned you were then aware of the difference between yourselves and your readers or your audience or those people who have been caught up or influenced by you. Do you sense the difference between yourself and let's say your audience who reads your poetry; are you aware of that?*

GS: I'm beginning to be aware of it. I had maybe kind of overlooked that for a long time, but I am actually becoming conscious of being older than my audience, of the fact that that does allow for certain differences. I am in a lot of contact with young people, not on the university teaching level, but like they're my neighbors. We do a lot of work together and so maybe I'm in more contact in some ways with them than maybe even with you. Because, you see, in the life I lead where I am, people don't think of me, people don't even *know* me as a poet, hardly. Or they don't know any of this history because they have no sense of history. We all just know each other for what we're doing, which is very nice. And consequently there's no shyness or hesitation on their part; like if I'm an old fuck, why then I'm an old fuck, you know; so they don't have any exaggerated respect. (Laughter) Which is charming. So like I live with a lot of people on a totally ahistorical non-intellectual level, that have only faintly heard about any of these things. So I have a good measure of where their heads are at.

JM: *Are most of the people at Kitkitdizze totally nonacademic, and have never had much contact with the university?*

GS: Oh, there's just every type coming out in the country nowadays. Some of them have just barely graduated from high school, and some of them are local to the ridge and were born there—not just at my place but like around the area as a whole. Some of them had incredible academic backgrounds—like one of my best friends, who's also one of my gurus in a way, stopped just short of his Ph.D. in biophysics, and now he fixes trucks. But whenever I have a really difficult question I go to him, on the scientific level. And he recommends books to me which I recommend to Michael sometimes, which you saw reflected in the talk at noon today.

ML: *So if you're living with people who don't have that sense of the*

Standing: Michael McClure, Gregory Corso, Miriam Patchen, Kenneth Rexroth, Allen Ginsberg, and Lawrence Ferlinghetti. Sitting and kneeling: Shig Murao, Gary Snyder and Peter Orlovsky; Grand Forks, ND. March 1974. PHOTO BY DENNIS SORENSON.

past, then do you turn to yourself and to books for most of the explorations that you're doing? You see, the way you're setting yourself up, you are apart from this community in certain ways.

GS: On some levels, I am, yeah; which is my choice: to continue in my own growth outside of the academic and the urban intellectual world and see what happens.

JM: *This whole turn in the discussion brings up a question about how you perceive the university world, or the academic world, functioning in a society in process. You've purposely disassociated yourself from it for a long time. I suppose it goes all the way back to what you were talking about earlier when you left Indiana University.*

GS: Well, I think actually it concerns me a lot. In the first place, it's my major source of income and you know I don't say that as a joke; in some ways I'm a good Maoist.

JM: *In* Earth House Hold *too, you say that some of your friends might be in the academies.*

GS: Sure, it's an existing structure in society which is certainly one of the most creative and potentially revolutionary structures in this society, perhaps *the* most, as we have seen.

JM: *As structures go.*

GS: As establishment structures go. And it is very clear that the kind of work that I and the rest of us have done, the kind of lives we're leading, has a relationship to what that structure is looking for. There is an ecological niche for us in that, so that all of us have an ongoing dialogue with the universities. Like they are one of the points of contact for me, the universities are, and I think that I would be less valuable in that dialogue if I did not choose to live in the back country. The very fact that I speak from such a completely different place . . .

ML: *But you've integrated some of the university too into yourself, the discipline.*

GS: Oh, sure. That isn't necessarily university either. I have, but that makes an interesting play, you know, and I have great respect for the possibilities of libraries, for the storing and transmission of lore. Actually for universities as a place of discipline and like nobody ever even talks about it properly to my mind and I'm thinking about it, maybe I'll try to write an essay about it myself if nobody else does. To try to put in a 40,000 year anthropological perspective what universities are. They're like giant kivas that people descend into for four years to receive the transmission of the lore.

JM: *(Laughing) My experience of the university seems so far from transmission of lore, you know, and a kiva, that I just . . .*

GS: (Laughing) Well, it should be closer.

JM: *That's what it* should *be, you're right.*

GS: But that's what it *could* be. (Pause) Also, there are some things you don't have to learn in universities. But, like, universities are valuable as, like, shrines, like libraries are kind of shrines, and the librarians are priestesses in which an eternal flame is always burning. And you have to learn the rituals to approach the layers of knowledge. And the rituals of approach are how to use a card catalogue for example, and I suppose nine-tenths of your university education is finished when you learn how to use the bibliographies and the card catalogues. And you learn that there is a method of approach to any piece of information you wish to get—and you *can* get it. Like if you want some information you *can* get it, like that's *right there*; if people would just learn that, then they would have something. And then what goes with that of course is that in the right time, at the right place, a piece of information can move the world. The right piece of information at the right time is a key tool. The other things that universities do is they can provide learning situations that we cannot provide for ourselves, like we can read philosophy and literature of all sorts, but very few of us can maintain a botanical collection, or a working chemistry laboratory, or any other kind of scientific laboratory. So to have working laboratories available in which one could see how experiments proceed is valuable in the physical sciences—in other words, and in engineering and so forth. It's invaluable.

ML: *You mentioned thinking of writing essays about something. Do you conceive of any dichotomy between what you would put in an essay and what you choose to put in your poetry?*

GS: Well, yeah, there is a dichotomy in that I put things in essays that I can't put in poems.

JM: *I know you keep journals a lot. What's published from them is really interesting, and you work in the Japanese journal poet tradition, but how do you know, or how do you decide when you're writing a poem, or when it's going to be just a journal jotting?*

GS: I don't know at the time; sometimes . . .

JM: *Which may relate to another thing you were just talking about.*

You said in relationship to the university that you think that it's very vital for you to remain in the back country to make your connection with the university, the kind of connection you make, and one of the other things that you mean by "the back country" I think, is the subconscious. (G.S.: Yeah.) I'd like to get back to the Earth House Hold *essays, especially "Poetry and the Primitive" and what you say about experiences of contact with the muse. Is that an experience that you sometimes have in writing some of your poetry, and other times don't?*

GS: Well, the simplest way to answer that is to say that every poem that I write that I trust (and I know right away from the beginning whether it's that or not) comes from a place that I can't control, or call on, or make demands on. It comes from a place in myself which has its own life and requires its own kinds of respects. It demands absolute equality with my intellectual and analytical mind, and manifests itself according to its own whims, and that's one way of talking about the muse.

JM: So that means that a poem that you really trust and respect is one that you didn't have to choose to write.

GS: I never choose to write a poem.

JM: So the question of whether it's a journal or a poem is not really a question if it's a good poem, because you just know it's going to be a poem.

GS: Well, that's true of some poems. There are a few things that take place like in journal writings which I write almost automatically, where I don't see what's happening until later; for example a line here, a line there, six months later another three lines. I don't see it mixed in with other things. A couple of years later I look at it and say Oh, that was one poem and here was the first line, here was the next line, and here are the last three lines, and I see it as one. So sometimes it spaces itself out and it's not quite as clear.

JM: But sometimes it's also the kind of experience that you talk about in Poetry and the Primitive in which the muse just takes over.

GS: Yes. Very definitely. And then, like, working with a lot of   **17** fragmentary and intractable material as I do when I'm working on poems that go into *Mountains and Rivers without End*, I work on that on every level I can, intellectually and so forth, until I push it to those limits, and then I just have to wait for the creative integrating force to come into it. And, like, I wait, that's all, you know; I just give myself the time.

JM: I wanted to ask you about Mountains and Rivers without End. *You started on that a long time ago; Kerouac mentions it in* Dharma Bums, *I know. Is that something you still see as a viable ongoing poem?*

GS: Well, I expect to finish that after I've finished a couple of other things. I'm working on a prose book right now which I have committed myself to and I have a deadline, so to speak, although the deadline is already two years in the past, and out of a sense of responsibility I'm giving all my energies to that, and then I'll return to *Mountains and Rivers*, and I have that pretty well blocked out now. I'm very glad that it's taken so much time to do it because it gets richer and riper by allowing more time to have taken place. But I have some other ideas about what I want to do when I finish that too, so I'd like to finish it.

JM: Would you care to comment on how you see it blocked out, or is it still too inchoate, because it implies that they have an end instead of like those scrolls that you talk about.

GS: Oh, it does have an end—absolutely. Like those scrolls all do come to an end. Yeah, it has an end. It has an end, and it serves a function—and it will have a use and a place. Then I have some other poems I want to write after that, like my head is leaping ahead of the structures of *Mountains and Rivers* to some extent. Or maybe I won't write any more poems after that, I don't know. It depends. I'm going to be reading from a lot of new poems tomorrow night that are genuinely ecological-political, illustrating every point we've talked about with clarity. (Laughing) Poems of real clarity, Don Juan type clarity.

JM: Castaneda's Don Juan?

GS: Yeah.

JM: (Laughing) That's one of the enemies. Clarity is the second enemy on the way, you know.

GS: Well, that's why you have to write a lot of them and, you know, get them out of the way. So then maybe *Mountains and Rivers* will be power. That only leaves old age.

JM: *How much longer do you see* Mountains and Rivers without End *being?*

GS: Well, after I finish the book I'm working on now which is about Japan, and wilderness, and the history of Asian thought then . . . (Laughter)

JM: *He said modestly . . .*

ML: *You've only gone around the hemisphere a couple of times.*

GS: That's why it's taking me a long time. (Laughter) I took on more than I realized when I took on that assignment, which originally was an assignment for the Friends of the Earth. They asked me if I would do a book on Hokkaido, which is the northernmost island of Japan, and the most wild, where the Ainu people used to live, a few still live there. They asked me if I would do a little book on that; not so little, you know, large format, with photographs, for their . . . what is it, *Wild Places of the Earth* series. So I said I would. And so it's become a fascinating project that is going to be like a circumpolar bear cult; questions about the nature of civilizations colonizing primitive people, and the questions that arise in one's mind whenever that happens; a look at Zen Buddhism in its rich temples in the capital from the position of greasy shamans on the margins; and a look at the actual place as it is today; a look at the background and the future of Japanese industrial civilization trying to address itself to the question of how come a traditional Asian country with a Buddhist background could end up being the most ecologically self-destructive in the world. But what I'm learning from the Hokkaido book is all going to be useful in *Mountains and Rivers*. I went to Hokkaido two summers ago and travelled in the wilderness there, and met some Ainu, and one thing and another, and a lot of research since. And it's taken me to Pleistocene studies, and geology, and botany to an extent that I hadn't gone before, but I really wanted to go. I mean, everything I'm learning, I wanted to study.

But I think that by this intense focus on a place across the North Pacific, I'm going to really have the conceptual tools to come back and look at North America with a really fine eye. Like I'm really getting my geological understanding, and earth history understanding, and organic evolution, and botanical taxonomy, and ethno-botany, and I'm really getting those tools down, and I see all of those now as tools.

JM: *So that the garden that your Zen master mentioned is the world, you hope.*

GS: Right. Well, it's not the whole world. I mean you've got to be realistic; it's western North America, the North Pacific, and the eastern coast of Asia. That's the territory that I have come to know. I pretty well know the plant life, the bird life, and the annual climactic changes of that whole space of territory: the north Pacific, what you call the North Pacific rim and Pacific basin. I'm completely at sea on this side of the Rockies; I don't know the trees or the plants very much.

JM: *Well, it's good that you came to North Dakota.*

GS: Well, I don't know what the use of that's going to be, really, except that it's part of what I want, what I have a feeling that I need to do—which is to try to talk about North America in a credible way. Which comes to this whole thing about how do we spend our winters in Grand Forks, North Dakota. Like, how do we find the magic where we are, and relate to that, and make that part of our lives instead of feeling that we're off in the sticks somewhere where nothing is interesting.

JM: *Does what you said about* Mountains and Rivers without End *mean that you don't see it as endless cantos?*

GS: Oh, no. Not at all. No, I don't like that idea about endless things.

JM: *But you say,* without end.

GS: That's the name; the name comes from the Chinese scrolls. That's what they title them themselves, but only endless inasfar as they become cyclical finally. After that you can see where they go so you don't have to keep on doing it; no need to, you know, state the thing ad infinitum. Let the universe be endless, works of art don't have to. In fact, you know, craft-wise, I have perhaps an excessive sense of structure.

JM: *Yeah, I would certainly agree with that.*

GS: And bringing things through to a close.

ML: *You've been implying some of the ways in which your ecological interests might occupy you for the next few years, at least. I'm wondering especially because at least one generation was influenced by the way you chose to lead your lives, what kinds of personal growth you conceive of. I know that it's hard to separate that from your writing, and from the community you live in. Maybe I'm asking a question that includes all these things.*

GS: It really does. (Pause) My ongoing practice is Rinzai Zen Buddhism, with a big dose of Vajrayana Buddhism, and a big dose of native American shamanism. And I haven't by any means exhausted the need to do that practice, or what I want to learn from it, or how I hope to learn from it yet. And I share as much of that as I can with my neighbors. My wife and I work very much together on these things. One of the things I hope to do is be able to pursue that, to spend more time deeper in the mountains, farther away, you know, like from some people's standpoint where I am is at the end of the road. But from my standpoint where I am is at the beginning of the trail and . . . (chuckles)

JM: *I can't help but think of* Cold Mountain *and what Kerouac said in* Dharma Bums, *that you're going to end up, you know, like Han-Shan.*

GS: It's true. It's curiously true. But Han-Shan didn't live in a community. And another thing that is part of my personal world is erasing some parts of my ego increasingly into the cooperation of the group, and the decision-making of the group. And a third thing which I won't say too much about because it's too personal, is the ongoing erasure of sexual roles and sexual jealousies that all of us in our community are learning with each other, which is a difficult but very profound learning for all of us.

And I don't know where that's going to lead. And that involves my wife, and others who . . .

JOHN LITTLE: *Why is it too personal?*

JM: *Because the tape recorder is on.*

GS: You know perfectly well why it's too personal, John Little. (scolding)

JL: *Well, you see, I disagree with . . .*

JM: *If it takes two years to tell somebody that he drives his car too much . . .*

JL: *I'm disagreeing with the philosophy, is all. If it's valuable . . .*

GS: I mean it's too personal to talk onto this tape.

JM: *That may be how his poetic voice is different from Ginsberg's . . .*

JL: *But why? People can learn from what you have learned.*

ML: *It's violating the privacy of those people.*

GS: She's quite right, it is violating the privacy of those people.

ML: *They haven't agreed to this discussion; it's a community . . .*

GS: Like I would, if you turned off the tape, I would tell you everything and that's the difference. But the tapes go out into the university libraries and God knows where they all go.

JL: *O.K. I accept that—there are other people involved. That's fine.*

GS: And also that's a whole conversation in itself, but that is part of my personal growth. Very definitely. But you know, that's as much my wife Masa's territory as it is my territory. And we're very much together in that. It's very interesting.

JL: I want to reserve a few minutes of this interview to gossip about the Beats. I'm interested in Gregory Corso as the last of the Beats, and his life style. You know, watching Gregory is a good bit like reading On The Road, *and I detect that he is the last of the Beats. And I detect, seeing you all together, that Gregory has been the last of the Beats. There has been a separation in life styles for some time.*

GS: Yeah, that's true.

JL: How do you react to his life style? It seems to me like there's a great deal of distance between the collective group and Gregory Corso. Why? How?

GS: Well, this really is gossip, but Allen can probably answer that much better than I could because he's been much closer to Gregory and he's known everything that's happened to Gregory in a way that I haven't. Gregory has gone through a lot of stuff. He's gone through a heavy junk problem, which has been combined with a particular kind of ego sense, and his survival as a kind of hustler. Why that should not have happened to the rest of us in the same way, I'm not sure. Lew Welch died, and I'm going to read some of Lew's poems and speak about Lew when my turn comes to read poetry, because Lew was a very important person to us. He was a casualty. Gregory in a sense is a casualty, too.

JM: Kerouac was a casualty.

GS: Kerouac was a casualty too. And there were many other casualties that most people have never heard of, but were genuine casualties. Just as, in the 60s, when Allen and I for a period there were almost publicly recommending people to take acid. When I look back on that now I realize there were many casualties, responsibilities to bear.

ML: If you're talking about the change in time, though, I mean, what happened is everybody has seen freaked-out people on every single corner and it's no longer . . .

GS: Oh, that's a good point, Maggie, that's . . . well, excuse me. Let me go on with that. In the 50s we really did have to protect, defend, and nurture our freaks because they were valuable people. Something else has happened in the meantime. I mean, it's almost a matter of our sense of responsibility to project an image of a little bit more sanity. The Beats are responsible for plenty of freakouts.

JL: *O.K. Does that bother you and does it bother the collective consciousness of the Beats?*

GS: I don't know if it bothers anybody else but I take it into account. I mean, I see it as part of my karma. And I'll have to pay for it and I've had to pay for it. I've had people turn up at my door who are half insane, who told me that I had set them on their path. And I've had to deal with them, and it's not easy, because we're talking about real people, real situations.

JL: *How have you dealt with it?*

GS: As best I could. Which is to try to find out where the person is really at.

JL: *You spent time with them then?*

GS: Yeah. Sat down with them and talked and scared shit out of me and my wife one time, and my kids. And you know, like, not knowing really where these people are at, and trying to find out where they're at. You've got to realize that there's an underside to this, that at its bottom is Charlie Manson. But we have to live with that underside too, and in California we see that underside, and it's dangerous.

ML: *You were identifying with Gregory in a curious way, John, but I think the difference is really that what I felt was a lot of anger too in him, and that's very scary. It isn't always just a benevolent, crazy kind of thing. It really can strike out at other people.*

GS: Gregory has certainly done that, and I haven't really tried to deal with where Gregory's at; but he's had a lot of self-created hard times, and he's had incredible opportunities because of his grace and his gift for gab and his charm; he's had many, many beautiful opportunities. And then he's hurt a lot of people, you know; he's really shit on a lot of scenes, egregious shit, as it were. I don't want to get into having to defend Gregory either. Like he's got a karma which I wouldn't want to have; it is not my karma, fortunately, and I'm not responsible for it either. But we're all responsible collectively in some sense for Gregory, so what I would like to do is all of us (Lawrence, myself, and Allen and so forth) sit down and have a collective meeting with Gregory. That's what I'm going to suggest, too. I've learned how to do that where I live. Collective meetings of mutual and personal self-criticism.

ML: *What seems to be happening is he feels unloved.*

GS: Oh, he's always said that. That's just one of his arguments; "You don't love me." No, that's the bad little kid thing; you know, you do all the bad things and then you say, "You don't love me"—double bind. So I always tell Gregory, "Of course, I don't love you—you're not lovable." (Laughter)

JL: *Which is an absolute lie, and something that parents learn to tell miscreant children. He is lovable.*

GS: I know he is. But not when he fucks up *too* much, then you get mad at him. Well, now I'm going to be honest and personal with Gregory, too. When I get mad, I get mad. Why shouldn't I, you know, like that's my beat freedom, to get mad.

JL: *How much of a sense of competition do you have when you have five egos up on the stage? One of the things you want to erase is your ego. Does that come into play, is that more of a problem when you're on a stage with four other egos?*

ML: *You were running things, sort of. Allen sort of retreated into the background, and chose to.*

JM: *Yeah, he sure did.*

GS: Allen is like the president of the board. He listens to all the arguments, then he makes the summation. And that's, you know, beautiful, how he does that.

JL: *So answer my question. Is ego a problem with most of the panel?*

GS: I really don't think it is, John.

JL: *Does this turn in the questioning turn you off?*

GS: No. We've worked these things out over the years. Like Allen and Michael worked it out in the middle 60s. Michael and I and Lawrence have worked it out in the last four or five years. Michael and I are really strong allies, really close allies, and I feel as much fondness for Michael as anyone I know in the world, although he is very different from me in many ways. And of course, Allen and I are very close. We're all really very close in different ways. So I don't think (maybe I'm fooling myself)—I don't think that there is any significant ego conflict play in our relationships.

JM: *You said you were all very close in a lot of ways. If there was somebody else we should have invited here to this conference, would it have been Whalen? Or who?*

GS: I don't think Whalen would have come at this point. Although if he had come, he would have been fine. And that would be to my mind the only lacking person, for the peculiar focus of this situation. Creeley, if it were slightly enlarged, would be appropriate. And you know you can think of a few augmentations.

JM: *But you think that with seven people, these were the people that it should've been?*

GS: Yeah. Creeley or Duncan would fit in perfectly well. I'm glad that Shig came, and I'm glad that Gregory and Peter came. And I think that fills it out. Peter provides the craziness, you know, which is a very right craziness.

JM: *What about Burroughs?*

GS: Burroughs would have been appropriate in every sense except San Francisco. He wasn't in San Francisco to my knowledge. Or if he was, it was just an overnight stop.

JL: *Oh, a question I wanted to ask. I've had some friends in the past who tried to get me to think with Eastern thought, and I've struggled five or ten minutes, and sometimes as long as an hour reading this essay here and there and yonder, and really longer because I spent time with these friends who, one of whom is particularly brilliant and obtuse because he thinks in Eastern thoughts that are totally beyond my conception; I never know what the son of a bitch is talking about so I nod my head.*

GS: I'd kick the fuck out of him, that's all.

JL: *Well, hell, he loves me and I love him.*

GS: But he don't make sense.

JL: *Well, O.K., I never tried to kick the hell out of him but I'll keep that in mind.*

GS: Say, "Make sense, you son of a bitch." That's what I do with people.

JL: *I've tried, I've sincerely tried, to think Eastern and I have not made it. Have you made it?*

GS: I don't know.

JL: *Shit. You don't know. That's an Eastern answer, isn't it?*

JM: *(Laughing) John's got to categorize what he's thinking. He won't rest until you say Eastern or Western.*

GS: I really don't know. Because I don't ask myself those questions anymore. In fact, I don't know if I ever did. (Laughing)

Carolyn and Neal Cassady, 1948. "How it all began. A few weeks before we were married. This is my most prized possession. It was resurrected from a chopped up snapshot taken on the street in SF. Great Chinese technician did it for Annie." Carolyn Cassady.

CHAPTER 2

Life with Jack and Neal

Near the summer's end we heard that Jack had returned to San Francisco, but I rarely wondered anymore if we'd even see him. Neal showed no particular interest, either, as far as I could see, and since he was restricted to our county, it only made him grim, remembering past binges that had led to this.

So, it was a surprise one Friday evening when there was loud scuffling and banging on the patio door. Before I could open it, Jack staggered in, surrounded by a motley group of men. He was drunk and bellowing, but I greeted him warmly and put my hands on his shoulders, intending to kiss him hello. He shoved me away roughly with some rude remark, and I backed up, mortified, thinking my behavior must look odd to the assembled strangers.

These were sorted out as being Lew Welch, a poet originally from Reno and more recently a graduate of Reed College in Oregon; Paul Smith, a friend of Lew's from Reno who played the bass fiddle and sang, and a roustabout who had come to San Francisco in advance of the Barnum and Bailey circus by whom he was employed. I don't know where they found him, and I never heard his name. I eventually learned the visit was a spur of the moment whim of Jack's to see Neal and specifically to introduce him to Lew Welch, once again wishing to share people he liked with "brother" Neal.

Jack had been staying at the Big Sur cabin of Lawrence Ferlinghetti, and Lew had driven the others down to bring him back to San Francisco.

I told them Neal worked from six until two, but I would telephone him. Neal couldn't talk long on the phone with all types of tires to time in their cooking processes, so he suggested they come to the shop and talk or watch him work after the boss left around midnight. Meanwhile, I asked if they were hungry. The children had eaten early with their father and were now asleep. After taking a concensus of opinion and Jack had patted his pocket and embarrassed us further by loudly complaining to me that people only were interested in him for his traveler's checks, he nevertheless insisted on buying a dinner "to go" that they could bring to the house.

There were few such places in Los Gatos, but I called a nearby Italian restaurant that had been established for a long time and had a reputation for excellent food. I telephoned them, and they agreed to prepare a specialty to take out. The men were gone so long I feared the worst, and I was nearly right. When they returned, Lew, Jack and Paul tried to tell me about the chaos they'd created at the restaurant but were laughing so hard from the recollection, I'm not sure I know yet what happened. The restaurant was as "square" as is possible and the clientele quite elegantly so.

In walks this startling group: Jack in his checked lumberjack shirt, sagging rumpled jeans and hiking boots, his hair wild and falling in his partially closed eyes; obviously he was drunk and disorderly. Then there was Lew with thick red hair, also rather unruly, wide bright piercing eyes; slight of frame but wiry, and although clean enough, dressed in well-worn jeans, tennis shoes and a casual knit shirt. Paul Smith was the personification of a Roman athlete, and even though his appearance was rather the opposite of Jack's, he was nonetheless equally out of place. His golden hair was full and wavy and blended into a short beard; his eyes were gold as well, almost yellow, and he wore no shirt or shoes. His smooth, hairless, muscular chest and arms were tanned a deeper gold than his hair, and, his only visible garment being beige slacks, he was conspicuous as a tonal image of golden "youth," almost too clean, healthy and gleaming to be real. The fourth member, the silent roustabout, was of medium height, thickset and wore a tight striped t-shirt taut against bulging muscles. He had short curls over his forehead that reminded me of our white-faced cattle at home.

I thought afterward they should have told the management they were actors from some local play, rather than wasting so much time and energy in an attempt to impress the staff with Jack's fame and therefore the reliability of his check. Understandably, no one had ever heard of him and seriously doubted their story. At this particular time in our lives, our own name was also useless as a character reference. Perhaps the decision to trust them was taken when the scales tipped in favor of removing their noisy and colorful presence from the dining room, where Jack was earnestly engaged in an attempt to seduce a waitress while the others battled in his behalf.

While they were gone I built a fire and set out silverware, dishes and glasses for wine. The food was superb scaloppini, and soon I forgot the chagrin that had been caused by Jack's initial rebuff. They all made a game of honoring me as the sole woman among such attentive and attractive males.

Lew Welch was a great delight. He spoke with mock seriousness, yet a flicker of a smile or a glint of glee sparked his eyes to reveal that his intelligent and erudite patter was often the essence of satire. I was particularly impressed with his sharp insights, his quick wit and poetic imagery, even if an occasional earthy expression was added for spice . . . or to shock me. Jack tried to keep up with him, but too soon he was at the stage of being capable only of uttering unintelligible roars or grumbles. The roustabout never spoke, not even to answer my query if he wanted coffee. I passed him some anyway, and he drank it without a word. Lew assured me he was neither deaf nor dumb, so I concluded he must be as shy as I had once been. Paul said little, also; just sat smiling at me or hovering, his eyes waxing and waning, now shining gold, now shaded bronze. A disturbing attraction had ignited between us.

When we noticed it was nearly one o'clock, they all scrambled into Lew's "Willie" and rattled away to see Neal. I could imagine that scene well enough. I'd seen the tire shop, a pre-fabricated aluminum structure all open to the street in the middle of San Jose with a radio blaring country-Western music over the din of the re-capping machinery and

*Neal Cassady, drawn by
Carolyn Cassady.*

Neal's blamming and thudding of the huge truck tires from the piles to the floor, he looking like a creature from the deep in his goggles and grime.

While they were gone I did the dishes, straightened the living room and dug out blankets and pillows until I heard the roar of the two cars spinning into the drive. Lew was an acclaimed driver, like Neal, so no doubt some fearful competition had taken place on the way home.

Neal was exhausted, and the others both overstimulated with alcohol, tea and each other, so bed was all anyone wanted now. Neal went to shower, and I alloted spaces. Jack insisted on the back yard again, Lew would sleep in Willie, so Paul took the day bed in the living room, and I indicated to the roustabout he was welcome to the couch in the family room. Lew said, "Goodnight, Mommy" and kissed me on his way out to the car; Jack giggled and did the same, so I took it up, playing the mother coyly, and kissed Paul on the forehead as I "tucked him in." I went back to the family room so as not to have anyone feel left out, but the silent one was still sitting in a chair by the table in the dark. I leaned over to hastily plant the peck, when his great arms shot out and snapped around me, indicating better than any words: no cute games for this kid; he was all business. Rigidly, I disentangled myself and tried to laugh it off. He let go, silent and stern as ever, and I fled to climb in beside Neal, grateful he was there.

Next morning everyone slept late, and Jack came inside as I was making coffee. Now that he was sober, he seemed pathetically glad to see me, and I was relieved he appeared to have forgotten his initial encounter. He asked me to come out to the patio where we could talk alone. Once more we sat on the grass in the sun; he was full of clinging nostalgia as though he somehow knew we would never get back to the simple pleasures and sweet dreams we'd anticipated ten years ago. No longer did he make staunch vows to stop drinking; he knew he was being slowly pulled down into the quagmire, and his will was too weak to resist. His tormented eyes foretold the future; his face like a character from Poe. The usual answers from my metaphysical studies blinked on and off in my mind, but I knew now they were useless, the shame and isolation he felt deep within were too powerful to uproot with overworked admonitions. All I could do was sigh and wonder at the sense of it all, saying, "Ah, why do we settle for pleasure when we could have bliss . . . and you, who've known what it is. . . ."

Jack groaned a Dantesque wail, "I know, I know. What'll I do?" We talked of the faithlessness of men, the easy way out. "My unbelief is a belief to be transcended," I quoted aloud, and he said, "Well, I know now my Buddhism doesn't help . . . and why Buddha forbid alcohol . . . but I just *can't* stop. Thinking of those critics and the rubbish I've gone through with publishers starts filling my mind, and I reach for the bottle. . . ."

"But these past three weeks you've been at Big Sur . . . didn't it help at all? Though I know you don't like being alone."

"Naw, you know how it is. It was okay at first, then I got bored. Why is that? Why can't I be content?"

Lew came bounding out the door in some hilarious charade concerning "Aunt Harriet," his equivalent to Mrs. Grundy, and the scene exploded into slapstick shenanigans between Jack and Lew until my stomach ached from laughing. The roustabout had to get back to sign in with the circus, and Lew wanted to see his girl, so they were eager to return to the City. First, however, Jack needed more wine, so I rode with Lew and Jack in Willie to show them the nearest liquor store. All the way to and from they kept up a fast and witty dialogue replaying a mythical baseball game that did nothing to ease my stomach pain. Returning home they collected Paul and the Quiet Man and said goodbye to Neal, who was still in bed.

That night when Neal came home from work and I got up to get him something to eat, he told me he had been laid off. The boss had financial difficulties and had to let some men go. Neal, as the newest employee, was the first. Now what? It was the first of the month and the house payment was due. Though I objected, Neal thought it was right to ask Jack for a loan, so the next afternoon he called Jack in San Francisco. Jack was willing and gallant this time and said Lew would drive him back down with the money.

On Friday evening two Jeeps appeared in the driveway. Lew and Paul were in Willie and Lawrence Ferlinghetti drove Jack, Philip Whalen and Victor Wong in his. Victor was the artist-son of a prominent Chinatown family and delighted me with multi-colored felt-tipped pen drawings. His technique fascinated me, and I sat beside him on the floor watching him. I liked Phil Whalen very much too, although I was unfamiliar with his poetry, and he certainly didn't look like a "poet" . . . a professor, maybe, being rather stocky, tweedy and pipe-smoking. He struck me as an extremely kind and gentle person, quiet yet openly friendly and definitely not "beat." His presence was reassuring to me.

Since Neal had no work to go to, and since they were all on their way back to Ferlinghetti's cabin, they mock pleaded with "ma" to let him go off

Arthur Winfield Knight, Kit Knight and Carolyn Cassady, Los Gatos, CA, August 7, 1976. PHOTO BY YVES LE PELLEC.

with the boys for the weekend. This time I found it easy to be gracious and magnanimous, glad for Neal to have a respite, a time with the beauties of nature and in company I approved. Neal was overjoyed, himself, yet full of conscientious promises to hunt for work "first thing on Monday."

First, however, they invited the whole family to share dinner out somewhere. Was there a pizza parlor in the area? I suggested Magoo's, where I often went with the Wagon Stagers. We piled in the Jeeps. As could hardly be helped, this large group took over most of the pizzaria. There were few other diners, but we occupied a long table in the center of the room, and what with the boisterous Jack, Lew and Neal and the echoing acoustics, we were a conspicuous lot. This time, perversely, I felt proud. We consumed platters and platters of pizza and tankards of beer, and no one seemed in any particular hurry. I wished Neal a happy

Carolyn Cassady and Yves Le Pellec, Los Gatos, CA, August 7, 1976. PHOTO
BY ARTHUR WINFIELD KNIGHT.

weekend with complete sincerity, and the children were glad to go with me
to Old Town for the Friday night production.

Jack and Paul stayed on at the cabin after the weekend, but Sunday
evening Lew drove Neal home alone, while Lawrence drove Phil and
Victor back to the City. Lew stayed a few hours with us to rest midway in
his journey. No longer was he the comedian, and I saw that he, like many
gifted "clowns," had a serious side as somber as was his wit sparkling. Neal
turned on the television to await the news, and Lew lay down on the bed
while I sat at the foot. No sooner were we settled than Neal realized he was
out of cigarettes and asked Lew if he could "make a run" in Willie.

Finding myself suddenly alone with this Lew I didn't know, I was
overcome with sudden nervousness. Worse, I sensed a male-female
tension, and I became as gauche as a schoolgirl, more so since he was
extremely poised. In an effort to cut through the sticky atmosphere, I heard
myself inanely "making" conversation. "I understand you write poetry,

Lew." Was that my voice? "Ah, yes," he replied, "Would you like to hear some?" And he began to recite, completely at ease, unnerving me all the more, yet I admired his lack of false modesty. His poetry surprised me, in that I understood it, or at least enjoyed it. "Why, that's beautiful!" Ugh, how phony the tone. "You seem surprised," he said flatly, a note of sarcasm. "Well, of course, I'm no judge of poetry, you understand. Allen's is all I've read for years, and his is not so lyric . . . uh . . . which I prefer." I was practically fluttering and I was miserable. He still gave me the impression I should be trying to seduce him or offer myself for a "quickie" while my husband was away. He said no more, and I tried to become absorbed in the television until thankfully I heard Neal return. With a third party present, I could relax and be myself again.

I left them together, but I overheard bits of Lew's remarks to Neal which sounded as though he were commiserating with Neal on my being such a frigid and unresponsive female. I regretted his censure, not because I thought him particularly mistaken, but because I liked him so much and wished for his approval. However, if leaping into bed with every available male was the requisite for his friendship, we would never be friends.

On Monday morning Neal went to the Los Gatos Tire Company on the recommendation of a friend, and those wonderful men agreed to hire him, even though they were not particularly short-handed. It was a great relief. He was close to home, his hours were the regular day shift and we could live a more normal life again. As usual, Neal astounded everyone with his speed and efficiency. Employers, employees and customers stood by and watched him unabashed. But when he came home so physically exhausted, I feared he was using this manual labor to work out much of his bitterness as well as a penitent flagellation of himself. How I wished he could find an occupation that would employ his remarkable mind. No hope for that, now that he was a felon; even more doors were closed to him, and his faith in himself even less likely to bloom. All I could do to help was to try and keep the homelife as peaceful as possible. It encouraged me when most evenings after his bath, he'd take a beer and completely relax by floating around in the pool in one of the huge innertubes he'd brought home.

Our Rambler wagon was finally in bad enough shape for Neal to admit it was useless. We hated to let it go; it had served us long and well, and . . . it was paid for. But, now that Neal had a driver's license again, he was anxious to use it, and the first chance we got after his return to work, we hunted another car. To our joy we found a Jeep, just like Willie, only maroon instead of blue, and we got an exceptional deal with our trade-in.

To check it out we decided that Friday after work, we'd surprise Jack in Big Sur and show it off. I made a picnic supper for us to eat on the way, and the children and I sat on a mattress on the floor in the back, which was low enough so I wouldn't see the cliff-hanging roads of Big Sur. Neal's driving terrified me enough on straight flat roads, and I seldom went anywhere with him anymore, but this trip was too good to turn down. When he turned off the highway onto the dirt trail that led down to the cabin, I looked out once and only once. The road was chipped out from the hillside at a downward slant; one lane and no guardrails.

"Sure hope we don't meet a loggin' rig, Ma," Neal cheerily yelled back to me, not watching the road ahead, "'cause I'd have to back up all the way back to the highway to let him pass." "No, Neal, don't. . . ." I moaned, and prayed.

On flat ground at last, Neal parked beside a barbed wire fence near an iron gate. He explained we'd have to walk to the cabin to get the key to the gate, but it wasn't far. The sun was hot on the sandy trail that led through a pasture, but we soon saw the cabin nestled in the pines by a rushing mountain stream that seemed in a great hurry to get to the ocean. It splashed noisily close by the porch and then slithered off like a green and black snake through the trees.

Neal lustily knocked on the cabin door, but before there was a response, he flung it open. I could see nothing but darkness and the dim flicker of a fire; the brightness of the sun had weakened my vision. A second later we heard Jack roar, and he bounded toward us, laughing. "My God! It's a band of *angels* . . . with St. Michael at the head!" He couldn't get over our unexpected appearance. He had been sitting in the dark room, and the sudden burst of sunlight with all the blond heads shining in it kept him exclaiming for many minutes, and referring to it ever after.

Inside the cabin was one large room. In the center near the back wall a fireplace had been built by elevating an oil drum on a platform of bricks, the front cut out. A flu had been welded to the top side and continued up to the roof. The smell of the wooden cabin and the burning pine logs perfumed the warm atmosphere. The only windows were on the front, shaded by the porch.

"Yessir, Ferlinghetti built this in four days, Carolyn." Jack noticed me taking it all in, "Imagine that, *four days!* There's no bathroom; we all use the beautiful outhouse in back, and Neal and I have taken care to put a can of water and some soap out there, so you needn't worry . . . We'll teach these heathen yet about proper bathroom hygiene . . . like us

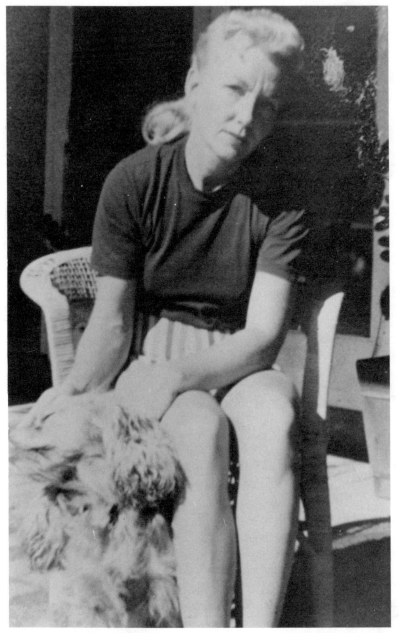

Carolyn Cassady, Circa 1958.

Sissy Spacek and Carolyn Cassady, 1978.

French have always known forever, right?" This feature of the accomodations intrigued the children since they'd never seen a real outhouse, and they ran right out to investigate.

Paul Smith had stood up from sitting near the hearth and now greeted us, quiet and smiling, his eyes still melting. On one side of the room, against the wall, were some folding cots, and on the other side I could now see a small table and chairs. At the table sat a pretty darkhaired girl in tight jeans holding a small child, and beside her sat a slim young man with black curls framing a handsome face. We were introduced to Mike McClure and his wife, Joanna. Mike had been discussing a poem with Jack, and Neal was now asked to read it and give his comments. Both Jack and Neal expressed extravagant praise and approval, and when they'd finished, they handed it to me.

The title was the first jolt: "Fuck Ode," and about halfway down the page embarrassment and revulsion caused me to barely scan the remainder of the rather long poem, hoping no one would notice. Luckily, they were busy talking about the gate key, and no one was anxious for my opinion. I looked sideways at the lovely delicate girl and her cherubic child and wondered how she felt to have her husband describe in such relentless and gross detail sexual acts between them that to me would be cherished as too personal and private, the meaning too internal, to be translated into common vulgar language of the street . . . all *too* common. Was *that* what sex meant to him? To *her?* Yuk. "Poetry" my foot. Seemed to me anybody could describe sex realistically like that, and was it "poetry" because the lines were chopped up? Well, I was seriously biased, no doubt.

Neal and Jack took the children to get the car, the McClures went ahead to the beach where we would join them later, and Paul poured me some coffee. It was flattering yet somewhat uncomfortable for me to be alone with Paul. He was such a pleasure to look at, I would have liked to paint him; every movement was harmonious and graceful, and he was such a perfect "specimen," it was all I could do not to touch him as one would a piece of sculpture, but I knew it would be like putting a match to tinder; together we created that aura of magnetism that made conversation halting.

So it was a relief to hear the rattle and bang of the jeep as Neal backed it close up to the stream and the porch. He and Jack stomped up the steps, and it was evident even before I saw his bloodshot eyes, that Neal had indulged in tea. The children ran in with them, and all eagerly told me of the mule they'd found in the pasture, whose name, Jack told them, was Alf. Now they were eager to see the beach.

"All right, children, come along." Neal took command. "And just wait till I show you the fantastic wreck . . . ugh . . . come on, we gotta go by the stream here . . ." and the little group clustered around him as they started down the path. Jack grabbed my hand and pulled me to the door, quite purposely away from Paul. "Come on, ma, I'll show you my meditation cove." Paul merely smiled and ran ahead to catch up with the children.

Jack and I ambled slowly beside the stream; he was telling me incidents and observations from his previous stay there, and I was sopping up the smells and sights of the sun-dappled woods. The stream opened out and spread itself over a clean, sandy beach in a secluded broad cove far silver bridge that made me shudder . . . with good reason, it would seem, when Neal pointed out the remains of a car lying upside down, rusted and mute on the nearby rocks. Neal joined Mike, seated on a large rock in the shade of the cliff, the wife and child digging in the sand at their feet. Paul took my children to explore caves further up the beach, then helped them build dams in the stream and find pieces of driftwood to sail down the strong channels.

Jack led me around a jut of rock in the other direction. We sat in the warm sand in a snug little cove while the reddening sun slid into the water and stained it and the surf a brilliant pink.

"Did you do any writing while you were here?" I asked.

"Only poetry. I wrote a great poem to the sea . . . Cherson! Cherson! Shoo . . . shaw . . . shirsh . . . Go on die salt light, you billion yeared rock knocker . . . Like that, see? But I haven't been able to write much else since all this awful attention—everybody at me."

"Do you still carry those little notebooks everywhere?"

"Naw . . . I forget . . ."

"I have an old one of yours, did you know? You left it at the house one time. It's a charming story . . . what I can read of the French . . . about your aunt in Canada. It's a story that reminded me of Dickens. I've kept it, hoping you'll write more like that . . . more like you. I'm sorry, Jack, but On The Road and The Subterraneans . . . they just don't sound like the Jack I know. Who are you trying to be? You're not all that rough and vulgar, are you? You're not that much interested in sex . . ." Jack interrupted laughing, "Hey, you know a funny thing about that? When Neal and I went to the hot springs with the boys last week, he and I were the only guys there who wouldn't take off our shorts. I thought at the time, Ha, the big "Road" heroes, and they're the only modest ones in the bunch." He shook his head and chuckled.

"I guess Neal is pretty much like the way you portrayed him, though I like to think deep down he isn't really . . . and of course he *is* hung up on sex, but that's part of his neurosis . . . and *you're* never like that, except maybe when you're real drunk. I wish you weren't afraid to be yourself . . . write about yourself honestly, I mean. There's nothing to be ashamed of . . . I don't mean everything should be sweetness and light, when it wasn't . . . just *honestly* you."

"Yeah? Well I been looking at myself 'honestly' down here, and I don't like what I see." He looked at me suddenly, pulled me to him and kissed me in a desperate sort of way. Then we lay back, my head on his arm, and we watched the sky cool and the stars pop out one by one. It

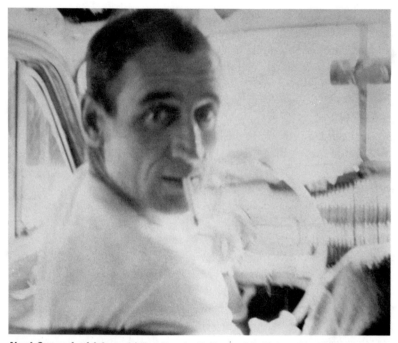

Neal Cassady driving old Pontiac to Bolinas, CA. Taken by Allen Ginsberg from back seat. Circa 1963.

became too chilly to sit longer, and the tide was creeping up, so we searched our way back to the cabin, clinging to each other in the now dark woods.

The hot coffee by the fire was welcome. I sat down in a low-slung canvas chair on one side of the fire, Jack in a chair opposite, and Paul folded himself cross-legged on the floor beside me, leaning against my chair. Neal went to lie down on a cot by the far wall, his hands under his head, while the children found some cards and sat at the table to play. Mike and Joanna announced they would return to the ocean and sleep near the beach.

Paul began to sing softly. He had a low mellow voice and a technique much like Mel Torme's. Absentmindedly, my hand strolled through his hair from time to time as one would acknowledge a pet. Everything seemed content and cozy. Then little by little, Jack began to fidget, now and then grumbling or spitting out a remark I would either ignore or try to answer, pretending I didn't notice his tone. I couldn't figure out what was eating him until he got up and, fiercely throwing a piece of wood at the fire, he burst out with, "My God, Paul, haven't you got any consideration for Neal, man? How can you be so unfeeling?" and he smashed another piece of wood against the first. Paul stopped singing abruptly, and I tried not to laugh. "Neal?" I said quietly. "If you look closely, Jack, you'll see he's so concerned he's fast asleep." But Jack growled and stamped over to the kitchen area to look for wine. There was none. He hesitated, then went over to Neal.

"Hey, Neal, Neal? Come on, man, drive me into town for some wine, okay?" He was gruff and angry. Neal stirred and sat up, good natured as always when awakened. I spoke up, "You men said you wanted to build a big bonfire on the beach, remember?"

"Yeah," Jack retorted, "well . . . you and *Paul* do that while we're gone, and we'll join you later. Come on, Neal." "Right," said Neal and got up, calling to the children to come along if they liked, and everyone scrambled to the Jeep and rumbled away. For a minute I'd thought of objecting to the children's accompanying them. Both men were churlish, and I feared Neal would be more careless, smoke more tea . . . but, too late, they were gone, and there was nothing I could help by worrying. I mentally put them in God's care and stopped thinking about it. Besides, I'd need all my wits about me to resist Paul.

We put on sweaters, collected matches and paper and walked back to the beach with a flashlight. The waves were now rhythmically lapping and shushing among the rocks and smoothing the sand in glassy reflection of the moonlight. I'd rarely seen a night on the ocean without fog, but tonight the stars hung over us so glittering and close it looked almost artificial, like a ballroom dome. We stood close together for a minute for warmth while absorbing the wonder, but when Paul's hands began the restless seeking of the male, I hastened to our stated purpose, the fire. It kept him busy until it was lighted and roaring. We looked about for the McClures, but they were nowhere in view, so we sat by the fire back to back, hugging our knees, our heads on each other's shoulders, while Paul sang for me until there was only a bed of coals. Neal and Jack never appeared. My anxieties surfaced again, and we hurried to bury the fire and trudge back through the cold woods.

The Jeep was parked beside the porch, and inside it I saw the children snug and asleep. Jack was a lump in his sleeping bag on the porch, and inside the cabin, Neal slept on a cot. I was relieved but also disappointed and a little angry that they had left me with Paul. Paul got his sleeping bag, and on the way out to the porch kissed me goodnight, properly this time, in spite of my resistance, which was only half-hearted. I climbed in with Neal and the smoky aroma in the stuffy warm room soon put me to sleep.

Next morning Jack and Neal were grouchy and furtive, and I was annoyed. When Paul left, I asked Jack, "Why didn't you come back to the beach? Here we had that big fire going, and all for nothing." My tone was petulant, but his was harsh and accusing. "Neal thought you and Paul wanted to be alone." "Oh, Neal did! That's just dandy. He might consult me once in awhile instead of pushing me off on any male who happens to look interested. Why doesn't he protect me from wolves, not encourage them?" I meant him to know my protest included him, too, but my outburst served only to brighten his mood, though he was still suspicious. When Paul returned, Jack stopped him outside on the porch, and I hurried to fix breakfast for the children. In a few moments Jack came in all smiles again; Paul had banished his fears, but his doubting me didn't improve my disposition. As for Neal, he didn't care enough to even ask; he just assumed what he wished to . . . another act of "sharing," I supposed . . . which now looked to me more like cowardice, or at least an inability to stand up for his "rights."

The McClures returned for a late breakfast, after which Joanna and I cleaned up the dishes and the cabin, and we all climbed into our respective Jeeps. I had to be back for the Wagon Stagers performance, having missed the night before, and the McClures were headed for the City. They did ask if we could stop en route to visit friends of theirs, an artistic couple who lived in the Carmel Highlands and to whom they wished to introduce Jack.

The men sat about an umbrella table in the yard and discussed literature over their beers while Joanna and I toured the beautiful modern home, all wood and glass, and admired the wife's paintings on the lofty walls. Then the McClures bid us goodbye as we each took our separate routes.

I was excited about sharing my new enthusiasm with Jack. Not since Denver had he participated in my theatrical activities, and I knew he and I and Neal shared similar tastes in drama, because we'd all three so often watched plays or Westerns together on TV. They were as sensitive to quality and authenticity as I without their ever having studied it, and I could hardly wait for Jack to see what Margaret had accomplished. I expected Neal to support me, since he had already come to the plays with me and applauded them with generous approval and real enjoyment.

It was too late; the timing was all wrong. Jack had his jug of wine, and after the beer at the artists' home, was well on the way to his now daily intoxicated condition. We had stopped at a roadside cafe near our destination, when we found we were both ravenous and early, and I hoped it would sober Jack. Instead, he refused to eat. Neal was still being distant to me and chummy with Jack because of Paul's attention to me, so I accepted Paul's company gladly. We were lingering over our coffee when we became aware of a commotion outside. A siren wailed and a fire engine screamed into the open parking lot. Paul and I hardly looked up from our engrossing conversation until the children came running to me out of breath to say our car was on fire.

"OUR car?" We all ran outside, and I felt a moment's panic. We could hardly afford to lose our new car . . . and certainly not before the show, which must go on.

Fortunately, the fire was out by the time we got there. It had been mostly smoke, anyway, caused by a smouldering cigarette in the mattress. Jack had been sitting on the tailgate with his jug, so the finger of suspicion was pointed at him, but no one voiced the accusation; we were so relieved it was no worse, and it added to our weekend adventure. The mattress was now thoroughly soaked and the smell horrific; we were glad we hadn't far to go.

By the time we arrived at Old Town, Jack had reached the stage of singing with half-closed eyes, so all I could hope for from him was that he'd be subdued. Neal parked the car by the back gate of the stockade while I went to find Frank Dean, the owner, and ask his permission to admit them. I found Frank putting up the flats on the station wagon stage, his wife, Bernice, practicing her part of their Oleo act. They readily gave their permission, so I sought Margaret to obtain hers. When I returned as far as the stage, Jack was standing in the middle of it barking some story at Frank in an exaggerated Western twang. I cringed and made sign language of chagrin and contrition to Frank behind Jack's back and ran to get Neal for help. He and the children collected Jack to take him on a tour of the town, and I ducked into the wagon dressing room, now quite late for work.

The actors were all good friends and kidded me about Jack's behavior as I applied their make-up and beards, and I knew they sympathized with me although they were disappointed not to meet the great writer themselves, which now appeared unlikely. Yet as each one finished dressing, he'd go out to hunt Jack and see what he was up to. In a way I was glad I

Carolyn Cassady and John Clellon Holmes, July 26, 1982. PHOTO BY ARTHUR WINFIELD KNIGHT.

couldn't do so myself. The children had taken him to the old saloon, and on seeing the piano, Jack had pounced on it and started banging out great dissonant chords while bellowing tuneless Western songs, his behavior still smacking largely of mockery. The audience was beginning to straggle in, and Frank came to ask Jack not to play the piano and disturb the other saloon guests. Jack became defensive and defiant and yelled back at Frank about his "rights" as a customer in his most obnoxious way. Frank had something of a temper, it now rose, and he ordered Jack off the premises.

Neal had taken advantage of my absence to go back to the car and smoke more tea, and now Jack strode angrily out to join him, growling, swearing and grumbling. When one of the men reported this to me I hurried out the back gate and around to the car, sick with disappointment, chagrin and fury. "Is it that I demand so damn much of you guys that just *one* time in all these years you couldn't manage to do me the courtesy to even *act* interested in something I care about? Oh no, everybody's supposed to fall all over *you* two . . . just give, give, give to you . . . but *you* . . . oh, to hell with it. . . ." I had to stop to stem the tears, and Neal looked sheepish but said, "Uh . . . maybe you could get a ride home with somebody? Don't you think I'd better take old Jack away . . . so's we won't bother or embarrass you further, my dear?" The last bit allowed sarcasm and ridicule to enter his tone, and I was hurt and disgusted. I slammed the car door and ran back through the gate. I glanced back to see the tires spin in the dirt; and then the Jeep swept out of the driveway with a cloud of dust peeling behind it. So now they'd managed to have their time alone together. "Huh, you deserve each other; good riddance," I said aloud.

There was no problem in finding an actor who'd take us home, and now I was the more grateful for Paul and his warm adoration. On the drive home he told me how much he'd enjoyed the evening, and it struck him as a sort of celebration . . . for the next day was his birthday. "Your birthday? Why, Paul, why didn't you tell me sooner? How old will you be?" I expected him to say twenty-five or -six. "Seventeen," he said shyly. "Seventeen! *seventeen?*" I couldn't get it to fit in a slot. Nobody was seventeen . . . least of all Paul. Why, he looked older even than the Santa Clara boys who were at least nineteen and twenty. I sat stunned. The actor laughed and said with a wink at me, "I'd never have guessed it."

Neal did not return with the car the next day, so Paul was stranded at our house. Without the excitement and activity, the rose color began to fade from his glasses. I could see it, even if he couldn't yet, and I had known from the start it was inevitable. To help his growing restlessness, I painted a quick oil portrait of him to keep us occupied . . . one of my best, I thought.

The next morning Neal still had not returned, so Paul set out to hitchhike down the coast. The next I heard of him was a letter from Gavin some months later when he was visiting a commune near Santa Barbara: ". . . had a wonderful Xmas lunch at my nephew's mother's and a fine bearded friend of yours was there among the 20—Paul Smith and his red-headed chic. We talked much of you and Neal, and came to complete agreement. *You* are the saint. But Neal, in spite of the fact he has never realized that it is inevitable that one horse (or car) can run faster than another—remains one of the great human beings that we have ever known—a kind of *wunderkind*, as the Germans put it. If we didn't love him so much we wouldn't worry so about the seeming inevitability of his going back to the Big House."

When Neal returned, he blamed his absence on Jack, of course, and told me he'd taken Jack to see a girl named Jackie, whom I learned had been one of Neal's former lovers. It occurred to me this idea might have been behind the whole fiasco, consciously or unconsciously. Neal was telling me about it to prove to me that he was through with Jackie. I clutched at the reassurance, even though I knew it proved nothing. I foresaw as well, that his restriction to our county was at an end and my peace of mind with it.

The following Friday evening Jack and Lew appeared again at the door, this time accompanied by Lew's girl, Lenore. Her appearance surprised me. She was about twice the size of Lew in all dimensions except height, with a much larger ratio in several areas, very Latin looking and definitely female. "Fertility goddess" registered in my mind. Jack had been drinking but was still coherent. Conversation centered on their plans for the coming week at Big Sur, and I wondered why the threesome. As with errant schoolboys, the truth leaked out finally that Jackie and her child were outside in the car. I was horrified.

"Now really, Jack, how could you do that? Bring her in at once. You can't let her sit out there in the freezing cold. What is the matter with you?"

"Are you *sure* it's all right?" Jack actually looked fearful.

"Why, of *course* it's all right. What can you be thinking of?"

"Oh, oh," Lew sing-songed, "Bring out the saucer of cream!" I could hardly believe my ears. "You guys are nuts! Or you watch too many soap operas. Do you really think we're going to tear out each other's hair? It isn't Jackie's fault . . . or mine . . . that Neal and Jack are interested in both of us. Honestly, it makes me boil when women blame 'the other woman' for taking her man . . . that simply is not possible. No woman can *take* a man who doesn't want to go. It's *his* choice, not theirs . . . for the woman who's most attractive or has the most to offer. The women can only look to their laurels." Could these bright, worldly men still be so deluded? But now Jack had gone out and sheepishly returned with Jackie. I asked her to sit down, and we had a perfectly ordinary conversation about children like two normal adults.

Now Jack began unmistakably to send me soulful looks and make suggestive remarks . . . more than that . . . outright invitations, and he irritated me further. I did my best to ignore him and my inward sobs of regret and keep my attention on Jackie. Neal, meantime, had started pacing, growling, breathing hard, humphing, glaring . . . the old familiar symptoms of jealousy . . . not for *me*, I knew . . . but for Jackie . . . giving her the agony act because she was going off with Jack. I didn't know whether to laugh or ring for the men in the white coats, it was all so insane.

Lew became bored and anxious to get on their way. At the door, Jack said to me, "Now Neal's mad at me because of Jackie, I can tell . . . but it was *his* idea!"

"No, Jack, no . . . that's not the reason he's angry . . . Oh, never mind, run along, but it isn't *you* he's angry at."

The whole scene depressed me, but it eliminated my need to condemn Neal; Jackie was punishing him for me . . . and he had asked for it again.

Little did I know this was the last time I would ever see Jack. A year later I got a letter, the first of many more throughout the remaining years of his life that continued to tell of his ever-present but never-to-be-fulfilled wish to return. "Dear Carolyn: Not writing because I dreamed of you last night, and quel dream! but I was planning for weeks to write and explain my months-long silence.

"I in fact wrote you a big letter from Mexico City saying 'How about me coming up to Los Gatos?' but I tore it up because the Mexican fiasco made me wonder I might get all hung up in Frisco again instead of just at home with you and Neal. So came home. But that too was favorable in the stars because after 6 weeks at home thinking and reading Balzac and working and throwing away writings suddenly, boom, I just finished my new novel, Big Sur, about the summer 1960 you remember.

"In it, as a matter of fact, I sort of answer to your letter of last summer. You know, that old idea about you and me meeting in Nirvana later at which time Neal will be perfect, etc. you remember. Anyway, pretty romantic. [The "Nirvana" idea had been all his.]

"I just want you to know that I cherished your letter, and I cherish you, in that special way you'll realize when you read the book. Later I can send you excerpts off this typewriter, if you want, in November. Like when we all walked down the Big Sur path to the sea, you and I talking as of yore, and Neal had his new magenta (?) jeepster stationwagon, and the kids, and McClure, and then that awful night I brought Jacky to your house. So ashamed of that I never came back for my old shirt you'd sewn for me so sweetly (as I say) but you never were even mad.

"Anyway at this time, naturally, having just written a book in which you figure (and don't worry, you come off just like you are, which is moral and clean) (as a contrast to all the big lewd Lew Welches and Jacks and Paul Smiths whoopee) you're so on my mind I wish you'd write. Not only telling me every detail whatever you wanta say, about you, me, but I want to know if anything's wrong with Neal. And news of Jacky would interest me and might help me put the final touch in there. You see, if I were a big Russian novelist writing fiction it would be so easy. I hope you appreciate the fact I feel, well, shamed? awful? shitty? for writing about everybody as they are. I always make an effort to clean up the mess by changing names, times, places, circumstances. But in years from now no one will see a 'mess' there, just people, just Karma, the gaging Karma of all of us. And in this case, of you and me, the soft and gentle Karma that aint even started. (wow, that dream last night). But Carolyn forgive me also for intruding on your gentle home life and for all I know you've got something new to absorb you but just write me letter on typewriter like old days.

"I'd like also to come out Calif. right soon. Sigh, pain in the ass Jack.

"In fact, wait a minute, I aint finished . . ." He excitedly recapped the events that led up to our arrival at Big Sur on our surprise visit, ". . . climaxed by the most marvelous sudden booming open of the cabin door allowing golden light to burst in on me and McClure and what do we see but five angels, Neal the archangel standing arm outspread, you next, golden hair, the kids, the jeepster outside, that surprise visit? The talks and walks, and that funny evening I got thrown out of the Hiss the Villain play?

"Boy do you realize how many books I could write?

"Well, your part in the story is you talk to me quietly and sadly about the old days, the new, I describe the children, what you're doing for them, your home, but there's that undercurrent of strange muted romance between us. So please don't get mad.

"What I'm really worried (about somebody's getting mad) is Jacky; I come right out and say she bores me whereas you (Evelyn) never do—O it was horrible—well—it ends up that terrifying night of Sept 3 when I went mad for the first time, while Jacky slept and her kid slept, Lew and Lenore slept, but I had nightmares the likes of which I only barely can describe . . . It was the night of the end of Nirvana, in fact—I realized all my Buddhism had been words—comforting words, indeed, but when I saw those masses of devils racing for me—but Buddha did ward off devils under the Bo tree before he knew & understood—but I'd like to tell you all about it when I see you—At least, one of these days, we'll have one of our old quiet religious arguments by the fireplace as Neal sits there playing self-chess saying 'Hm, yass, got ya dirty pawn' . . . 'You old Queen'. . . . A Dieu, or as the Mexicans say, Okay Memo, JACK"

Jack wrote several more letters describing his work on *Big Sur*; it evidently excited him a good deal, and when I read the published book, I, too, felt it had been a turning point for him in his writing. He was far more honest about himself and able to be more objective without sacrificing his real emotions. I couldn't see he wrote much more about *us*, as he seemed to think, but I understood why he'd always kept it quiet, after all, I was a *married* woman! But I did hope this breakthrough would start him on a new regenerated tack in future work.

Railroad tracks near San Miquel de Allende, Mexico. COURTESY: STEVE DOSSEY AND DONNA WOOD.

CHAPTER 3

Pierre Delattre Remembers Neal Cassady

While doing research in San Miguel de Allende for a story on the later years of Neal Cassady's life, we were directed to Pierre Delattre. Mr. Delattre has lived in this charming, colonial Mexican town on and off for the past sixteen years. He is presently head of the Writing Department at the Instituto Allende in San Miguel.

Our interview with Pierre took place on March 17, 1981, in the library of the 300-year-old stone palace, which serves as an artists' school for the multi-national community.

Our first glimpse of Pierre occurred when we attended a Poetry Reading at the Instituto in which he was appearing. Pierre brightened the stage as he wove a story about his friend, John the Mouse, accompanying and accentuating the tale with flute tunes, yodels, and Scandinavian jigs.

Pierre is fifty years old, and has published two novels, *Tales of a Dali Lama*, and his most recent, *Walking on Air*. He feels he is just now at his creative peak. In his writings, Pierre's intent is to lift consciousness and to open up the possibilities of what can be done with this earth.

In Pierre's own words:

> "If you're going to fly, you must first be
> grounded. Love of the earth comes first
> before we can transcend or leave it.
> We must put our planet in order."

Steve Dossey and Donna Wood

INTERVIEWER: *Your book* Walking on Air *was recently published. Would you provide some background on your profession as a writer?*

PIERRE DELATTRE: Well, I started to write seriously after I left the area of religion. I had been working in San Francisco—North Beach. I was very involved in mystical, religious movements—counterculture—and had been for many years. I wanted to bring this into art. I've always wanted to be a writer, but I wanted to have something to write about; so, I decided to spend the first 10–20 years of my life involved in social action, trying to encourage what I felt was a very important movement—the counterculture, which became the beat, hip sequel. And, out of that came much of my writing. Having been a minister in North Beach, a street priest, I was the one they usually brought the bodies to. I dealt with many casualties; so, for me, a lot of the experience of the Beat Generation was one of picking up the pieces. In fact, Neal Cassady's body was brought to my door here in San Miguel. He was kind of the last of those glory figures of the Beat Generation. So, that seems to be my particular destiny; to try to understand and deal with the tragedies which affected many of us.

INT: *Can you tell me a little about how long you have lived in Mexico and what brought you to San Miguel?*

PD: I came to Mexico because I didn't want to pay my taxes on the Vietnam War. I think I came here the first time 16 years ago. There happened to be a job at the Instituto, so I started teaching writing. I have taught writing on and off at the Instituto for the past nine out of sixteen years. But, I came here mostly because I felt it was an energy center for a

Neal Cassady and unknown merry prankster, 1965-6?. RON BEVIRT PHOTO.

lot of exciting activity that was going on in the counterculture. I felt there was a major movement against the main stream of American culture in the United States; and that, during the Vietnam War, and after the so-called Beat period, it began to spread out; and, as somebody said, it was no longer on the road, but it was off the road and into the woods. One of the places into the woods, though this is a desert, was San Miguel.

INT: *How do you think Beat Literature will hold up over time?*

PD: I think that it is an insignificant force. I think that it was a cultural, a sociological expression that is interesting to sociology. I think a great deal of literature is interesting ju.t for that reason; but, as art, I can't think of a single piece of the so-called Beat Literature that holds up very strongly as what you might call great literature. Maybe you can suggest one and I might agree with you, but I can't think of one offhand. For example, as much as I love Allen Ginsberg, to open a poem by saying that he has seen the best minds of his generation destroyed by madness, is itself a completely fatuous lie. First of all, to presume that he knew the best minds of his generation just because they happened to be his friends; and, secondly, that he saw them destroyed by madness as if madness were an impersonal force that acts upon us—not to realize that the problem was self-destruction, not destruction by some external force out there. That kind of lamentation, as if there were some almost paranoid vision of something at work that is destroying the intellect or destroying sensibility, was the weakness of the Beat Generation—and was the weakness of a great deal of its literature. Victimization, a sense of being the victim, and I think it is what we have to get over with—the whole countercultural movement realizing it is no longer a question of the destruction of various sensitive, tender and loving souls, who must somehow defend themselves against this onslaught of the materialistic, earth-destroying forces. It is a question now of realizing we are those forces, and we have to muster our courage and our strength and not take such a weak and self-pitying position.

INT: *How and when did you first meet Neal Cassady?*

PD: I first met Neal Cassady when I had a television program in San Francisco called "Against the Stream," where we were trying to show what some of the currents were against the mainstream of American culture. It was on Channel 5, and I asked Neal to be on it. He came on with his wife, Carolyn. It was an interesting program, because, first of all, Neal was very miffed at Kerouac, or pretended to be. Because, after all, he had landed in jail as a result of the great publicity that he had gotten out of that book. Neal felt he had been singled out as some kind of token image because of that book, and spent a lot of time in jail paying for the publicity. Neal decided to come on very straight. He had a crew haircut, and was doing his respectable number. So, the first time I met Neal, it was kind of funny, because I had heard so much about Neal Cassady from reading *On the Road*. And then here comes this guy in a blue suit and a red tie, playing it very straight. Well, the next time I met him was years later, and then he was back to being the Neal Cassady I associated with Neal Cassady.

INT: *Tom Wolfe characterized Neal as "a monologist who didn't care whether someone was listening or not." Was that the Neal Cassady you knew later on?*

PD: Well, just to give you an example of the way Neal was, the next time I ran into Neal after this television interview in '59, must have been maybe 1965, and the first thing he said to me was KPIX, Channel 5, corner of O'Farrell Street and so and so, 9:30 a.m. . . . Then he proceeded to tell me everything that we had talked about. He had a photographic memory for everything, including every conversation he had ever had. While it is true that you didn't converse with Neal so much as listen to him, at the same time, he remembered everything, he remembered everyone. You could say that he did more talking than listening in a sense; but, on the other hand, he was a very fine listener in the sense that he picked up on, I guess what you could call, people's vibes. He was very psychic, very intuitive. Much of what he understood about you, he understood without you having to say anything. You felt that about him, and that is what made you feel so affectionate toward Neal Cassady—he was "there," he just wasn't there in dialogue a lot of the time.

INT: *Would you describe your association with Neal Cassady during his visits to San Miguel?*

PD: Yes. Again, I had this role I have been cast in. You see what happened to me was that I spent four years studying comparative religion at the University of Chicago and had planned to go on and be a writer. When I found myself making speeches against the organized church, and was very involved with race relations and civil liberties, somebody asked me in the Congregational Church, which is a very liberal branch of Protestantism, what I would do if I were in the ministry? I said there is a very powerful, spiritual movement in America today; but, it's not in the churches—it's out in the streets where a whole group of prophets and singers were energizing and coming together. Singers, poets, jazz musicians and so forth. You should get out there and encourage this in any way you can. So, they said, you have a Bachelors of Divinity Degree, let us ordain you into the ministry and we will let you do whatever you want. So, I opened up a coffee house [The Bread and Wine Mission] in North Beach. So I became a street priest, though I wasn't preaching to anybody. In fact, more of my congregation was Jewish rather than Christian. I became cast in the role of a priest in the sense that when people needed comfort, or they wanted to get married, or a christening, baptism or celebration, they came to me. And, when they were in trouble, they came to me.

Neal was one of these. So, when he met me here, he already saw me

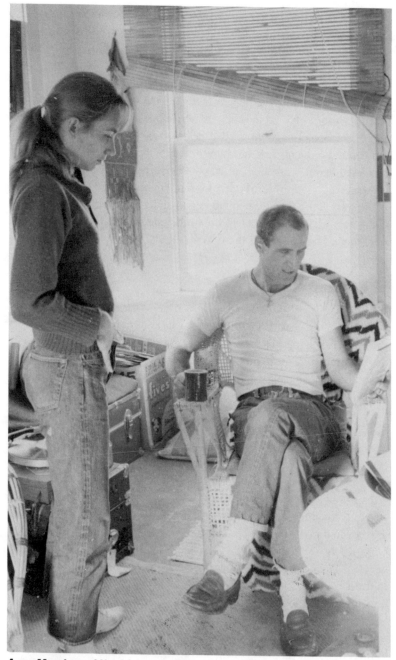

Anne Murphy and Neal Cassady, Bolinas, CA, 1963. TAKEN BY ALLEN GINSBERG.

a little bit like I was his priest. He would come to me to talk over his troubles. Most of my relationship to Neal Cassady was hearing him tell me about the troubles he was going through. Though I also participated in a lot of the fantastic nights where I saw the other side of Neal. Neal was very ambiguous. If there was anybody whom you could imagine as a shadow figure of Neal Cassady, it would be Herman Melville's Billy Budd. He looked like what I would imagine Billy Budd to look like; a muscular, sailor type. You could picture him in a striped shirt. He looked Australian; in fact, he always seemed to have a slight foreign accent like an Australian. I never really saw him as an American. He seemed like a foreigner, more like an Englishman. He was very formal. He was intellectually brilliant and his brilliance consisted of the ability to speak without reflecting, apparently. He was fascinated with speed.

I always felt there were two major movements in the States at that time. There was one that was trying to slow everything down; and their drug was grass. There was another that was trying to speed everything up, and its drug was speed. Those who were trying to speed everything up were trying to run their lives out as fast as possible. They had a Rimbaud complex and they wanted to burn themselves out, and many of them did. The greatest poet on North Beach, and he wasn't all that great, but he was a great poet, was Bob Kaufman, who was a neighbor of mine and a very good friend. Bob burned his brain out on methedrine, on speed—and only now is just beginning to recover to an extent to be able to articulate again. For ten years, he was totally out of it. One whole group burned itself out. Christopher McClain, who was an editor of some fine poetry magazines, and read some of the early poetry to jazz, burned his brain out. As far as I know, he has never recovered, or maybe he is not even alive now.

Anyhow, when Neal arrived in town, he was the celebrator of speed, and people who were into speed would flock around him because he was sensational. We used to go out and sit in a room with him in San Miguel; there would be 30 or 40 people, most of them stoned out of their minds, watching Neal. A guy named Paul Santoro played away at incredible speeds on his guitar, backing up Neal, who began to speak. He would do these raps where he would make incredible connections between Melville and Whitman and Baudelaire, and race car drivers and Bohemia 200 years ago, and God knows what. The connections he made were just impossible to conceive. They were so brilliant, like one flash of insight after another, but they never occurred with any pause. I think the best example I can give you was this one I told Neal about a race car driver who had died. He was

59

fascinated by race car drivers, and he asked me what country he was from. I said I didn't know; so he said, well, I'll name the Italian drivers and b-r-r-r-r proceeded to name something like 50 or 60 drivers in a row without even pausing long enough to think up the next name. It was just one name after another, full speed. I said it doesn't sound like any of those, so he named all the French drivers, all the American drivers, and he went through this incredible list of drivers as if he were reading at accelerated speed off a sheet of paper without ever stopping for an instant. He drove the same way; he drove at incredible speeds and people loved to get in the car with him. I heard many tales of driving down to the beach with Neal. He drove so fast that you should have been terrified out of your mind; and yet, everybody had complete confidence that he would get you there, and he always did. He was a brilliant driver and very responsible; but, through it all, his complaint to me, and the reason he would come and talk to me on occasion, was that he felt that he had been cast in a role. He often said to me that he really didn't want to be this hip hero; that being a hip hero was bugging him and causing him a lot of pain and suffering. He didn't know how to get out of the role that everyone wanted him to play. It was noblesse oblige. In fact, the last thing he said to me before the last time I saw him, he said, all I want to do is go back to working on the railroad. And that is what he actually ended up doing, is walking down the railroad tracks to his death.

INT: *During these times of complaint, did he put the blame on either Kesey or Kerouac for the role he played?*

PD: It's hard to tell to what extent he was serious. He may have been playing, joking when he said it, but he did several times say to me that he resented this role. And yet, he obviously courted the role and went out of his way to make sure he was there creating the scene at the right places. He was obviously torn between the attraction of being this charismatic figure and the revulsion at what it was doing to him. It was obviously driving him up the wall. So, I don't see how he could have . . . he loved Ginsberg especially, and Ginsberg loved him. The relationship those two had was much . . . I don't know as much about his relationship to Kerouac as I do to Ginsberg. He and Ginsberg had an enormous love for each other and appreciation for each other.

INT: *Did he continue to express this love, even later in his life?*

PD: Yes. I never heard him say and I didn't know much about his relationship to people like Kesey; but I do know that he always expressed a great deal of love for Allen Ginsberg. Kerouac, as I say, I didn't know. He didn't speak much about him around me.

INT: *I understand Neal was involved with the Instituto Gallery Players. What do you know of his role with them?*

PD: He didn't play in the Gallery Players. He had,—there was a woman named J.B. [Janice Brown] here, a very powerful, wonderful woman who ran the Gallery Players. It was a little repertory theatre we had here, and she was in love with Neal. After he died . . . according to her, Neal had come to see her, here in San Miguel. I guess he had come back to see her . . . she had gone to see him. She took his death very tragically. For several years she sort of carried the torch for Neal. Then I realized there were several women carrying the torch for Neal. But, she was certainly one of them.

INT: *Would you characterize the nature of and the length of Neal's visits to San Miguel?*

PD: I don't think he was ever here for more than six weeks at a time. He didn't spend much time anywhere. He was always very restless and on the move.

INT: *Is it true that Neal initiated or participated in a rock 'n roll band while in San Miguel?*

PD: You might say that wherever Neal went, music moved toward him; he was a magnet for music. Music was played around him; he was a rock 'n roll talker. He just rapped and people made music around his rapping. It's hard to describe, but when Neal started talking, people picked up guitars; they started playing flutes or banging drums. His voice flowed through the whole thing. He was the connecting link to all these instruments. He is the only person I have ever run into who could create astonishing poetry on the spot. The poetry was one that gathered together all the major cultural, political and social impulses of our time; and he tied them together and gave them meanings. He was capable of making endless meanings; and, it's strange because he was uneducated in any formal way.

Yet, the people he brought out in these connections just blow your mind. You couldn't figure out where he got it all because there were a lot of esoteric references. But, he was not the character at all I had read about in *On the Road*. Though I don't doubt Kerouac's experience of Neal Cassady, my experience of Neal Cassady was closer to an English or Welsh coal miner-actor. One of those types like Peter O'Toole. In fact, they have certain resemblance. Neal was much more refined in a strange way than the image generally conveys.

INT: *Tom Wolfe wrote the following about Neal's death: "Some local Americans said that he had been going at top speed for two weeks and had walked off down the railroad tracks one night and his heart just gave out. Others said he had been despondant and felt he was growing old and had been on a long downer and had made the mistake of drinking alcohol on top of barbiturates." What do you know about the circumstances surrounding Neal's death?*

PD: Neal had been off speed for awhile and was trying to stop using speed because it had just been bringing him down too much afterwards. He was kind of exhausted when he was here. He was spending almost all his time with J.B., so I didn't see much of him the last round. But, I'd heard he was in town. I saw very little of him, and the story that I got was that there was a wedding down at the railroad station. There was a bunch of like gypsy people living down there. They had a wedding party that night, and Neal went down there, and I take it that he was on some kind of drugs, and he mixed it with alcohol.

INT: *Were these Americans?*

PD: No, they were Mexicans, and I was told gypsies. I know there used to be a lot of people living down there in the railroad cars with those potted plants hanging on the side. That's the kind of people he loved. He had a mystical connection with the railroad. He always talked about wanting to be back on the railroad. As I understand it, he went down there and having popped a lot of reds or whatever, he then proceeded to get drunk and he announced that he was going to walk the railroad ties from San Miguel to Celaya, which was about a forty-minute drive from here. He made it about one-fourth mile up the railroad track and collapsed. The first I knew about it, the police arrived at my house and they had his body.

Ken Kesey and Neal Cassady, 1965 -66? RON BEVIRT PHOTO.

I think in the truck, but I didn't go out to see. They told me that a guy with my address in his wallet was in the truck. They told me his name; they had his name; that's when I knew about it. So, I went and found other people.

INT: *Was he dead at that time?*

PD: Yes. He was dead on the spot; apparently he died immediately. Then, later on J.B. and I went out and we took a walk along the railroad tracks. J.B. was trying to see if Neal was still around somewhere up there, but the definite feeling was that he had taken off and was far away. There was not a feeling of a lingering ghost.

INT: *Does anyone know why Neal was going to Celaya?*

PD: Just, I think, because the railroad track was there and it's the next town over.

INT: *Did you participate in any of the acid tests with the merry pranksters?*

PD: No, I didn't, and I always had the impression that Cassady was not terribly into acid. I didn't feel that acid was his thing. But, maybe I'm wrong about that. I'm giving you impressions. I'm not an authority on Neal Cassady. I wasn't a travelling companion of his. I was just a casual friend. Actually, I think the thing that's least said about Neal Cassady is that he had a very serious moral side to his character. He wasn't what you would call a merry prankster type at all. He was a sober individual and his raps, if you wanted to compare them to anyone at all, you would have to compare them to Lenny Bruce. They were moral raps; he was making statements about the cultural situation. They were short moral perceptions, and also there were a lot of poetic appreciative connections to it. What imagination was all about. What was fascinating about Neal was that he was making constant pleas for the awakening of the imagination. In that sense, I suppose he might have wanted to use LSD as a tool, but his primary interest was less in the drug than in stirring imagination, and he knew that he was an example of that, like a specimen of what could be brought forth.

INT: *At one time, Neal was involved in the studies of Edgar Cayce. Did he ever elaborate on his theosophical convictions?*

PD: I have forgotten what he said. The only point that I could reinforce is that he himself was some kind of practicing psychic. He had arrived at some means of communicating, some means of transmitting and receiving images and connecting them on a level the rest of us hadn't caught on to yet. He was definitely psychic—that's why I say if someone thought he didn't listen, he didn't have to listen. I used to work a lot with psychotics in mental hospitals. He had a psychotic mind in the sense that he would pick up on all these vibrations that often only psychotics can pick up on. But, he managed to function at the same time. He would quite often answer your questions or say something to you that indicated he knew what you were thinking when you had said nothing at all. And, that's why I say, to say you weren't talking to Neal is well . . . you were always talking to Neal.

INT: During your association with Neal, did he ever appear preoccupied with a death wish?

PD: Yes, pretty much all the time, and I think everyone was aware of that. He said right out that he wanted to die, that he was tired of living. He was very tired of the whole thing. He had just worn himself out; he had raced his brain and his body. He was just shot.

INT: Do you have any other anecdotes you would like to relate about Neal?

PD: I suppose one of the things that also made him interesting was that he was erotically attractive to men and women. And I don't know much about the erotic attraction he held for men, but he was, I know, with women. He had a fantastic power of attraction, but there was a lot of poignancy in it, because he could never complete whatever it was that he was trying to complete. It's as if he was running fullspeed ahead, you could see it. One woman who was a lover of his described him to me like . . . she said that he makes love like an engine, a piston, just firing away for an incredible amount of time. Then he would collapse, and sleep for maybe 24 hours. And through it all, I don't think he ever arrived at the end of the line, so to speak. And, I think that was one of his problems, that he could never actually explode, he could never let it go. He was in a perpetual race for a release which he couldn't find, and I think that because of this he very much longed for death. But, I have also got to say, for me he was a pathetic figure. I saw Neal very poignantly, as someone with a brilliant mind, who was being exploited, not really able to resist it. He was being romanticized for things that he was suffering a great deal from. When you see a mind like that, you like to see it burning a slow flame and lasting a long time. But, on the other hand, if you want to go out fast, I guess he did it as well as anyone could do it.

15.
*Allen Ginsberg (in tree), Robert LaVigne and unidentified woman,
Berkeley, CA, 1955.*

CHAPTER 4

From My Last Two Thousand Years

I discussed St. John of the Cross and the problem of religious versus secular life with Allen Ginsberg. We sat at the West End Bar and shouted at each other about crime, Rimbaud, Wilhelm Reich, and weeping saints on bloodied crosses, and swore never to meet again—our characters and causes too disparate—and met again devotedly.

I watched my wife walking toward me on campus, and thought: Well, she's pretty, she's smart, she has a nice walk, and I'm married to her. We were like incestuous brother and sister, not yet sure whether we liked or disliked each other, not yet blaming each other for any ill or evil in our lives.

I envied Morgan Delaney, who adored his wife, all his wives, cared only for them, each one of them in turn, and wanted to swallow his life wholly into theirs. I was looking for a community other than marriage, but believed that if I failed with this one, I could not succeed with the other, no right to claim it. Love begets love, and only love begets it; but the duty to love begets dry boredom, which begets anxiety, which begets the desire to destroy.

I wouldn't have won the Clear-Thinking Returned GI Prize. My head was crowded with words like "illusion," "need," "hero"—Nietzsche, Freud, Carlyle—and coziness was far from my idea. Yet in fact I was trying to make cozy when I required depth in love. There were worse casualties of the time, but I was one of them. It was the age of togetherness, tract houses, and the baby explosion, and although we lived in a Manhattan slum, our romance was dimmed by family intentions. Sometimes one of us sulked over a failure to share the housework. Sometimes the sulker gave up sulking and made toasted cheese sandwiches, followed by conjugal love. I tried to think it through: Like me, she's midwestern, Jewish, goes to school, and speaks languages. She sews. Good with her hands. She dances a little tensely, but she dances. Probably I'm not so loose myself. And when I touch her mouth, I'm touching the mouth I most want to be friendly.

Good friendship was not my best dream, but it was the highest possibility of the fix we had chosen. We were sharing a life in the new postwar Bohemia—there's that healthy but creative couple, confident yet not disgusting, serious not solemn, a pair of genuine laughing free spirits, honest, friendly, reliable . . . Marvelously tolerant of weaker souls than their own, even ardently admitting to flaw while somehow managing to be treated as the hope of Morningside Heights . . . There they are again, the two of them walking together down Riverside Drive and through life, making likable jokes while they search for the Truth—*a burden to everyone.*

Unknowing, obscurely fettered, I sought community in the memory of Hart Crane and Plato, Whitehead and Blake, Homer, Dostoevsky, and Kafka. And Rudolph Carnap, the logical positivist. And Ernest Nagel, the symbolic logician. I drifted through the vocabulary and disciplines of philosophy, looking to become wise because surely I was not. I felt hair prickle and skin crawl at simple lines and phrases—"vexed by a dream," said Shakespeare, and I was a child again, vexed by repetitive dreams I could barely remember, and by the memory of those dreams. I had doubts. I needed to find my history and its meaning, and to give myself something beyond idea and self. Instead, I just went from day to day, cheerful and fretful.

Allen Ginsberg, Mexico, 1954. FROM ALLEN GINSBERG'S COLLECTION

One night we were invited to Allen Ginsberg's cold-water flat on the far East Side, across Harlem. Allen understood about my wife. He had great resources of tolerance even then; but I was early married for a graduate student in those years, and the others in the rat-tracked rooms stared—a couple? a couple? a *couple?*—as we pushed the door aside and entered. Oh Lord, here they come, one husband, one wife, the spouses. There were mattresses, orange crates, and extension cord rootlets striving out into the hall for the nourishment of sockets. (Bohemian bulbs are hungry and must eat, Bohemian radios are thirsty and must drink.) Some of the men in the room were poets, also a recent profession of mine, and they stared from their safe Parnassus as if my new fulltime occupation was husband. Oh, but I'm not, I'm not! I wanted to declare. I'm married, but all I am is not what you'd call a husband!

"Why do you talk so funny?" a furry plump little non-versifier asked me.

"I'm from Lakewood, Ohio," I said. "That's a suburb of Cleveland." I skated on Rocky River. I sat in trees, looking at Lake Erie. I longed for Susan Norton.

The poet bugged out his big brown eyes.

You can speak freely, tell your secrets. I won't pass them on to the other husbands.

"Moshe Pupick the All-American boy," the poet said.

I decided to destroy him with a look. He didn't melt or faint, so I tried words on this early hyperthyroid case: "You're Jack Armstrong," I said, "if Jack Armstrong used a dildo."

When disappointed, I sought to be abusive, like native New Yorkers. One thing I had trouble learning: the friendly street gaming of it under all the crowded rage. When I was abusive, I was really nasty—Dick Whittington studying Manhattan ways, which are not so simple as a shove and a curse.

"I'm beginning to get you," said the poet. "You make yourself clear. You're a cunt."

Allen threw his arm around both of us. "Come on, come on, come on, you're two of my dearest friends, come on now."

Passionately I wished to understand Manhattan.

Red wine and some healing herbs. We lay on mattresses. Everyone seemed to settle into ease. My wife was unhappy.

Her unhappiness was gradually transmitted to the young men lying about and waiting for something to happen. To be the lonely only lady was not her dream at that moment—not in this place carpeted with extension cords and empty Saltine boxes. Nor was it the young men's dream that she be the only lonely lady. She sat on a lurched, bitterly arthritic mohair couch with an Esso map of Africa tacked to the wall behind her. Allen was saying, "I'm going to Africa this summer. I'm really going this time."

"Where?" my wife asked.

"Like Rimbaud, I'm going. I might not come back. Africa is the cradle."

"Where? Where in Africa?" my wife asked.

"I'm going by freighter. I don't know what I'll do when I get there."

"Where, Allen?"

He seemed to be starting to point, but then his arm changed its mind and drew back and a glass of wine started on the long voyage to Africa, past my wife's shiny dark hair, smashing against a cluster of French colonies on the west coast, sending shards of glass and streaks of wine down Esso-modified Mercator projection and clean, well-brushed lady's hair. "There," he said, "that's where I'm going."

"Christ!" I said.

Young men on mattresses as still as a bas-relief. Someone giggled. Allen looked morose and pensive, not quite proud. My wife aimed a steady righteous ire straight into my heart, wanting me to hit him, but a fellow doesn't do this to an old friend, a fellow poet, given to mysticism and the wisdom of the body, who surely wouldn't strike back. I knew him: he would suffer my assault with the forbearance of Alyosha.

"We're going," I said, trying to make this sound masterful. It was not masterful.

Allen stood courtly at the door to bow us out. In the green plastered hall, vines of extension cords led out to the place where a light bulb had been removed and a dense nest of double-sockets had been planted. The revolution against Consolidated Edison was off to a slow start. Allen watched us down this sad corridor.

We quarreled that night, my wife and I. She hated my friends. A smell of red wine arose from her hair as her wrath mounted, and I wanted to love her, to bury my head in her red wine, to say Never mind, you're my only dearest friend; but instead I only promised never to inflict embarrassment upon her again. Another promise I didn't keep.

Nelson Algren and John Clellon Holmes, Broadway, NYC, 1963. COURTESY: JOHN CLELLON HOLMES.

CHAPTER 5

Crazy Days, Numinous Nights: 1948–1950

J
O
H
N

C
L
E
L
L
O
N

H
O
L
M
E
S

AUTHOR'S NOTE: The following journal entries, selected from hundreds of pages written during the period, are a random mosaic of life in New York in the brief period between World War II and the Korean "police-action." They are a record of one young man's transformation, at the behest of new experiences, from a cautious and politicized intellectual, whose first novel is rejected herein, to the rash and earnest writer, who is flinging down a second, *Go*, as these pages come to a close. The mood, the events, the people, and the set-of-mind that fueled the novel will be apparent here to those who pay attention. Revelry, drugs, drink, the despair out of which, alone, hope can be born (and finally, a hint of the madness that accompanies all important self-moultings) darken the lens through which I began to glimpse a way out then, a way forward.

John Clellon Holmes and Jack Kerouac, Old Saybrook, CT, November 1965.

I was 22 at the time of the first entry, and 24 when I passed through the depression dealt with in the last. I have made no changes in these fragments, and emandations of extraneous material are indicated by three dots. Capturing the deeper drift of the times, as I had lived them, was my sole criterion for the selection.

March 10, 1948
Masaryk leaps from his window in Prague and is one more casualty along the course. The reports are so conflicting one is loathe to believe anything. . . . It really does not matter much. I do not think he was murdered. I think he could not live anymore in this new, rather terrifying world which is dropping down everywhere . . . Suicide is becoming so common in our high places today that we need to understand it more, not less.

June 22, 1948
I've stumbled across the concept of the authentic. I can't define it . . .

There are people who are fine people, they are intelligent, they are sincere, they please, they don't tease. Everything about them adds up, superficially, to a gigantic plus sign, but something is missing. They are second-teamers of the spirit, they louse up the better part of the world. What is wrong? Why is this so? It's simply that they can't tell what's authentic. What is the concept of the authentic? It is this, although I can't decently explain it: It is a way of looking at things that goes to the core, that tries to get below the surface, to keep going down. A man who knows what is authentic for him, has a sense of reality that is . . . etcetera, etcetera, etcetera.

July 15, 1948
Re: Nihilism: Towards a working definition for our time . . .

July 18, 1948
Went with Christian Chapman to a penthouse flat in Tudor City and saw three of his friends. The young professional set without a profession. A "war widow" and two "jokester" friends, one of whom is sleeping with her. How I dislike the wife of the dead hero! Her foot quivers when she speaks of him. Her lover must be respectful, must wax serious and meditative; we must all heave a sigh . . . A taste of Celine or Miller or Cannastra would do them good. They would puke on the floor from seemly horror . . .

August 9, 1948
I am starting to see the situation just a little more clearly as it has reference to my work . . . It is as Auden has said: "Nothing can save us that is possible, /we who must die demand a miracle." . . . If we were told by both sides (the U.S. and the U.S.S.R.) that on Christmas Day, 1948, the world was going to burn itself to ashes . . . in other words if the global death sentence was pronounced, we would then, and perhaps only then, go about trying to find a solution. We would go on until the last minute trying to prevent the holocaust, even though we knew that it was impossible . . . The knell is sounding of the old way and now we must do things, not only because they can help, because something will come out of them, but because it is necessary for us to do them to exist . . .

September 8, 1948
The whole world is going berserk and I'm going too, just for laughs . . . I think myself into straitjackets. I wake up yowling out of my dreams. I stay up until two every night and scrape myself out of bed at seven in the morning. It's the binge of the New Age, our Brave New World . . . I don't

listen to quite so many news broadcasts anymore, and I've cut myself down to two papers. It was the least I could do to save my stomach . . . I've been listening to bebop. It's the new insane music of this world. It's like the configurations of a wild mind. It pounds on and on, mechanical, disharmonic, the abstraction of an abstraction . . . Look at the young men go off to war! Singing their songs, making their obscene jokes, laughing and uneasy in their hearts . . . Now they go off, without memories, without regrets, the boys who always turned to the sports sections of the daily papers, who went to the shows, who fucked their girls in back alleys or under the stairs in the tenements. They learned to smoke at seven, had their first woman at the whorehouse on 161st street when they were fifteen. They wandered around this city, beating up old men for a lark, writing dirty words in the subway, posting no bills. Now they are finished. Where in hell's name does it lead? . . . There are those of us who don't give a good goddamn anymore. We're sick and tired of caring about the whole rotten swill of life. The boiling cities of the earth swallow us all and masticate us with their cement jaws and spit us out when they can't digest or destroy us . . . Why shouldn't we take what we can get, possess it absolutely?

An old man wanders by, down there in the street, staggering down the pavements, his feet faltering, his face grizzled and vacant, his eyes red-limmed and staring. He goes no where and has been no place. I tell you I am obsessed with this old man. He is my spectre for today . . . Lost in the Village tonight he will be set upon by the pack of street-wolves who beat up people out of a kind of nihilistic pleasure at the sight of pain. They will bring blood to his shaggy chin that will clot and dry and turn black, they will rough him up in the darkness, stifling his cries for help, kicking him efficiently in the groin, bruising his withered body with their aggressive feet, laughing crudely and running off when the job is done, leaving him panting and ableed on the pavement, one bruise closer to his grave. He will stagger into the nearest saloon where the laconic bartender will give him a shot of rawhide whiskey on the cuff, sneering when he gulps it down with that pathetic shamelessness of the needful drunk, and then when he is finished and leans exhausted and relieved and still bleeding against the bar while the bored freeloaders and steady lushes look on, secure because of the five bucks they still possess to drink through, he will be hurled back into the street, his head thudding on the curb, his breath exhaling like the stale air from a punctured balloon. The bartender will wipe the smell of the old geezer from his hands and go back to his work

Jay Landesman and John Clellon Holmes, Kerouac Conference, Boulder, CO, July 1982. PHOTO BY ARTHUR WINFIELD KNIGHT.

again, and the old man will be left to gasp his way back to consciousness in the swill and garbage of the gutter. He will stagger to his feet, and lurch down the street in search of somewhere to lay his battered head. He will be ejected from cheap hotel after hotel, flophouses will refuse him, missions (filled with the human refuse of his kind, the drunken debris of the roaring city) will have no lice-crawling berth for him to relax in. He will near the river, the bargelights will glimmer like the lost Christmas lights of his youth and in a sudden fit of longing and despair and weariness he will slip over the parapet into the black, rushing waters that receive him without a murmur, a curse, or a cry. His life will be over; the long aching years, the constant scrounge, will be over and he will rest in the womb of the river, lulled and swung in a deeper current, his broken head resting somewhere in a watery slime, and all his dreams come true. . . . Those of us who can invent escape hatches with a manic fury.

September 9, 1948
Our life is the spaced interval between drinks, our evenings the hurried dash from ice-cooled bar to bar where the beer is cheap. The bars are filled with others like us. . . . How I could use a completely insane two weeks right now!

October 30, 1948
Kerouac was reading out of Melville, talking about America, and Stringham said that "America was sick," and, when I argued, he went on: "What do people in Berlin know about any of this? They know that nothing means anything but getting along, but being yourself. That's all there is. The rest of this is sick, that's all, neurotic. Why does it mean so much to you?" I told him that it was 'my thing', and I did not see the relevance of his remark until today (right now, seeing the movie, A *Foreign Affair*). He is, in a way, quite right, half-right anyway. It is something that is changing in the world today, this Berlin business. Our generation is the one that is growing to full maturity wanting to go to Berlin, instead of Paris; feeling the center of something is there, rather than in France. Stringham is openly fascinated by O.'s move of going to Germany to work with the army, just to be there now.

November 10, 1948
Kerouac came over last night stark raving mad with a new theory about the sexual regeneration of the world.

November 16, 1948
. . . Sometimes after hours of talk, I wish I could reach "the understanding" with people without a word and be done with it, but realize that this is impossible, and say that I shall never want it again, that to be alone, lost, ravaged by your own work is the only fully safe state. This is not objectively true either. Kerouac emerges in these journals of his that I am reading, and I can't deny him or my desire to know him better. I feel him thru them, his own pain, his great mad thoughts . . . I know these moments he has put down in his rage. I do know them! How I fought to reject them that one mad winter, our first here in New York! How I fought to give them over and be rational! Where have I come to now?

December 10, 1948
Kerouac speaks to Harrington (in a letter written and mailed from here) about "the beat generation," the "generation of furtives" . . . They are breaking the laws of this country, almost every one of them. They are drug

addicts, or they are drug peddlers. Many of them are thieves, some are murderers . . . But it is interesting to note that Huncke, a street-arab as a child, a junkie, a thief, a second-story man, a miserable derelict, listens to Ginsberg, with interest, and comprehends him in a way. Their experience is the same, they recognize the same mental reality, they have been thru it. They comprehend subtleties that are Dostoyevskian, but only because they are "underground" and know what "the man" is talking about . . . I am called out into the street to try to understand the above-mentioned things, to fit them into my patterns, to change my patterns where that is necessary.

December 15, 1948
As far as bop: I have stayed up very late with Jack, listening to Symphony Sid ("the all-night, all-frantic one"), who plays six solid hours of bop "at your request and in our groove." Even his sponsors are record shops specializing in bop, and haberdashers and clothiers who will supply you with "those real gone clothes and flipped-out getups that'll make you the hit in your gang." I'm still puzzled by it as music, although I hear plenty of fine things in Dizzy and Parker, and there is no doubt in my mind that it is an authentic response to this postwar (or is it prewar?) world.

January 4, 1949
You remember little pictures that broke through the haze and etched themselves sharply on your memory (of New Year's weekend). The tiny little-apple breasts of Gana under the cherese dress and her Georgian-piled hair and her telling you about acting in psychodramas, and finally passing out on a bed and going to fitful sleep. The horror of the Chinese girl called Elizabeth when she found that we were offering her some marijuana and not just a regular cigarette. The countless times that Neal and Luanne danced stomach to stomach, her arms flung about his neck in abandon, both eyes closed, the pelvis alone carrying the beat, the feet still. The smell of a broken benzidrine capsule as it fouls the air sweet, and the slight discoloration that comes to the lips of the addict after several hours of it; and the frantic incoherence of speech after further hours, when everything is incomprehensible and somehow profound. There was a sinister spontaneity to everything, and yet everything was tinged with a sort of preordainment. People called at the right moment, the loosest of arrangements sufficed to bring about re-meetings, plans hastily constructed seemed to work out, people spread widely over the city found one another, places constantly turned up for us to go, there was never that terrible

hesitation which breeds social disaster, no one ever asked that recurrent and destructive question: "Well, where now?"

February 24, 1949

How to explain this kind of creative fervor that I have now, that demands that I write something down at top speed that I do not even recognize, and yet will not allow me to actually get into the chapter that has to be done? My life seems to be disorganized again and I look to the end of the novel with hope and expectation. Perhaps a kind of sanity again, an end of worry for the time being, the graceful careless reading, the indolent days. But certainly an end of this particular kind of madness, like "Sweet Georgia Bop" that screams on the phonograph near my ear right now . . . I can't make any sense out of it, but for the pulse of the blood.

March 4, 1949

Projected title: FRANTIC SEMANTICS, a Lexicon of Basic Bop.

March 28, 1949

Exhaustive weekend spent, but one which succeeded in getting my mind off my pending interview with Glauber of Knopf. And that was purpose and excuse enough . . . Friday at ten-thirty, Fred and Rae called and said they wanted to have a drink with me . . . I finally just walked out when they looked the other way for a moment and raved over to the river, knowing that I was very drunk, and knowing also that I could not successfully walk this one off. I babbled miserably to myself, and finally lurched home where six-fingers-down-the-throat were necessary before I could sleep. The next morning Stringham and George Wickstrom came over, having walked across the Park . . . We went out drinking, having one at Clarke's and Glennon's, and then heading Village-wise . . . We were hungry and Stringham suggested going to Hoboken to a clam house that he knew over there . . . It was four-thirty or so and we sat and had drinks . . . The same people came and went and came back again . . . We drank beer and wine mixed, the "dialectic delight" from Paris as the stories go. George gave Marian [Holmes' first wife] and me benzidrine, and this picked us up and kept us going. We talked on and on . . . lonely off-center feeling that invades me when I go to the latrines of bars . . . the gnawing loneliness that New Jersey sends upon me . . . I listened to George analyze me and talk about "the little man" who sits on his shoulder . . . It is something that I need . . . Rest and feeling and an end of the round of drinking et al that I have been lost in lately . . . I say this so often, meaning it sincerely each time. Right now I am nowhere, although as I write, the benny-strangeness is eaten away by time and an old, recognizable warmth, my own self again, comes back and I feel some relief.

March 30, 1949
I saw Glauber for lunch and It was a painful affair for us both. They will not take my novel. He lectured me for a long while on structure and style . . . I badly need honesty from whomsoever will give it to me, I need nothing *polite* right now . . .

May 27, 1949
Marian asked me quizzically, after reading Rae's note, "Have you been thinking about your other novel?" I think even she is worried. Well, I have been thinking about it and maybe it is coming along. But I doubt my sense of sureness about it . . . If these people run through the book ranting and raving it will be better than what I have done with *Frankel* and friends . . . But do I know enough about Ginsberg to write a novel about a guy like him? I don't know. I've got to make myself mad to write this book.

June 10, 1949
The trip from Providence to Hyannis was exciting with expectation for all, and some memories for me . . . Provincetown and its obelisk tower lay at the end of the road, and it was a trim, white, evening little town with square houses and long piers . . . We found a party in progress at the cottage when we finally arrived . . . The cottage was a shambles, a dirty pot of uneaten spaghetti sitting on a butt-littered table . . .

June 14, 1949
George told me last night that he thought I got much more pleasure out of experiences that I enthusiastically anticipated remembering. *Ist possible?*

June 27, 1949
"The Game of Hearts"—Possible title for someone's life work.

July 3, 1949
. . . An Eckstine record was playing on the jukebox in the Old Colony, and everyone took this as a moment to scoff because bop is unpopular up here and everyone laughs nervously when they hear any of it. I excused myself and made for home . . . The dunes, our great salt desert wherein I constantly expect to meet John the Baptist, were hazy with heat, great shimmering headlands of sand, tufted with eel-grass, and, bearing my burden of groceries and mail, and bearing inside me an idiotic, beery joy, I

Left: John Clellon Holmes. Right: Allen Ginsberg at Kerouac's Funeral. Lowell, October 1969. PHOTO BY ANN CHARTERS.

flew over them, falling, tripping, cackling to myself. I sat down in a gulley, shoes full of sand, clothes limp with sweat, and read some of Jack's letter again, and ran the next hill, shouting: "Everything's going to work out!" Like a dervish driven mad by the sun, I made for the sea and the distance.

August 20, 1949
I have been working at night. Since the third day of August, I haven't missed a day. Wonderful feeling, complete concentration, cooler then, nothing to distract. I begin about eleven or twelve, go on sometimes until after five. I go out for coffee and long walks about three or so. I have thrown over everything else, do not read the papers, scorn Partisan and the other organs by which the self-doubting literati receive their instructions, and feel, at last, absolutely self-sufficient.

October 14, 1949
We saw Cannastra, who is back in town from being a scallop-fisherman in Provincetown. He drinks every night in the San Remo. Before he got back, the people to whom he had sublet his flat gave a party—the finale of which was a fire which ate away most of his roof. He is living under canvas now and thinking vaguely of sueing somebody. Bruce is trying to get a job teaching in a University in Baghdad, and if this succeeds Cannastra may go with him. Ginsberg said to me, when I told him this: "That's really exactly what should happen, you know. I've always thought that Cannastra should disappear into the East, like Richard Halliburton."

November 17, 1949
Ginsberg was here, arrived chastised and gravely smiling with embarrassment. Before I could say hardly a word, he announced, without bravado or as if he was bearing momentous tidings: "Oh, I'm sane. I've broken into the world of sanity!"

December 2, 1949
As I am learning more and more what I am capable of, more in some things and a lot less in others, I am correcting my reserve. The lonely, introverted, cautious boy, given to scorning what he could not have, or adoring it; the big bulging head and the anemic arteries; the forlorn kid with the harsh words and airtight definitions, facing the world that seemed to confront him with an arsenal of deadly weapons and a concept of the Enemy: all of this is drifting off somewhere. . . . That's why I'm accepting lots that I couldn't once and putting it in this book . . . I proved that I could write an intellectual novel, a book so intellectual that nothing in it lived, no guts or breath or life at all. But Christ how well I *understood* what it was all about! I'm through with all that now.

January 12, 1950
. . . We staggered into the Lyndon's car and roared uptown to Stringham's, missing trees by inches in the park, and having at a bottle of wine, two opened quarts of beer, and the remains of the whiskey. It was light and greyish when we staggered into Edward's. He was in bed, surprised to see us, perhaps a trifle angry and after a few minutes slipped away again without being noticed. Kerouac was crawling about under the rugs, Susan flopped on the bed and put on the radio. I was still going at the bottle and Jack attacked E.'s piano and was playing sloppy bop chords on it and frowning violently. When we all realized that we had driven Edward away, we somewhat sobered and the Lyndons gathered together all their stuff and

we started to leave. Jack fell backwards from the piano, knocking over a bookcase and laughing thickly, we gathered up the Lyndon's two cats (who had been staying with Edward) and started down the stairs, Jack vaulting over each bannister, and finally, on the last, falling down a whole flight of stairs. A man opened the door and sneered at us: "I want to thank all of you for giving me such a pleasant morning!" The cats escaped on 113th street, but we finally got them together and . . .

February 3, 1950
I will only know my place in this Dostoyevskian world when I hurl myself fully into it, without an escape, without a chance, making an irrevocable leap. I have had a sad, grey vision of my life in the fathomless Petersburg of my imagination, in which everyone that I have ever known lived. They were scattered in endless, tottering, labyrinthine tenements, quartered all over this thronging city. There is no rest for me but to rush from one to the other—without time for pause or reconsideration—rushing pell-mell (for my life depends on it) in search of some vague message . . . There is no time in this vision; the day, the never-ending day of my life goes on and on . . . Sometimes I think that I shall end staring at a pile of broken stones in some Middle European twilight, and there, totally alone, but not sorry, I shall know. I have felt this strongly; the concretization of a sense of doom that has possessed me, no matter how fast I have striven to outdistance it . . . a knell for all our extravaganzas . . . the death of the spirit. . . . Perhaps, it is just death itself . . . But, no, it is in America that it will be done or found or known. It will be when we are no longer on the road to it, but finally reach the Forest of Arden, which may not be gay or verdant or restful at all, but must certainly be an end . . . simply a green death perhaps . . . I am now alone, staring stunned with shock through a fabric of appearances.

March 24, 1950
It is the infinite, small cruelties of people that have suddenly been revealed to me . . . Someday I will have reached a point of perfection, or depravity, when no one will be able to make a mark on me, when I give myself to no one. . . . Yesterday on University Place, I could have pulled the city down with my frustrate hands. I could have swollen to explosion with some deeper, grimmer anger than I have ever felt before—and bewilderment and disillusionment. When will we all look up, and accept, accept! Or be alone. There is no logical reconciliation of our desires and our world. . . . Perhaps Ginsberg is right, however, that beyond our wrath

and passion there lies an eastern passivity. This has been a near-fatal week. I have killed again and again. I am blood-bespattered, with the gore of others and of myself. I am horrified by the power I sometimes feel in myself to smash everything. I am aware that I sin and deceive and lie and procrastinate . . . But even that does not matter. When will we all be desperate enough to drop the poses . . . How can others know of this, and why can't I finally accept their inability to comprehend my own ethical turmoil? This is the hardest thing of all.

March 28, 1950
To decide that one is unlovable: perhaps the most appalling discovery this year! . . . We go down in the city and drown. I think of Lucian, so rumpled and weary and set in his ways this morning. How long will this go on for him? And for the others? I do not know where to go or what to do. . . . Marian tells me that I am naive about people, some bum-fun, plaster Assisi who invites the put-down for having kissed the Leper. It's a joke, because I don't want to be a saint, only to find out how to live, as Jack writes on the first page of *On the Road* [an early version]; to find the moment when "pride shall fall". . . . *Goodness!* Not the saccharine sweet, too-rosy-to-be-real goodness of parlor Teresa's and blind priests, but something workable. I think of these kids who are today everywhere, organizing their Non-Virgin Clubs. . . . Perhaps it is some malignant fascination I have for things that are twisted, sick, malformed. . . . I'm willing to admit that I feel like a metaphysical scatologist sometimes . . . Why do I abuse myself? Why do I say that sordid, end-of-the-night things are real? Why does my heart go out to people who are everywhere alone, everywhere lost, everywhere wild? Perhaps because I seek a team to play on. I only know that I am saddened somewhere inside where only thought has gone before; and the streets dull the ache. . . .

April 3, 1950
These last weeks! Eck! I have been living at the exact geographic center of a Dostoyevskian situation, or shall I say situations . . . I have become convinced of my own fatality! I once compared myself to a contagious disease. One cannot brood infinitely on the problems of human goodness and frailty. . . . I have prayed to be left alone; one never is. I have made my bed.

April 28, 1950
I rush from place to place eagerly, meeting new hordes of people, engaging

each in feverish conversation, only to discover beneath the shiny, fetching surface, the same fears, the same insecurities, the same resolve never to show themselves or what they feel. That is why I have given my heart to our generation, because though it is black, lost, wild and headed toward the deepest corner of the night, it faces itself in a grimy mirror and laughs and laughs . . . I grew up on horror at the sight of life. . . . Now I look up and out my window, and see the same old, cruel world, driven by indifference and fear, and I say to myself: "Well, *this* is the Forest of Arden!" And it is true, this is all we have . . .

June 10, 1950
Then again I often think sadly that the drive has gone out of our madness of last year . . . Of course our obsessions are not so hollow as were those of the Magnificent Debauch of the Twenties. Our search is, I firmly believe, a spiritual one . . . Our search is for the Rose that we insist must dwell, or at least become visible, after the end of the night has been reached, and by the end of the night I now think we have meant the total breaking down of oneself, the process of *admitting!* How strange if the end should be, as in Yeats' refrain: "Daylight and a candle-end!" It has relevance.

June 13, 1950
It seems very paradoxical, but the utmost "carnality of mind" hovers on, and often becomes, the greatest "spirituality of mind". What physical love is striving for, in its intensest moments, is the sexual transformation of flesh into spirit. "The body is the socket of the soul" through which the current necessary to bring light must flow. Who said this? . . . two angels having sexual intercourse . . . It may be that homosexuals are robbed of this intensity, too many pressures of guilt and shame operate at the sublime moment for them. . . . A shudder passes through us, the profoundest shudder that man can experience. It shakes him down to the centers of his nature, it is the earthquake that unclogs, frees, opens up; and it reveals to him his being, his spirit. He finally recognizes his divine creatureliness.

July 10, 1950
My generation will be pretty well finished if the war, of which this Korean thing is the first engagement, comes off . . . For a brief period after the last war many of us became left-wing, even pseudo-communist—like me. Our youth, our passion, our outraged idealism: the sum total of lives without real hope was poured into this belief in a better life. It mortally twisted us. The lucky ones got out before they died spiritually. The Czech coup was

what finally severed me. It occurred to me then that the philosophy behind Communism was a kind of intellectual disease, the virus of which was the simple moral contradiction: *the end justifies the means.* Something ethical inside me was wounded by events. History wouldn't allow me my little dream. I ran for my life. But it had injured me. I have still not got rid of the sneaking suspicion that (modern politics) are the crowning achievement of the whole of Faustian Western Civilization, from Plato's Republic to the New Deal. But I can't see that Western Civilization can be saved by sacrificing the humanist principles upon which it was founded. Those arguments that say, "We must hit them before they hit us," or "You've got to fight fire with fire," or "The only thing to do is wipe them off the face of the earth": These arguments sound very much like the same old *realpolitik*, and I can't buy that any longer, no matter who is selling it . . . I've lost faith in politics, I don't believe that real justice can be legislated, that goodness and equity can be established merely by putting them on the statute books, and that human laws will always operate for the majority merely because you write them down . . . If I could only be a decent anti-communist, or even a decent anti-fascist, that would be something, that would be a position after all. But I find that I am only pro-life, pro-human and nothing else. . . . Can we really live without hope based on reason? I only know that somehow we must.

August 21, 1950
With Harrington and Kerouac the other night, I gave it up. They are born to misunderstand each other. Why fight that any longer? Ego drives the one, and insult the other. They fear for themselves, out of that fear they are willing to turn on each other . . . It is such sadness as this which makes me wish to make a getaway. It is brutish and hateful to stick around to witness greater confoundments, further reversals. Where will we be in ten years? Can any man truly say now: I do not hope to turn again. The times have made us turn so often before. Perhaps it is only the impossible position that can be maintained before the massing of the Enemies. That is my position, as of now at least. I will be good or die. I cannot seem to live in this century, in this terrible year, any other way. . . . But unlike Bartleby, I do not know where I am. . . .

August 27, 1950
The depression continues, softened somehow. I do not have the crises anymore . . . The worst was Friday night. It was that suddenly everything had lost *meaning*. It has never really happened to me before. Very often, I

would feel friendless, I would feel that the values I had once believed in, or values generally believed in by others, were illusory: but I would, at the same time, find myself filled with a *fervor* of disillusionment. I would be saved by a certain bitter cynicism. Friday night, however, this did not happen . . . I suddenly felt sweep through me all manner of evil, black and Raskolnikovian ideas. Murder, suicide, vandalism, lust and depravity: all this seemed equal to everything else . . . If I had perished in that minute, that would at least have been an illustration of the weight of the perception I had had. But nothing happened. That was the horror: I had to go on living in the face of this fact . . . I knew, when it had passed somewhat, that it is out of this perception of total, atomized meaningless-ness, which exhaustion, confusion or anxiety can bring one, that saintli-ness and crime are born. I was forced to accept my own perception or break everything in sight . . . I would either fill up with love and understanding, or become a thing of unreasonable rage and wrath and vengeful glee . . . It was the absence of meaning that really terrified me . . . I could not search for anything meaningful, because I seemed to have seen that *nothing* had meaning or value; that there was, in fact, no such thing as *meaning* or *value* at all. My only hope is in the second reaction to it: that admitting it all, accepting it, living on, loving all things because of their vast impersonal democracy of existence, is the way to keep from perishing in your mind, or going mad.

AUTHOR'S NOTE: the novel, *Go*, was finished a scant year after this last entry, and is tinged at its end by the dispersal of many of the people mentioned, and the knell of what we had called "a new season." My marriage to Marian was finished, too. Ginsberg was "sane" and employed, Kerouac was disconsolate over the first rejection of *On The Road*, and about to take off on another of those flights of his, which inevitably turned into searches.

The disturbed young man, self-revealed in these journals, had become a writer-of-sorts, discovering, in the toil of novelizing, the ground on which to begin a reconciliation between his world and himself, and he can testify today to the simple truth of William Carlos Williams' avowal that "the earth is black and it is there, only art advances."

CHAPTER 6

Jack Kerouac Letter to John Clellon Holmes

6100 W. Center Ave.
Denver 14, Colo.
June 24, 1949

Dear John (and Marian dear, and Ed, and George):–

Just got your vast letter and read it once over, and am starting in this reply right away out of SHEER EXUBERANCE. (Exuberance-bone, that is.) First off, I can't hide the following fact from you any longer: turns out that my big ideal Homestead idea, which wasn't a bad idea at all is collapsing around me. It seems that I had underestimated the madness of everyone. My mother is bored and wants to go to Radio City, and wants her job back in the Brooklyn shoe factory; so she wrote, and they gave her the job back, and she's leaving for New York next week to go back to work. My brother-in-law doesn't know where the good fishin' is in Colorado, so by God he's going back to North Carolina. I have spent my entire one thousand dollars in this huge madness. I am so hog-tied by all this that I am not doing anything, just sitting in the sun while my sister and brother-in-law work. I am doing a lot of writing however, and my editor Giroux is flying to Denver July 15 and most likely will have me fly back with him (or something) because he's only coming for 3 days, to stay at my house. I will have to sublease this house to some sucker, and then take it on the lam to Frisco, where Neal is hiding on Russian Hill in a queer house with crooked roofs. There, I will get a job as a fry-cook and dig some bop (there's none in Denver). After that I am going to Pharr, Texas, which is way down near Monterrey, Mexico, to see Burroughs who is there, at present, as he says, "immobilized in this valley of heat and boredom." I will set there awhile, and make runs to Monterrey. Also, I have to go to the Southern Colorado country, somewhere near Alamosa, to see Hal Chase, who got a $1000 grant from Columbia to dig. If I can, I'll go to Butte and get a job as a fry-cook or student miner, and gamble awhile (for material.) Then, in September, I'll come back to New York, where my mother will already have an apartment (through her shoe factory lady friends) and become a bloody New Yorker again. But I'm glad. It's my forest of arden, after all, right?

You remember my telling you, John, about the great classless mass of Americans who never read the papers? Here in the foothills of Colorado I have been running around with a bunch of them. One day I went riding with a group of mad middleaged women and a little boy. One woman had flaming red hair, no teeth, and rode a snow white circus horse. She says to me, "I hate these goddamn women who don't say SHIT when they have a mouthful of it." Then a cowboy who joined us in Horse Heaven hills began doing tricks on his pinto, such as standing up in the saddle. She shouted in a loud voice, "By Christ if I tried that on my stallion I'd land my ass on a rock!" There were tourists, women and children, gaping at us. "The dumb sonofabitch ain't got no more sense than a mule. He'd soon SHIT in my face as look at me!" This went on all day. We made plans to go riding to Arizona this summer, although I haven't seen her but once since, and she didn't really recognize me. I saw her this second time at a Tex Ritter movie. It seems there's a huge class of Western madpeople out here who go to Class C Westerns just to hear Tex Ritter and Roy Rogers sing "Twilight on the Prairie" and to watch the horses and the gunplay. In

Jack Kerouac, 1942.

their conversation they continually made allusions to "Roy" and "Dale Evans" (his leading lady) and "Trigger" (his horse) just as we make allusions to Dostoevsky and Whittaker Chambers. They sit there and watch the Myth of the Gray West, on rainy days in Larimer street movies. Drunken cowboys snore in the balcony; little kids titter and throw popcorn. Everybody believes in Roy Rogers and Gene Autry. It's very beautiful. Then I start thinking about the mad beret-characters who actually make these movies in crazy California (the tea-head Mitchums, the horn-rimmed directors, the bag-eyed leading ladies who lead dissolute lives in motels, the seedy beat-up companions with their mad Neal stand-ins who leap from horses to railroad cabooses)—it's crazy. I have come to believe now that life is not *essentially* but *completely* irrational. I should like anybody to challenge this CLEAR idea. I have seen proof of

Jack Kerouac, Old Saybrook, CT, November 1965. COURTESY: JOHN CLELLON HOLMES.

this. Ginsberg is right: everything is a big balloon. Some of us take ourselves too seriously. It's all very beautiful because it isn't moribund, this "irrationality" I speak of. They are, for instance, holding a Goethe Festival in the mountains this summer. Think of grave, foolish Goethe; and this foolish, serious-titmouse festival, and all the incoherencies that will ensue. It reminds me of what I heard once about Carl Sandburg, that he appeared at a wartime dinner of some kind, and made a speech which no one understood or listened to, and looked sad while everybody ate and chatted through his speech, and finally giggled. (I think.) I may not have the story straight. Or the time that Thomas Mann took Allen Temko by the shoulder (this insane character who thinks life is a Hemingway dialog and is indeed a very funny guy)—took him by the shoulder, and turns out Mann's only a little guy, and a little cross-eyed I understand, and says, "In youth lies the future." Do you mean to tell me he was serious? or that he believed such guff?

Everybody's hiding something.

That's what I'm after.

Consider this for irrationality which reached a point of mystery:— One night I went to an amusement park with a widow and her 14-year-old boy. This mad widow likes me, for some reason. Coming back from the park with the boy (she had left), hitchhiking in the black Colorado night, a man gave us a ride in his little truck. He had his whole family with him. The boy and I sat in the back with one of the man's little boys. The little boy was wrapped in a blanket, although it was not cold. Just then a car came out of the dark, with no headlights, and came straight for us; just missed, swerving, and disappearing in the dark, no lights. No sound, nothing! The two boys with me giggled. They thought it was funny. At that moment I looked at them and they were both wrapped in the blanket, as in a shroud, and I yelled: "What the hell is this, a foreign country?" Turns out, all of life is a foreign country. This incident I have just described is one of the great mysteries of my life. Nobody can help me to figure it out. I just couldn't understand what was going on. Can you? The dark car, the soundlessness, the incomprehensible family in the truck, the night, the blanket-shroud . . . just like I say: America is an Egyptian land.

Many things like that have been happening. I walk along the country roads and all these incomprehensible people—these members of the vast incoherent American Fellaheen population—give me rides in their rattling trucks and almost break my neck. Fellaheen people never fear to die. I begin to learn all this. When they talk it is impossible to understand what they're saying. When you say to them, "What did you say?" they reply: "I dunno." Meanwhile, along they fly, jumping and bumping through the mysterious night. It's just like Dagwood Bumpstead, great hordes of strange little children appear out of nowhere, and walk with you.

I rode in a rodeo. We ran around like an Indian attack, in a wild circle. I went to the movies of this rodeo to see myself ride. There I sit, in a big sombrero, like a imposter Hipster smoking a weed. Honest. All hunched over the saddle, leering at the air. There's a closeup shot of me drinking from a beer bottle in the saddle. It's ridiculous. I have been hunched over my typewriter since I was eleven, that's what it is. I don't

Caroline Kerouac and Jack Kerouac, Lowell, MA, Circa 1940-41.

Jack Kerouac, September 1951. COURTESY: ED CUFFE COLLECTION.

think I'll be a rancher. I'll live on a barge in the Hudson River, right by the Fulton Fish Market, and play my chromatic harmonica which I will soon buy in a Larimer street pawn shop.

Sometimes I go out in the alfalfa field and sleep. I take walks with my dog and throw him in the irrigation ditch just for kicks. I buy eggs at a farm for 24¢ a dozen, and heavy cream. There are sunflowers and prairie-snowballs and long green fields, and snow mountains: as I said to somebody, "I am Rubens and this is my Netherlands." I've been drawing pictures of the scene. I hitchhike to Denver and lurk on Curtis street, in the poolhalls and the 10¢ movies, and drink huge beers in Larimer street saloons. I go riding around at night with Justin W. Brierly, the great figure of Denver who runs the Central City opera. He has a great car, with a spotlight. He's straight out of Sinclair Lewis. He's an English Lord but prefers teaching in Denver High School, running a law practice, running the mountain opera, a real estate business, and being godfather to all the "talented" Denver boys like White and Chase and Jeffries and once upon a time, Neal. I went to the high school and saw him in a class, telling his 14-year-old pupils they could play hookey if they wanted, he didn't care. All these little boys admire him. He winks at me. Ginsberg calls him Dancingmaster Death. He once sent Neal to high school but Neal finally stole a car and rushed off. He has a picture of Neal at the age of 16, a huge portrait. This guy is a big Andre Gide, you see; a Denver Edouard . . . Uncle Edouard of Counterfeiters. He is going to take Giroux and I to the opera, free. One night he drove me around Denver (the first night, in fact) and he had one of his bright boys with him, and spotted the damn spotlight

Jack Kerouac and fans, Northport, Long Island shortly after publication of "On the Road." COURTESY: ED CUFFE COLLECTION.

of his into people's windows to explain the Denver interior decorating trend. "Provincial," his bright boy sneers. They show me castles in the night, bought by fabulous mining barons; explain everything to me. I prefer talking about Neal and the others. I told them (in Lucien's words) that I was not a big writer, just "The Queen of the May," and they thought I was indelicate. I have to make my choice between them and the Rattling Trucks, and I chose the Rattling Trucks, where I don't have to explain anything, and where nothing is explained, only real. REAL REAL, see? Shee?

I haven't had a cent in my pocket. Maybe Giroux will soon give me an advance on "On the Road," which is become a novel by now. In any case, enough about all this, and on to other matters.

But first let's consider this matter of "unseriousness" finally. It's not a lack of respect that makes for this—as in the cases of Rabelais, Swift, Celine, et al. Like Eliot said, rhetoric is allowable in a drama only when the speaker of the rhetoric is "aware of his dramatic position." Then, it is not *all* comedy, but part tragic—like a Polonius speech. It seems that a soliloquy is also a kind of "awareness of drama," as if one addressed the immortal Auditor, who is Beelzebub, and Beelzebub is But the Lamb. But nothing is more absurd (and many other things) than a serious speech addressed to a serious audience . . . or even, perhaps, to a single serious human auditor.

Hal Chase, for instance, told me seriously the other day that he was going to climb a mountain. From the back porch of my house, eleven miles away, I can see the big red rocks, just over the washline. Turns out this is the "mountain" he climbed—and got fagged out doing it to boot. There's something so pathetically tiny about those rocks, and so back-yardish, and so near to my garbage pail, it just tickled and amazed me when I discovered his mountain after all. How can I take such a thing seriously?

Perhaps the greatest thing I ever learned was from my Lowell boyhood buddy George Apostolos. George was the funniest guy in the world, and still is, I think. I mean, I really *learned* things from him—style, tone, the way to look at things. He himself is just a dumb Greek, you see. We had a pal called Iddyboy . . . a huge moronic French-Canadian built like a bull, who [had] the kill-instinct in him. George had practically hypnotized him, and sometimes would go into a wild witch-doctor dance to get Iddyboy excited, and then turn him on me. (When George had a bone to pick.) I would have to defend my life with this bull. . . . he would froth at the mouth in direct ration to George's white eyeball-poppings. (never mind, never mind, the words.) So one time George and I promoted a six-fight boxing card in the yard of a parochial school. Iddyboy was in the main bout. Geo. and I went through many crazy preparations to be his "seconds" in the ring, that is, we got striped polo-shirts, cigars, derby hats, pails, sponges, blackjacks, everything to look the part as we had seen it in B-movie boxing pictures. We were going to really give him the works in his corner; splash water, puff on cigars, jam the mouthpiece in his teeth, swagger, lurk, dart in and out of the ropes, count money. George (to show you his utter and complete wonderful madness) was even going to imitate the sound of the warning buzzer ten minutes before the round. You've heard those on the radio. "Ba-a-a-a-a-!" Only George used to make this buzzer-sound last twenty seconds. "Ba-a-a-a-a-a-a-a-a-a-a-a-a-a-a-a-a-a-a-a-a-a-a-a-a-a-!" even until the round started.

Iddyboy knocked out his adversary in .21 seconds of the first round and there we were, no chance to perform before a screaming mass of children. I remember this with amazement. Why did we want to do this? What is meant by "B-a-a-a-a-a-a-a-a-a-a-a-a-a-a-a-a-a-a-a-a-a-a-a-a-a-a-a-a-a-a-a-a-a-a-a-a-a!?" What is Rabelais talking about in his Crazy-Book? And the Decameron? What got into Celine when he wrote the first chapter of "Installment" which ends with him lifting his mother's skirts and roaring with rage? What is Shakespeare talking about when he has those mad servants singing crazy little jingles? Or Lear's fool?

You shee, there's something to it.

All my serious passages in "On the Road" (and in Town & City), as I re-examine them, turn out to have this crazy "Ba-a-a-a-a-a-" sound—I noticed this very strongly last winter, even in my "Rain" chapter which has a funny sound, as if saying, "Oh mother I can't dance" or more accurate: "And this, and that, and this, and that, and all that shit, you see." But with an undercurrent of truth, in that, after all, it's all true anyway, and the main thing is that I took the trouble to say it all, "and this, and that, and all that shit, and even this, and that, you see how it is?"

It's like Neal says—"Ah yes, ah yes." Only, Neal's sound is lazy, "Ah yes, ah yes, I can't dance," and that's why he'll never write. Now Harrington has this awful Ba-a-a-a-a as much as anybody, if not more. And I'd give my left tit to know what's really going on behind his sound. Because we all know something and don't admit, and that's why we keep on living and don't die of boredom.

This sound-business is not exactly Ginsberg's, because what he wants to find out is something else, not funny at all. But we won't discuss this now. Just remember that Ginsberg is always posing . . . ALWAYS, even with me, and what he really thinks he never even manages to show by making noises. The only way to know Ginsberg is to drill a hole in his head and crawl in, and catch him when he's sleeping . . . then, as he himself says, you can have "a long serious conversation in the same head." And then you wouldn't [have] any "serious hidden invocations," as he says he needs to put in his poetry. Why should they be hidden? What's so serious about them? Death is about the only serious thing, because it puts an end to all the unseriousness anyhow, and it's too late to laugh, though not always; and in any case, all I mean to say is that the dividing line between

Jack Kerouac and Joe Sarota, Fall 1938.

Jack Kerouac and Elaine Markson, NYC, Circa 1962-63. PHOTO BY DAVID MARKSON.

seriousness and unseriousness is almost unknown, and is where our best knowledges take flower.

Et cetera. Your request for objective information on Allen is really a big order. You ought to just invent them out of your own larger naturalistic fund of information than he has. In any case I may see you soon—if I go back with Giroux, I'll definitely go to Provincetown, and I can answer your questions one by one. If in the Fall, and if that is too late, let me know in your next letter and I'll prepare a special brief on A.G. The only trouble is that if I ever prepared such a brief, I would immediately want to use it myself, as I always come up with such Golden Bones. One thing I have is several score letters from him full of information at various points in his life.

I've been thinking about you and have come to a pass where I feel qualified to suggest that, among other things, you should write immense novels about everybody, using the New York scene and the New York types (that is, us.) But on a more social plane. Do you think you can write accurately about a madman like Allen? I should like to see you invent a potpourri out of Anson, Cannastra, Allen G., Durgin, the people who come to your parties, the San Remo, the bars, the mad parties, big swirling vortexes like The Possessed, not concentrating too much on one individual, but painting a large impassioned portrait like Dickens, only about the crazy generation. Because this is the Crazy Gen. If you do write the Allen novel . . . revelation is revolution . . . be sure to introduce everything else you can think of. This I believe to be your special genius: to see everybody as a whole. That's why you listen to everybody at parties. What Allen does at parties is wink at everybody. He's up to something else. But you're concerned with the Canvas of it. Now if you really think I ought to send you objective information on Allen, tell me outright. What can I say? Born in Paterson in 1926; his mother was a Communist who went mad; spent childhood at crazy Communist picnics upstate; his father a school-teacher. Saw green faces in his window at night. His bucolic life consisted of one little arbor near the Paterson Gas Works where he hid every afternoon, trembling. Burroughs is his Father. Neal is his God-Bone. Lucien is his Angel. He goes around looking for confirmation of his coy loneliness, as we all do. He is justifying his mother by playing madman. His father represents hateful sanity. In one of his visions he heard a great machine descending from the sky. And all that. It can be invented. The thing you've got to worry about is, i.e., why do I, John Holmes, do this?—what do I mean by saying these things? Do you understand what I intend to mean? you shee.

Oh balls. I'm a bigger bullshitter than any of them.

What's this about you people running around naked? Believe me, if and when I go there, I won't make no dangling cock of myself, I've got a bathing-suit. Those things are reserved for certain state occasions and are not to be aired abroad like flags—unless you want to try to screw the cosmos, which I have found to be too large an order. The state of nudity is no longer nudity when you do it on purpose; and when you have clothes around. I find it as dull as charades, and mainly embarrassing because of a general consciousness of the fact that you *mustn't* be embarrassed. Pfui! I frankly am embarrassed by those things . . . (what things?) The best nudity of all, on a beach and all that, is a couple—but no more; the rest is

Jack Kerouac and Jerry Newman, NYC, Circa 1962-63. PHOTO BY DAVID MARKSON.

show. On account of these sage remarks of mine, I hope you will be wreath'd in pelvic garlands when I get there, and that includes your shameless wife Marian. Tsk! tsk! You *mad, Pagan* fools! I am struck dumb! I'm appalled, I'm become pale, precisely.

So my itinerary is: get things done with Giroux, sublease the house, travel, and get back to New York in September and write on the road this Fall and Winter (the rest of it), and collect my royalties in April, and go to Paris in ze spwing. In Paris I'll write Doctor Sax, which is going to be my Ulysses, my Pierre of the Ambiguities, my indulgence in mystery and poetry.

Here are some stanzas I'm sending Allen for our poem . . . the "pull-my-daisy, tip-my-cup" one:

"Be my fowler,
    bird I'll be:
    pry the air for me.

Kiss my eyes.
    Make me May,
    make my bones
    be golden

Close my flaps,
    rack my lacks,
    make me wreath'd
    and viney.

I'm a hawk—
    Oh my hood!
    my claws are only
    water.

Just a rose,
    just a lamb,
    just a rosey
    lambey.

Crack my brains,
    melt my bones,
    make my flesh a
    flower.

Make the night
    my red dragon,
    make it follow me

Pull my daisy, tip my cup, all my doors are open. He-he!

* *

I've been writing extensively to Harrington, and will see him also before I go back to N.Y. He's sending me some chapters here which I will show to Giroux, who will like them. If Tommy visits you make him write to me. Anything else? Okay, I hang up. Write me another long letter, John,—See you this September. If I overlooked anything in this letter I'll catch up to it next time. Have a drunk on me.

Take it easy George,—
hello Ed!—
see you soon.

Jack
(was only kidding,
Marian, about your
nudity

CHAPTER 7

Jack Kerouac Letter to Allen Ginsberg

about May 1954

Dear Allen [Ginsberg],

Starting last Friday afternoon drunk on wine, and ending this morning sober, with bat in between in town seeing Kingsland, Anson, Holmes, Cru and Helen Parker, here's a big semi-silly letter; reason I wont throw away silly parts is because they may amuse you and you would be amused instead of not amused. They were written drunk, are gossippy, but maybe funny; first 4 pages.

Your letter was happily received, as I thought something had gone wrong and you wouldnt write me big letters any more. I felt a warm glow of pride and happiness reading it, that you should write it to me.

And I wanted to tell you many gentle and brotherly things.

I recently had an affair with a junkey girl call'd Mary Ackerman that you may know of, friend of Iris Brody's, saw me and Kells in his yellow jeepster in Cuernevacas in 1952; knows everybody, but is so hot and so Camille like suicidal and crazy I cant follow her around; she just went to hospital for an overdose, for instance. And it's too late anyway for me to love, to love love, that is, or love women, I mean, I mean sex and involvement and commonlaw marriage like, or i'm talking thru my hat. I saw yr big letter to Kingsland.

I see Chester Kallman all the time now, and his Pete. I've been getting sillydrunk again lately in Remo and disgusting myself a la Subterraneans. I want to live a quiet life but I am so weak for booze. I am very unhappy and have nightmares; when drinking; after a week of abstinence, i am happier than ever before in life, but slowly become bored and wonderin what to do now; am writing two big books only because have nothing else to do and it would be a shame to waste all that experience in "talent"—as Carolyn says—and generally speaking, I have crossed the ocean of suffering and found the path at last. And am quite surprised that you, innocent, novice-like did enter the first inner chamber of Buddha's temple in a dream;;; you're going to be saved—There would be rejoicing and hossanahs in heaven if anything once in heaven WERE a thing, or could rejoice, where rejoicing is a naught—heaven is nothing—

let me see you conceive of nothing while you live. and I give you heaven

Silly begins here:—

WALTER ADAMS I aint seen

DIANA HANSEN CASSADY I seen, on the street, she showed me pictures of Curt and she said she got big letters about Edgar Cayce, is this giving something away? but she cant find the books he alludes to and anyway she doesnt care and she stood on the sidewalk goofing but I was late and she was the same.

JOSE GARCIA VILLA was on the village sidewalk and as Lucien and I strolled along he came up, sad, Phillipino, and we talked, and he said "How are you "Lucien?" and then he gave us address of his new magazine. . . . but I didnt send him any pomes.

> Little anger Japan
> Strides holding bombs
> To blow the West

To Fuyukama's
Shrouded Mountain Top
So the Lotus Bubble
Blossoms in Buddha's
Temple Dharma Eye
May unfold from
      Pacific Center
Inward Out and Over
The Essence Center World.

This is from my new book of poems *San Francisco Blues* that I wrote when I left Neal's in March and went to live in the Cameo Hotel on Third Street Frisco Skidrow—wrote it in a rockingchair at the window, looking down on winos and bebop winos and whores and Cop cars—and I quote it to draw your attention to the fact, we have consistently been clairvoyant of each other's minds for years now, this poem has "bubble" in it which you used with Buddha in your letter (tho you deleted it for "balloon")—and it hints of the temple, the inner chamber, of the Mongolia wall, of which, incidentally, I too have a dream, in *Book Of Dreams* (which I'm now finishing the typing of)—

the dream, is, "Dreamed of being in some kind of hardship pilgrimage with a man and woman in some Mongolian harshland and when we got to the Fellaheen town of the rippling-tree which had a gray cement factory color and dismalness I said "However in your town here I could pose as a prisoner of yours, in fact, in reality, I am your prisoner, according to the facts,"—"Yes, that's a fact," they said much and innocently pleased, especially the woman—they might have been Mongolian—I walked on the sidewalk ground carrying my rifle stock down as befitting a prisoner and they rode the point of our vehicular or animal travel-gimmick that had carted us across the Siberian wastes—I secretly mistrusted their joy, we had started on some Jesus pilgrimage by the wall, now they were letting their thoughts be affected by matters of war (there's a war), —but I trusted them finally."

A thousand other examples of our clairvoyance oneness later.

LUCIEN I saw, as I say, went to his house one Sunday afternoon, bringing a pint of whiskey cause I owed him 3 bucks from another night, and tho Cessa was like displeased, I insisted we mix it all up with ice in a bottle to take to the park with us, where she wanted to sun child, so on the park Lou and I are belting from this magnificent huge cocktail and here comes HELEN PARKER and BRUCE AND TOMMY and sits with us, and then I got to go for a leak in Washington Park toilet so I walk with Tommy across, and we pass STANLEY GOULD who says, "Who is that, Tommy Parker?" and here comes GREGORY CORSO with black skin tan of Scandanavian ships and cut his hair off in crew cut and looks like great beachcomber poet and he takes my Buddha book and reads one line coldly, but then says, "I know it's great, you cant lend it to me can you?"—"No, I gotta have it by my side all the time."—"I know," he says, and we talk about you, and he says "When Allen gets back I wont pay no attention to him, fuck him"—I say, "Why do you talk like that about Allen, whatsamatter with you and Allen"—"Fuck him" he says, like agonized over something. . . . I warn Mary Ackerman not to hate Gregory, like she wants to do, I tell her, "He's no different than you, all is the same essence." and over comes hepcat to talk to us.

I was at HELEN PARKER'S and had a ball and then ALLEN ANSON came with WILLIAM GADDIS and I didnt like Gaddis cause it seemed to me he was making Anson unhappy . . . I put my hand on A's head and rubbed his head and he went off with Gaddis and came back again to me'n Helen and we got drunk in the night and danced the mambo. . . . sweet Helen in the morning put on her easter bonnet and went to work down the streets of Village—good brave gal—Finally got rid of JACK ELIOT the singin cowboy who apparently was costing her a lot of money but poor Jack, he cant work, he's like the robin, he sings . . .

So I walk down the streets of the village with JACK ELIOT and we just been bangin two colored sisters all night, and he's playin the Memphis Special, and other songs, and we run into BILLY a great 5 string banjo genius from N'Awrleans, and bang? BILL FOX drives by and I stop him by yelling at his car, and he comes out, and I say, "Bill, give these boys an audition for Esoteric" and we have a songfest and a hundred and two school children gather around to listen and up comes an old frisco wino with his bottle and broken pulpy nose and he likes Jack Eliot's singin so much he says, reachin in his shirt, "By god, boy, i'm gonna give you my lass sandwich."—"I'm from Oklahoma meself"—and the sun goes down —and I have a pimple on my nose—

Mardou Fox calls me on the phone, it seems she's now a hardworkin waitress at Rikers restaurant on Columbia campus at 115 and broadway, so I go to her house, bringing ms. of subterraneans, as promised, and I tell her i still love her and we hold hands goin down the street, cause you know, boy, i love all women . . . but instead of being big swain I get drunk with JORGE D AVILA Ed White's boy and his great buddy from Porto Rico HERNANDO, who is the very firstperson I have met in this world who has completely and instantly understood the words of Buddha. . . . a great cat, you meet later, architect, so far. . . . You see Allen all there is to Buddha, is this,—All life is a dream—but later, I'll explain later. . . . it isnt AS IF it was a dream, it IS a dream . . . see? So I get drunk with the boys in the west end and JOHNNY THE BARTENDER is still asking for his copy of the town and the city, and at midnight I take a peek in Rikers, and there's Mardou rushing around on little twinkling legs with her arms sawing along her thighs, real intent on being "Sane" and just madder than ever if you asks me. . . . all this tainting and defiling these lesbian psychologists are putting down on these poor innocent avant guarde negresses, really my dear, the things I could tell that little cunt and wont.

JOHN HOLMES, I rush up to his place at 123 Lexington and ring the doorbell and he's laboring up the stairs with a bagful of gin, and we go in, there's Shirley, we get drunk, I rush out and fetch Mary, she jolts, we go back, we play old Billies, old Lesters, it goes on, we pass out, next day when Shirley goes to work me and mary and John go to a 3rd avenue bar and drink and talk all that day and I say to John Brothers Forever, and mean it.—Shirley comes home at night, sees three drunk lushes bums in her room, sighs, leans against door just like Marian, and it's the same thing again as Marian, and John "writes" during the day, and they havent published go in pocket books, for some reason, and he's "broke"—he says, "In 1952 I had a lot of money but now. . . . " and he is sad. and for money I guess, but we talked, and made up okay, and of course he asked about you with concern & intelligence. But he is suspicious of the reason for my visits—so I'll leave him alone.

JETHRO ROBINSON I havent seen.

HENRI CRU is back, has a pad on west 13th street and Mary stayed there awhile and regularly on Saturday afternoons he goes out looking for stray furniture in the streets and lays $50 bills on bookies in front of Remo (keeps losing on Correlation) and on Saturday nights has barrels of beer and Mucho Coukamongas, Kerouac, dont you DARE bring any males to my party, you know I'm not fruit dont you, I want you to bring every last couckamongo you can find to my beer party but god help you if laike the last time you bring these fruits (i had brought Pete Butorac and Chester Kallman, at 4)—Kerouac, I'm going to have to REPRIMAND you, do you hear me, I'm going to have to etc. 'n Mary was taking nude baths in front of him, and he does an imitation of it, and he keeps drinking beer in giant glasses a foot tall and has cases of it around and is constantly eating and fat and when he has his blessed couckamongos at night he never touches them and when presented with the opportunity as Mary and I done, when we turned on 2 mexican 16 year old sisters in the dark room, he blushes and makes jokes, poor old lost Henri

SEYMOUR I done heard about, from SAM KAINER, I was over to Mark Van Doren's house to pick up Doctor Sax where I'd left it, with his son CHARLES, Mark wasnt there and had already written me a note saying that Sax was "monotonous and probably without meaning in the end," saying, at first, "quite a work but I dont know where to place it," whereby I realized he is really nowhere, face it, but Charles was friendly, he is having a novel published by Giroux soon (my dear) and he had his sweetheart with him VARDA KARNEY who is all gushing and fascinated in my Talk about Buddha and wants to know how to practice dhyana and Samadhi and Samapatti and in comes a gang of young kids, and Sam Kainer, I say "Sam Kainer, where'd I hear that name?" and of course!! it's the cat who lived in Seymour's pad in St. John's wood all this time, blasting with him, conducting bop session, he wears a goatee and is very cool and Phillip Lamantia like and hep—and says Seymour for awhile was Ted Heath's band manager, Ted Heath big band like Woody Herman in England

JERRY NEWMAN I went to Sayville with him and we cultivated his vast crop of couckamonga green and corn, and I went with him to antique shops where he got lamps for his huge new CBS style by-his-father-billfooted studio which is the most beautiful, vast thing you've ever seen with soundproof walls so we could have screaming agonized orgies in there and nobody'd ever know (right around the corner from Holmes) and where he is makin big records and big money now—and says he will have big sessions with Brue Moore and Allen Eager and Al Haig

BRUE MOORE I finally met, with Gould my Buddy, and Brue says he's from Indianola, Mississippi, not far from Greenville, on River, and says "Lets you and me drink wine, you think I drink whiskey, you ought to see me drink wine, we'll go down to the Bowery and light a fire in the alley and drink wine, and I'll play my horn"—with Gould, we'll do this, in October. Be sure to be with us, Melville. I'm in Love With You Always.

NOW LISTEN ALLEN, do NOT FAIL to look up, if possible, Al Sublette, at the Bell Hotel at 39 Columbus St. Frisco, with, or without Neal, so Al can take you around the Great Frisco and show you, remember and dont fail . . . he's a great boy, and sell me to him, please, he mad at ma, at me—big mad good boy and maybe the first hep Negro writer in America maybe, if he digs—Not that he's avant guarde, he's, understand, a straight simple hepcat with a GIANT FLAIR FOR WORDS, a wordslingin fool, dont know it, a real POET in the sense in which it was known in Elizabeth's time, and, not surprisingly, a wino, and jolts too. I just could write epics about his vision of america,'s, what I mean, Al.

PHILLIP LAMANTIA, Ed Roberts, Leonard Hall, Chris Mc-Claine, Rexroth, look them up while you're in Frisco. Its your big chance to dig the Berkeley axis,—Is Saint there?. . . . Jaime de Angulo's house . . . big peotl heroes like Wig Walters obtain from there; dig Wig if you can, the "Cash" of Bill's JUNKIE novel.

Batteries of ad men
Marching arm in arm
Thru the pages
To Time & Life
And M C A

Rhetorical Third street
Grasping at racket
Groans and stinky
I've no time
To dally hassel
In your heart's house,
It's too gray
I'm too cold—
I wanta go to Golden,
That's my home.

Okay.
There'll be an answer
Forthcoming
When the morning wind
Ceases shaking
The man's collar
When there's no starch in't
And Acme Beer

Runs flowing
Into dry gray hats.
When
Dearie
The pennies in the
palm multiply
as you watch

Van Doren. . . . I had these San Francisco Blues poems tacked on to the ass of Doctor Sax, and in his note he only alluded to the dulness of SAX and never mentioned the poems at all, I suppose he either dint see them, or read them, or thinks they're not poetry. Ring or iron indeed. There's a hole I found in the master. He aint even there. I dont have to whittle sticks with Yeats, Frost and William Carlos Williams and in the same wood, to know that Mark Van Doren is a pretentious little pugnose dutchman anxious to envy whitman.

t'envy melville.
Fuck these little editors
of America.
these pissyass misinformed minimizers
—

Tragic burpers
With scars of snow
Bound bigly
Huge to find it
To the train
Of time & pain
Waiting at the termin-nell
MONDAY MORNING (AFTER BIG USELESS BINGE)
Your dream of the Cross is a Great Dream of the Europe in you . . . you must go to Europe fairly soon, before communism makes it impossible for Americans to get in. Bob Lax, the Catholic poet, editor, roving reporter, buddy of Bob Burford and Bev, has written me a strange little postcard from Paris. He was in New York last month and I met him three times, we talked about religion. He is good saint. You remember him, the friend of Giroux and Merton, in their class in '37 or '36. He is inviting me implicitly to go stay at a monastery 30 miles north of Paris, call'd L'Eau Vive, on Soissy sur Seine. So if i ever go to paris i go there. it

is financed by rich jews. very likely you could go too. it is not a monastery but a retreat for international religionists, like hindus go there too and oxford educated burmese mystic and americans of all kinds and priests wandering the roads of your europe, which i hope to see with you when i go myself.

let me discourse on your cross. In the firstplace, what a malady for you to assume that there is any such thing in this emanated-from-ignorance world, as anybody's "desire" and that it could or should be emobided in a symbol or cross. beastly wrath sits at the base in the form of that 13th century tho strangely leering dragon with his pterodactyl leftover ooze wings . . . at the heart of the world is the reptile, where is this big desire of yours and why shouldnt the god malevolently egg you on and leer at your templar armors? I had a dream too about the cross, god it would kill you. . . . a picture depicting Christ Crucified tearing and straining off the Cross but nailed tight so in a gigantic agony pose hanging golden and mustached from the wall of a Cathedral and the reason the picture is so "valuable to Ginsberg" is we see his large penis balling up in a loincloth and as viewed from below very erotic . . . the picture is captioned "By Elmont High School gang 19 . . . , and is marked J. Kerouac under to show who drew it, a great thing which I leave in Gene Pippin's apartment in the Caribbean (or Charley Peters', one) for the occupant's edification of concern showing spirituality of his rapacious-seeming visitors, you, me and Lou, who've just rummaged thru all his junk and pants and books and paper clips while he's out. . . . .) . . .

Your cross, your darkness around it, the golgotha gloom, wom, that marvelous ancenstral palace, the classic knight. Voltaire's interpretation . . . how can there be "eternal" desire anyhow, in buddhism your taught at once not to make any such arbitrary dualistic distinctions, such as that of eternity or non-eternity. . . . You were not even born, you dont even exist now, you wont even die, but a figment in a dream, as all things. . . . why do you persist in calling this a balloon, that is, a hot air in a bubble, the world is of course a bubble, balloon anyhow, but why do you make fun of my final emancipation from bondage to ignorance in this world? assuredly your cross and your knight is rich, like certain medieval paintings, but wealth of drapes and dark lap colors and rembrandt splendor cant make up (wealth of detail, les meubles) cant make up for simple line of clarity as elicited by a near-naked indian whose Crown of Glory far exceeds messianic hungup maniacs of Rameh, whose main ambition is always political and terrestrial otherwise there be no reason for multitudes and pharisses to give them political crucifixion——jesus got in everybody's hair, face it——Edgar Cayce is nothing but a jesus christ hillbilly who pretended to be ignorant of medicine, pretended to go into trances, was just apparently an extremely intuitional and classic physician who had a mystic streak and wanted to prophet-ize and so cooked up this bed-trance medicine. . . . it's as if you should say to me, Blueblue of Township Maine has phlebitis, what should we do O Guru, and I close my eyes and loosen my tie, and I say "Give him trypsin, it's the latest thing. I see him even now going down the riverbank for a piss, he was reborn years ago as an Atlanticean posturizer making milk bags for the lion ladies who came partying down his alley night and day looking for the roman cross that never was so agammemenon could wait at his ladies bone, still the rameh dkdout tcould fland." thank you, O gury. . . . Simon Magus,——Why do you ascribe to yourself "a fatal messianic role" when in actuality you can be, are, just a sweet kind mendicant, compassion sits at the center of the world, fatality is a dream. Curiously your 4-point Credo is like the Four Truths of Buddha . . . Love is the weight of the world is correct throughout. After that, following an apparent jewel-sleep-of-wisdom revelation, you tried to terrestrialize, advatage-ize, for your clinging earth-sake, the rest of it. I mean by earth-sake, that in you that is attached to Gain, of any kind, when all you do is love and lose . . . I like what bill says about human hieroglyphs of suffering, it is very close to Buddha, Lucien is in accord with what Bill said, in slightly different way..

I accused lucien of being proud of suffering, which, incidentally, is what Neal is, because the only thing, only reason why I couldnt make any impression on his intelligence with the doctrines of the east, was because he being a life-proud american like bill and lou, wouldnt accept the No. 1 truth of Buddha, the first of the 4 great truths, all life is sorrowful. . . . thinking that misery is grand, rupture's their rapture. . . . life is suffering, this youve got to understand, if you think it is anything but suffering you have lost completely the significance of even the need for emancipation. . . . First there is discrimination, then discrimination of form, then desire for the form, then grasping and acting at the desire, then the resultant decrepitude, decay and death. . . . You know as well as I do if you keep awake in this earth with a radiant mind, you can go beyond life and death, since all's in the mind. . . . . going beyond death you go beyond birth and any rebirth—going beyond these you go beyond manic manifested forms into the imagelessness of the golden and the silent the dharmakaya (The Truth Body).

But let me, say, "ah, lets wait till I see you, it's too long, too stupid in letters, and argument is not the soul of it, silence and example shall show you."

And of course, for your beginning studies of Buddhism, you must listen to me carefully and implicityly as tho I was Einstein teaching you relativity or Eliot teaching the Formulas of Objective Correlation on a blackboard in Princeton.

Here, first, is the correct bibliography. Do NOT read Bhagavad-Gita, it is a barbaric document of the early Hindu timeless ages, of whom Spengler said, "Compared to Buddha and his intellectual world-weary Rome-like disgust with Sorrow, the Bhagavad-Gita is the pulse of the blood of India" etc. etc. and so on with your Faustian bloodbeater and his multifold endless attachment to the millions of useless meaningless little details of what he calls world history. . . . why all this furniture, as Howard Mumford Jones would say?

The Gita opens, for instance, with someone recommending war and murder because "Nothing matters." In Buddha, because nothing matters, do nothing then. Same in Tao. Spengler in his comfortable man-of-letters study on a gray exciting German morn says this is the difference between Syncretism (late civilized disgust) and its opposite the Culture fury. If you see a half-dead worm being devoured by a thousand ants, what shall you do? Do nothing. You deprive the ants of their nature food and the worm's got to die—but that's not a consideration for us, since we should never have looked and discriminated in the first place.

TEXTS FROM THE BUDDHIST CANON KNOWN AS DHAMMAPADA Samuel Beal, London and Boston 1878

LIFE OF BUDDHA, or BUDDHA CHARITA, by Asvaghosha the Patriarch, translated by Samuel Beal (Sacred Books of the East Vol. 19)

THE GOSPEL OF BUDDHA by Paul Carus (Open Court, Chicago 1894)

BUDDHISM IN TRANSLATIONS, by Henry Clarke Warren (Harvard Oriental Series Vol. 3, Harvard Univ. Press 1896) Also in HARVARD CLASSICS

THE BUDDHIST BIBLE, Dwight Goddard (Goddard, Thetford, Vt.) This is by far the best book because it contains the Surangama Sutra and Lankavatra Scripture, not to mention the 11-page Diamond Sutra which is the last word, and Asvaghosha's Awakening of Faith, and the Tao. The Buddhist Bible uses sources—from the Pali, the Sanskrit, the Thibetan, Chinese, Burmese and modern.

BUDDHIST LEGENDS E.W. Burlingame, Harvard Oriental Series Vol. 28 30. These are commentaries on the 423 Aphorisms, very rich

THE DIALOGS OF THE BUDDHA, DIGHA-NIKAYA (long dialogs) Rhys Davids, 3 vols., Oxford

VISUDDHI MAGGA, by Buddhaghosha, trans. by P. M. Tin (The Path of Purity, Pali Text Society, Translation Series, 11, 17, 21)

THE SACRED BOOKS AND EARLY LITERATURE OF THE EAST Volume 18 India and Buddhism Parke, Austin and Lipscomb New York-London

* *

There's more and you will undoubtedly be telling me what to get if you get into this, which I advise and in fact insist on with all my heart heat and argument and brotherliness. I dont mean to put down Cayce, for after all he did say, "Practice, then, brotherly love, kindness, longsuffering and patience," he was no charlatan when it came to the business at hand, he was no charlatan anyway.

Now, Allen, as Neal or Car can tell you, last february I typed up a 100-page account of Buddhism for you, gleaned from my notes, and you will see proof of that in several allusions and appeals to "Allen" and I have that here, if you really want to see it, I will send it importantly stamped, it's the only copy, we must take special care with it, right? "Some of the Dharma" I called it, and it was intended for you to read in the selva. Some of it is now, I see, useless, because mistaken, or written on tea, or other faults, but it may really give you a send-off into the above tomes, which is my wish.

Your adventures in Mexico I am reading and re-reading, they are very sad, you only fragmentize, I cant wait to hear the Dakar-like details later, for poetry reasons. The House of Death is yr. subterranean prophetic Cave of Golgotha.

I know that now I am a dehumanized beast and maybe you dont unnerstand me any more.

Trapped in a Tea Shoppe is like Alistair Sims and would wig Seymour truly. . . . I hear he is . . . nowhere to be found.

My Brooklyn in the dream is true, because I often have such dreams of the vast brooklyn, I ride on endless els, and rust yards, etc. and (tell this to Neal) last week I worked 2 days on the New York Dock Railway as Yard Brakeman, right down on the Brooklyn waterfront, at Moore McCormack Pier 15,—switching cars off the floats, where railroad meets sea, it was my destiny to finally make that job—$18.35 a day—but that phlebitis junk bump is holding me up, my job is braking cars and the arm cant do it—so I took a months sick leave, must get some trypsin (parenzyme) the miracle drug.

Bill in Europe is really so sublime, so accurate,—we must make a movie, or better, more seriously? I claim you should sit down and write VISIONS OF BILL IN EUROPE, a la Visions of Neal, and we'll publish later when we get $500 to buy and maintain our handpress in Mexico City or Phnarktown. Incidentally, concerning the press, i no longer want to "run it," you run it, but I still offer my services as handset printer. . . . worries of business way beyond me now, only humble la-bours with hand okay, i have garden in my yard and beanfield now you know, and potatoes, etc.

Lucien in New York amazingly bright, like future glory when he reborn—a Super Liberace Billy Graham Nature Boy Prophet of Gold.

Your hieroglyphs of little boats and in the temple buddha are so great I think you should write a whole volume in that picture-writing, using the visions of Jamie and Cathy in crayola notebooks as yr guide, and dont think I'm not serious

Have you dug my Van Gogh jumping-out-at-you sofa in the study, or did someone take it off the wall—huge pale drawing with soft firepats falling on the couch at midnight

Your Mexicali lastdays, at rubbish cliff, remind me of my visit in January to Juarez, across from El Paso, where Taramare Indians walked around knee-deep in the dump looking for food

As for heaven, we're already there and always were, since all things in final reality are already delivered to Nirvana, are already of the essence of truth, permeating purely and throughout tho we cant with our sentience-be-clouded eyes realize that all the time—but as carolyn says, "you know all, and there just is no time or space"—"The air of life is permeated with roses all the time."—Visions of Neal

Your heavenly file of female angels tripping up to heaven is so beautiful, really, i wish I had such universal dreams as that, such visions of radiance. Point 2 of yr credo, "the mind imagines all visions," re-write as "the mind imagines all things which are but visions"—or, the mind imagines all things (to avoid misunderstanding in words) Point 3 should be, Man is already come and gone in a divine dream already ended

The world is made of water,
you only think its water

I dont have to write, I write to teach, I suppose I must teach, but like Joe McCarthy I'm getting awfully sick and tired of being reprimanded for loosing my hold on life's attaching apparati . . . it's as tho I'd committed some crime. . . . Nirvana means "snapping of relationship" and so naturally nobody'll like me any mo—Close yr eyes, cross yr legs under you, practice slow inbreathing and outbreathing, think, "I am breathing in, I am breathing out," then you think "There is the breathing in, there is the breathing out," and soon essential mind will begin to shine in you and you will begin to experience your first samadhi.

I suppose this is enuf for now, so goodnight my good one and dont be mad at me (none of ye).

Jack

CHAPTER 8

Jack Kerouac
Letter to Neal
Cassady

Sept. or Oct. 1957

Dear Neal [Cassady]—

Come on you ole sonumbitch and get on that typewriter and write me your first letter in 5 years, if not to me, who?—Tell me what happened after I left, Louanne, etc.—My mother and I rode 4 days and 4 nights on the bus to Florida and got a $45 a month pad a week later then I went to NY for publication of my book & everything exploded—To the point where, for instance, Warner Bros. wanted to buy On the Road for 110,000 dollars with me playing part of Sal Paradise and my agent turned it down because it wasnt enuf money or something—Everybody asking me "WHO will play Dean Moriarty?" and I say "He will himself if he wants to" so boy maybe truly you can become movie star with luck (tho my girl Joyce says not to wish that fate on you)—Allen in Amsterdam with Gregory and Peter writes that you should play the part yourself, and him Carlo, and me Sal—But meanwhile I was asked to write 3-act play for BWay, which I did, just sent it in the other day, big shot producers reading it, again a part in there for you, for me, Allen, Peter, etc. it's the story of ACT ONE You and Al Hinkle walk in Al Sublette's kitchen play chess while Al and I toast Khayyam tokay and Charley Mew figures horses, Connie standing around, finally you and Charley and me play flute solos straight off that Visions of Neal tape of 1952 . . . crazy scene. Second ACT: You and me alone at races, playing third choice, Pulido, dreams, talk, Cayce, girls, beer in cartons, etc. including the horse that spilled in the backstretch and nobody cared—ACT THREE the night of the Bishop with Donovan, Bev, Carolyn, Allen, Peter, you, me, Bishop, Bishop's mother and aunt but all of it changed to Lynbrook L.I. to New York Scene and the Bishop is "of the New Aramean church"—Nothing incriminating—I mean only grayfaces wont like it—Meanwhile magazines demanded shorts, so sold Baseball tale to Esquire for 500, article on Beatness to Pageant for 300, blues tale to Playboy for 500, and sold book to German and Italian publishers —Appeared on TV, John Wingate's NIGHTBEAT before 40 million viewers and talked about God monstrously had Wingate fluttering thru his prepared questions sweating I sprung God on him and he sprung dope on me—went out got drunk with him after show—Little Jack Melody phoned me at TV studio—Had hotel room with publishers drunk rolling out my roll-Road-ms. on carpet for screaming interviewers, —BWay producers bring beautiful models sit on edge of my (girl's) bed, ugh, wanted to make it so much with so many—Went on 2 wild weekends with Lucien and wife and two kids to upstate cold nippy Fall red-apple country, drunk— Everything happened and I was wondering: what has all this done to you, are people bugging you & chasing you in Frisco? Man, that Mercedes Benz ride of ours to Mexico City on El Paso Hiway not far off, I already (come next year) got enuf money to buy one!—Main thing, is, movie sale, Marl Brando definitely interested, soon's he crawls outa bed and reads ROAD he buy it, meanwhile Paramount and Warners bickering—gossip columnists report that Slim Gaillard will play himself in movie version! (we gets to get hi with Slim!)—This time I no make faggot scene, but girls, girls, girls,—only a few feelers from a few faggots in mail—Went out drank ate with Henri Cru, Bob Donlin (who was snapped by Playboy magazine 150 color photos with me, I feed him bite of spaghetti, he kiss me, we fall down in Bowery, talk to bums) (later Stanley Gould shown with me in front of San Remo)—everything happened—I was drunk all the time, no more wine, just whiskey, which by the way is much easier than wine—All the time wondering "What is Neal thinking?" and if I sell movie this Christmas, as likely, as I pray for, will convert 150,000 into monthly trustfund checks like Burroughs, not squander, will shoot right out to Frisco go stay with you at Los Gatos pad with money to burn on groceries, kicks, etc.—Promised Buddha would go meditate whole month in mountain solitude, eat no meat if sell movie spend whole month praying for all living creatures—Fathers of St. Francis of Assissi church 34th st. New York saw me on TV talk about God and Francis and are giving mass for my spiritual and temporal welfare—I also correspond now with mad nuns at a monastery who love me—Write! I tell you more! Buddy as ever.

Jack

p.s. After brot mother to Florida I took foolish trip to Mexico City, just in time for earthquake. Went to find Esperanza, couldnt, she must be dead, went to find Garver, he dead, died in July, alone. . . . Finally old Garver dead—I cried in Mexico, alone. . . . got drunk in Mexico, alone, stayed only 10 days and rode that bus again and again thru nightmare New Orleans again and again—Saw Dick Hittleman in NY and he says "Come on man go down to Mexico and make it with Diane, she needs somebody like you" I said "You tryna kill me man?"—wow—Had for awhile swollen balls and no sex, suddenly got letter from Gary Snyder in Japan saying "I pray to Avalokitesvara Buddha and you be well quick" and suddenly as I read letter my balls went down and I been straight ever since and went to NY and balled with chicks and am straight again—???—The chick I really need is Gary's sister Thea—question marks mean: How come Buddha answers all prayer? Man on TV (Wingate) said: "Can you tell us to whom you pray?" and I said "To my brother Gerard, my father Leo, Jesus Christ, Avalokitesvara Buddha, and Our Mother in Heaven." Meanwhile, man, here's what: when I get check for $300 every month trustfund I travel and ball all over world, to India, Japan, racetracks, Mexico, Europe, Paris, all over, I move fast and when I make a million my monthly check will be $8,000 and that's when you and I make time in your old plan that Lazy Charley was gonna bring you, no Lazy Jack is the system.

Please give my love to Charley Mew, Al Hinkle, and Al Sublette, hey?—if you see them—I saw Jane Belson at a mad party in NY too—she was scared of me, I was drunk—My exwife Joan got divorce in Juarez and now wants me to sign adoption papers so her new Arab husband Aly adopt..I will move me and my Maw back to Richmond Hill Long Island next spring and then build me a logcabin on Lucien's land upstate and them will be my headquarters.

Now come on, Neal, reason I didnt see much of you in Frisco this last time was shortness of money. . . . no other reason—so write and let's get on the ball here, HIBALL

Jack

CHAPTER 9

LeRoi Jones in the East Village

AMIRI BARAKA

I ring the doorbell to Amiri Baraka's (LeRoi Jones) home. A tall, statuesque woman greets me after the second ring. It's Amini, his wife. She smiles warmly and looks me directly in the eye. I tell her who I am and why I'm there. She welcomes me in and says that Amiri has gone to the store, but should be back shortly. As I take a seat on the sofa in the living room, Amini disappears into the back room to continue a telephone conversation. I look around the tastefully decorated room and admire the warm and earthy color scheme and interesting African artifacts. I overhear Amini on the telephone, "Well, right now we're trying to get funds to . . ." I decide to set up my tape recorder. "I told you she was pregnant," I hear Amini remark. My recorder is set and ready to go. Amini runs through the room and up the hall stairs while the phone is ringing. After a few minutes she returns and comes to keep me company. She apologizes again for Amiri's delay and adds that he has to pick up the kids from school also. I ask if she has two telephones and she says no, she ran upstairs to get something and the phone just happened to ring. Then she comments on how hectic things are when the kids are there, all vying for her attention. I tell her I understand; I'm from a large family myself. She says she is too; she was the eldest, so she's been raising kids all her life, it seems. She rises out of her seat slightly, looking out the window behind me, and announces that Amiri has arrived. "Oh, he forgot the kids," she says and excuses herself to go get them.

Amiri comes in with a box of groceries and disappears into the kitchen. After about ten minutes he comes in and looks at me with big ambivalent eyes and says, "Hello." I attribute the ambivalence to the fact that he has recently been a victim of police brutality; he was charged with assaulting a police officer and wife-beating. The wife-beating charge has been dropped, and Amiri has issued a press statement accusing the police of trying to "character assassinate" him and the Black Liberation movement before the world. He sits an unlikely distance from me and my recorder. I hand him a copy of *The Beat Diary* [Edited by Arthur & Kit Knight.] which he flips through briskly, telling me that we can start whenever I'm ready. I flip the switch of my tape recorder and we begin.

Debra L. Edwards
Newark, NJ
June 18, 1979

DEBRA L. EDWARDS: *What was your indoctrination into the Beat scene?*

AMIRI BARAKA: I guess I was just coming out of the Air Force, about 1957. Then I came back to Newark and then went to New York and got an apartment down on East 3rd Street and got a job at Gotham.

DE: *Gotham Book Mart?*

AB: Yes, and I was down there for awhile and I was aware or became aware of Allen Ginsberg, and I started communicating with him.

Bob Dylan and Allen Ginsberg at Jack Kerouac's grave, Lowell, MA, 1975. PHOTO BY KEN REGAN. COURTESY: FULL COURT PRESS, NEW YORK.

DE: He used to come in the store?

AB: No, at the time I got hold of Al, he was in Paris and I wrote him a letter there. I think I got in touch with him because I wanted to start a magazine.

DE: *Yugen?*

AB: Yeah, that was about '59, so I got in touch with Allen probably around 1958, and he sent poetry for it, and recommended some other poets. So that was the beginning of our association. Also my association with some of the other writers called the Beat Generation.

DE: *Like Diane di Prima?*

AB: Yeah, but I met her a little later, when I started to meet people who were in New York writing, principally around the Lower Eastside. As I began to meet them more, I came in contact with a whole lot of other folks who were down there.

DE: *Like Jack Kerouac and—was A.B. Spellman there?*

AB: Yes, Spellman came later. Kerouac I met about '59 or '58, whenever Ginsberg came back from Paris. I think *On The Road* had just come out and I met Kerouac through Ginsberg. He came in and gave a lot of readings. And I met Jack Micheline, Gregory Corso, Philip Lamantia, all through Ginsberg in that particular period. And they began to have public readings at a coffee shop up on 9th Avenue just about at 42nd Street. That was like a regular gathering place for poets. And as we were putting out the magazine, through Allen is how we met most of these people, either through letters—those who still lived in San Francisco, some of whom I met much later—or when they came through New York, I would get a chance to meet them.

DE: *Why did you start* Yugen?

AB: It was started because I didn't see publications coming out that carried poetry or writing that I was interested in. Therefore, I thought I should start one to try to gather that poetry that I thought was interesting.

Although I later found out that there were some interesting magazines, but they were like sporadic. Well, like there was *The Black Mountain Review*, which was immensely important at that time; I didn't know about it when I started *Yugen*, but I found out about it and got all the back issues; and *Measure* was another magazine that was very important. But these were . . . I just thought nothing was happening on the poetry scene as it should be so I started publishing.

DE: *Why did you discontinue it?*

AB: Why? Well, I think it just outlived its usefulness as far as I was concerned. By the time *Yugen* stopped publishing there were innumerable magazines that were publishing poets and writers that I had some respect for.

DE: *How did you get involved with* Floating Bear, *how was it started?*

AB: It was thought that there was needed a faster publication, one that would do correspondence, reviews, new poetry, that would come out monthly, that would be more flexible. So di Prima and I started that.

DE: *You left before it was discontinued?*

AB: By that time I had other interests. I had become more involved in Black Nationalist politics and those kind of publications became less relevant to me.

DE: *Who were your major supporters and subscribers to both particular magazines?*

AB: It's hard to say. I'd say in terms of *Yugen*, I imagine it was young writers and people who collect the work of young writers, young American writers. As far as *The Floating Bear*, it was probably the same people—writers, poets, musicians, dancers, actors, companies, anybody who was interested in poetry.

DE: *Painters?*

AB: Right. Lots of painters.

127

Amiri Baraka, Greenwich Village, NY, April 1979. PHOTO BY GORDON R. ROBOTHAM.

DE: You encountered censorship problems with issue number 9 of Floating Bear, *right?*

AB: The problem arose when we printed the . . . it was two pieces, one by William Burroughs—which was a piece on Roosevelt, which was really a kind of scatological piece, a satire on Roosevelt and Harry Hopkins—and then there was a thing on somebody else, I don't know, but I know the Burroughs piece was the principle piece.

And we got busted. I got arrested; they came to my house about 3 or 4 in the morning, and I was locked up for distributing obscene materials through the mail. It might seem strange now because some of the very language is in the movies, even some on TV, it's not a big thing anymore, but at the time they made a great deal of it and I defended myself before the grand jury with the decisions on *Lady Chatterly's Lover* and *Ulysses* and I was conversant with a lot of those facts and information. So I used that and they let me off. They found no reason to indict. What we were saying was this literature had socially redeemable value. Really, in terms of pornography, there was nothing in it at all to arouse anyone sexually; it was just the language.

DE: Were there any criticisms of your work?

AB: No, I was arrested as the editor.

DE: You also had censorship problems with The Toilet *and* Dutchman *in which you confront the issue of homosexuality and castration of black America by white America. Would you discuss the censorship problems you encountered with these plays?*

AB: *Dutchman* encountered censorship in various places; well, it did encounter censorship problems in Los Angeles, no, no, that was *The Toilet*; it played, then they closed it, then they let it play. *Dutchman* had encountered some sporadic kind of censorship problems but *The Toilet* and *The Baptist*, in fact there were two plays of mine that were opened, *The Baptist* and *Dante*, which was taken from this novel of mine, both of those were closed by the police. But later opened. But that was back in '64. Well, it's not too long ago, really, about 15 years ago, but that's when they did close them, closed them up as being obscene. And then I think we got a lawyer to intercede, and they raised up off of us and let us do it. I think that was much more prevalent then, the whole censorship bit. In the main, for literature mainly, I think that's been cracked, although you still see from time to time cases where in some little community there are little backwards groups that get together and they want to ban certain things. But now, I think, the censorship is much more ideological and it's much more subtle and it's continuous; they keep works whose ideology they disagree with, they keep them off the board or off the screen or off the set—and that's continuous.

DE: *Homosexuality consistently reoccurs in many of the works of the Beat artists; was it the order of the day to indulge and express this indulgence as some kind of artistic or spiritual freedom, some kind of process of self-knowledge?*

AB: In American life homosexuality has always been accorded some kind of shadow life, well, in western society generally since the Greeks when it was somewhat respectable; it has not been respectable since then, but I think with the Beat thing it was a question of people trying to be honest and forthright and I think that was the whole forerunner to the homosexual movement now, where they have Gay Rights. In the Beat period a lot of those people were gay, and they came out with it more directly than before. Allen Ginsberg, long before Gay Rights, was very realistic and expressly revealing about the whole thing.

DE: *So it was part of the general rebellion of the time?*

AB: Yes, it was a part of that. The whole question of people coming out with who they were. Like I think the whole drug thing became much more open, at least the marijuana people doing it. Then later the yippies developed out of that and the smoke-ins and things like that. I think the Beat period was a kind of egg for a lot of that stuff.

DE: *Was that the sustaining force of the Beat period, its historical and social contribution?*

AB: As far as I'm concerned the importance of the period is the transformation of the literature and more important, the transformation of a significant number of the American population in terms of their ideals because the literature that came out of there reflects the development of a particular life style, the development of particular ideas associated with particular people. Beat came out of the whole dead Eisenhower period, the whole period of the McCarthy Era, the Eisenhower blandness, the whole reactionary period of the 50s. The Beat Generation was a distinct reaction to that, a reaction not only to reactionary politics, reactionary life style of American ruling class and sections of the middle class, reaction to conservatism and McCarthyism of that period. Also reaction to the kind of academic poetry and academic literature that was being pushed as great works by the American establishment. So it was a complete reaction: socially, politically, and of course artistically to what the 50s represented. That whole opening and transformation of course had its fullest kind of expression in the 60s in the Black Liberation Movement.

DE: *What were your aesthetic goals or aspirations as a Beat poet?*

AB: First of all, the whole Beat thing I always thought of as a publicity gimmick.

DE: *At that time?*

AB: Yeah; no, I thought the press put a handle on it, Beat, because then it made it packagable, marketable and more easily put-downable. So Beat meant nothing to me. I mean it meant some identifiable area of life but that's about all. I mean I didn't identify with it as I am a Beat. I understood what they were talking about but generally my feelings were that it was a rebellion against those times which I mentioned. That it was people consciously trying to disassociate themselves with the reactionary ideas and life styles of America in the middle of the century.

DE: *So you didn't really have any aesthetic goals?*

AB: No, the goals we had were to break away from that kind of dead establishment literature and life style, those were the conscious goals that we had.

DE: *Did you achieve them?*

AB: I think the movement as a whole achieved them in the sense that there was a definite breakaway. It's more like a peoples front of opposition to certain dead ideas of the society. Now the point of unity was the point of breakaway, that all those people loosely associated as Beat, and maybe Black Mountain and San Francisco and the other groups like that, they all could be linked together commonly only to the extent that it meant they were breaking away from the established, traditional norms. It's as if, say, a group of people were united by their being opposed to another idea but once you went in to investigate their commonality, you would see most of their commonality consisted of their opposition to something else, rather than them having a consistent or monolitic aesthetic themselves.

DE: *What were some of the problems you encountered as a black writer trying to define society?*

AB: The problem being a black writer is first coming into consciousness of that, of understanding your similarity, say, with a disenchanted sector of American society, seeing your commonality with that but at the same time seeing that even in that commonality, seeing that you represent a particular kind of experience, that is the Afro-American experience. That's the first problem, which is mainly ideological.

The second problem is, once you understand that, how do you put that out, how do you begin to say that, what form do you use—I mean you need institutions, publications, you see, how do you deal with that? Which is mainly a political problem. We tried to solve that in the 60s but the Black Arts Repertory, the whole Black Poetry Movement saw itself as independent.

In dealing with the American literary establishment the problem consists of, number one, the racism, their racism in failing or refusing to understand the fact that there is an Afro-American nation and because of that there is an Afro-American culture, and Afro-American literature, like there is an Afro-American music and that these are particular entities with their own history, their own aesthetics, their own ideology and politics. Although they're related to the whole, at the same time they are a distinct aspect of it. So the question is one of being oppressed by the American establishment, by U.S. imperialism; whether that comes through literature or academic circles, or however you experience it, it's the same source, American imperialism. And then how do you combat that, what are your methods of combating that? First you have to combat it ideologically, that is understanding that you exist. Then you have to combat it politically,

Diane di Prima, 1954.

that is not only understanding that you exist but then struggling to survive and develop. And those are continuing problems.

DE: *As a Beat poet, were you primarily concerned with forming your own ideology or, rather, developing the basic fundamental skills of writing poetry?*

AB: The ideology question is constant whether you consciously deal with it or not because all it is is how you perceive reality. Now your perception of reality changes, just as reality changes. So that at one point you might define yourself as a Beat poet. Actually, that is an ideological concept, just like at another time you might define yourself as a black poet, that's an ideological concept. I think it has something to do with your perception of reality, how it changes. When I was more closely related to the Beat Movement I was much more interested in literature in general; in fact, I used to make statements that I was just a poet, I didn't care anything about politics. But the unique position of being black in that situation is that you might think that, but you are so constantly and blatantly affected by politics beyond and above what other members of that group might be, so that the whole question of making political definitions a reality became much more constant for me to deal with, it became much more of a consistent problem for me.

DE: Any specific events that brought this change on?

AB: The whole Civil Rights Movement, first of all. The intensification of the Civil Rights Movement, the emergence of Malcolm X, the African and Asian nations and Latin nations revolutionary struggles, the whole international situation, African independence, Cuba getting its independence. All kinds of things were happening in the late fifties and early sixties.

DE: Do you really think a black poet could survive spiritually or whatever, even make profound contributions, taking the attitude that "I'm just a poet" devoid of political ideology?

AB: The political ideologies are there anyway. What it would mean is you have a person actually making an idealist evaluation of reality, that is trying to say what matters is what is in my head. What's going on in the world has nothing to do with me is basically idealism. And even a person defining it in that way has made a political definition. Usually with blacks it tends to be more overtly backward because in the midst of their national oppression for someone to say "It makes no difference to me" is kind of . . . I mean a white poet can say the same thing you say, and it's still a lie but when a black poet says it right in the midst of a people being assaulted and oppressed, it highlights their distance from reality. In the 60s when the Anti-War Movement was going on and we were dragging even white students through the streets, for a white poet, I guess, that would be highlighted too. But for blacks and other oppressed nationalities it becomes particularly illuminating in terms of their social backwardness. Because so much is happening that does impinge upon their lives. And for them to deny that it does not have any relation to them is to deny reality.

DE: Who were some of the black poets you were involved with during the Beat period?

AB: Not many, actually. Well, I can't say that, not really. I knew a lot of black poets. Even from the time I got to Greenwich Village, actually I knew a lot. I used to publish the ones that lived down in the Village like Allen Polite and Bob Hamilton and, let's see, Ed James and Bob Kaufman. A lot of people came up later, like A.B. Spellman, Ishmael Reed, Calvin Hernton, Ted Joans, people I knew during that period.

DE: So Ginsberg was your first link with the Beat poets?

AB: Yeah, he was, actually, a good teacher. He had or has a really strong grasp of poetry, the history of poetry, American poetry, of Western poetry in general. And he was of great help to me in terms of learning about poetry in general and he was a great publicizer of poets, young poets and the whole Beat thing.

DE: How would you assess the avant-garde movement during the Beat period in terms of its impact, its contributions?

AB: One of its strongest moments was redefining what poetry was, redefining what art in general was. Questioning those things that had been put out, traditional values and academic values and, trying to put forward a more mass-oriented kind of art, a more people-oriented kind of art. For instance, during the whole Beat period readings became more important. People wanted to actually read poetry and the whole oral tradition was sort of reinvoked, to get poetry off the pages; because largely academic poetry is to be read in books and never heard at all. During the Beat period poetry readings came back in vogue. When the Black Poetry Movement picked up after that, readings were its principle form. Then the oral tradition became principle and the printed word secondary. That had a lot to do with reorienting a lot of people's way of looking at what poetry really is. The whole avant-garde movement in the 60s was moving much more towards a mass-oriented, a popular-oriented art. And this was its largest contribution.

DE: That it initiated this move?

Left to right: Gregory Corso, William Burroughs, Allen Ginsberg, Peter Orlovsky—Columbia University, NYC, April 17, 1975. PHOTO BY GERARD MALANGA.

AB: Yes, and that it moved towards American speech. It continued with William Carlos Williams' teachings and it went back to people like Whitman. It dealt with the question of writing in American language and used Charles Olson's teachings and went back to people like Melville and the American experience as opposed to the European experience or as opposed to the colonial experience, but America as an independent culture, as an independent nation. And then later on, of course, the Black Poetry Movement emerged, taking it a step further and talked about the Afro-American people's experience. So all of that was positive.

DE: *Were you emotionally, spiritually fulfilled by your work during the Beat period?*

AB: Yes, as much as anyone, I guess. I was always trying to do more, do different things, learn more, to create new things. Anytime you do anything, what it does is point out the need for you to do other things. You complete something at one level, then that reveals to you how much you have not done or how many more things there are to do.

DE: *It's like expanding yourself?*

AB: Right, like stages of a process. You complete one stage, then that allows you to understand the next stage when before you didn't even know there was another stage.

DE: *In the* Dead Lecturer *you deal with self-orientation and self-criticism, the obsession with death and the uses and constructs of image and idiom common to the ironic mode. But then you develop three basic new tendencies: (1) you attempt to construct new myths from a new language of symbols, (2) a growing concern with the social or public world and then finally (3) was a new tenderness and more freely lyrical tone. What were the stages that led you to this?*

AB: First of all, my earlier works such as *Preface to a 20 Volume Suicide Note* and *Dead Lecturer* should be looked at as an attempt of a young writer trying to be a poet. I was borrowing from other writers whom I was influenced by at that time, such as Eliot, Pound, Proust, Yeats, Cummings, Williams, Dante, and from Beat poets such as Allen Ginsberg; and I was borrowing from Charles Olson.

Concerning the *Dead Lecturer*, having learned the fundamentals of writing poetry, I thought, I began to try to find out what it was I wanted to write about. And even though some of these poems are somewhat derivative, I began to get my own tone. My own voice begins to emerge more. And I think that is what the lyrical aspect is attributed to. The *Dead Lecturer* is much more coming to grips with my own concerns, the key one of which was the question of estrangement, of being, say, a schizophrenic, being concerned internally with one group of ideas but at the same time, seeing other people's concerns were different. And being linked to other people's concerns by your being linked to other people, but at the same time having your own group of concerns. Which then makes you kind of schizo.

Then the black thing, being a black poet surrounded by a lot of white writers and artists, was put into relief even more intensely by the fact that my own concerns were more specific, growing much more political, while theirs were remaining generally the same.

DE: *Is this also the time you started trying to synthesize black music more in your work?*

AB: Yes, I think I wrote *Blues People* then, in '61. So it was all coming forward: much more political consciousness and much more awareness of the separation from my real feelings from, say, the feelings of the people I was with.

DE: *So you had arrived by the time of* Dante's Hell *at a purely black aesthetic?*

AB: No, what *Dante* actually did was move me away from the earlier derivative works. When I came to *Dante*, I then consciously determined that I was going to stop writing like other folks, like the Creeleys and the Olsons and all those other people. So what I did was write that book without thought to any kind of artifice but just straight ahead, whatever came to me to write. I used the Dante form because it was a form that I could quickly impose upon it. Yet the content would be as free as I could make it, but I thought I would impose this form so the book wouldn't just float away. I would at least try to construct some kind of systematic portrait of my own mind and life. That was probably the breakaway book, in terms of the breakaway from older, more derivative forms and getting more clearly into my own voice.

As I'm putting my recorder away Amiri looks through *The Beat Diary* again, but slowly this time, smiling to himself from time to time with big tender eyes.

CHAPTER   10

Anne Waldman
Talks with
Diane di Prima

Anne Waldman conducted this interview in Boulder, Colorado in July 1978.

ANNE WALDMAN: *Could you talk about that period in New York when you were running the Poets Theater and doing plays by Frank O'Hara and others? Had you worked in theater before? What inspired you?*

DIANE DI PRIMA: I began by being very interested in dance. I'm second generation Italian-American and my world was very restricted physically as a child. Girls didn't go out and play. When in my teens I came upon dance, it was an incredible release and it was a permitted physical activity. Up until that point I was really limited in my range of

Diane di Prima and Charles Olson, Gloucester, 1967. PHOTO BY ALAN MARLOWE.

movement, I mean, I spent my life reading and doing housework. Girls were supposed to be very smart. And there was no question about college and blah blah blah and careers, and final subordination to marriage. But, girls didn't do anything physical, the streets were for boys, not girls. So dance became for me a primary kind of release of my body, even before sex or any of that. Then through dance I met James Waring who became a teacher of mine, both as a dancer and generally in terms of how do you compose, how do you make the creative work happen. And he was working, making plays at the Living Theater on dark nights, which were Monday nights.

The Living Theater was then on 14th St. and was very active, and I began to be a stage manager and helped him do a Frank O'Hara play and

Herbert Huncke and Diane di Prima, August 1, 1982. PHOTO BY ARTHUR WINFIELD KNIGHT.

some other plays back then. So I had had that experience in theater, and when we made the N. Y. Poets Theater there was Alan Marlowe, my husband, myself, Jame Waring, Leroi Jones, and a dancer named Fred Herco. We were the founders of the theater. In '61 what we had was a gallery on 10th St. The back part of this gallery had a stage. Anyway, we did that season a piece of a book by Leroi Jones. It was called "The System of Dante's Hell." This was before he'd written any plays and I think it's what got him into starting to do that. He spent a lot of time watching the rehearsals, figuring out theater stuff. And we did a verse play by Michael McClure called "The Pillow," and a play by James Waring, and one by myself and several other pieces. Six plays that season—one-acts mostly. And then the following year we were away, and then the year after that we

Drawing of Diane di Prima by Robert LaVigne.

got a theater on the Bowery which we kept for a year or two where we did many plays by Frank O'Hara, Michael McClure, Wallace Stevens, an opera by David Walker, and others. We kept mostly to plays by poets and we didn't get set builders to build sets, we got the painters. We were thrown out of one theater for showing Jean Genet's movie "Chant D'Amour" which led to a whole court case, where the court upheld the right of the landlady to throw us out because we were obscene.

AW: *What year was this?*

DD: 1964. We moved to a theater we built ourselves in a loft in the Village on Bleecker St. Now, in that case, we had to pretend to not be a theater because there were strict rules governing what the building would have to be like if it was a theater. So we called ourselves a club, an arts club, and issued membership cards, obeyed all the rules for clubs, which were that you had to sell your memberships otherwhere than where the performances were, and keep a membership book, so that was easy. We worked there for a year. Red Grooms did a set for us there for a play by Kenneth Koch. And then we moved out from there to another theater, the one last theater, which had a Ukranian bar upstairs and was on E. 4th St. We mainly did plays on the weekend, and during the week we'd have other activities.

AW: *Has male energy and consciousness been dominating the poetry scene or do you find you can work with that energy? Have you had trouble getting your own work published in N. Y. for example, in big publishing houses which are on the whole dominated by male editors?*

DD: For the first 10 to 15 years I never really realized one way or the other or cared that much about what was going on in that way. It wasn't an issue for me. It's only more recently I've come to spend any time realizing or thinking about the fact that if the body of work I had done by '63 when *The New Hand Book of Heaven* was out and *The Calculus of Variation* was finished had been done by any of the male writers on that scene at that point, who were my close friends, I think the acknowledgement that a body of work was in progress would have been much greater. But, in those days, I was just expecting trouble all around, so it never occurred to me. I just kind of grew up with a tough back to the wall, ready-to-fight-anybody attitude. I can't really say why. I didn't distinguish which of these things is happening because I'm a woman, which of these things is happening because that's just the way the world is, and there was a lot of that's just how the world is, don't forget, in the air in the '50s, too. We all expected the worst. All of us . . . it's the Jean-Paul Sartre era. But, yes, I'm sure that a lot of stuff, like not getting published, is traceable to that. There's another thing there, which is not only am I a woman, but I'm a particular kind of woman—I'm not apologetic. I'm not sad, you know, if. . . . Maybe if I was drinking a lot and writing miserable poems about some man and trying to kill myself every three years, maybe that would be okay, because, that makes guys feel okay, too, you know. But, I think it is that I've actually had the balls to enjoy myself. I'm a woman, I've enjoyed myself. My politics is ridiculous, it's not establishment politics. And, although my parents were sort of on the lower edge of the middle class, I'm definitely a street person. All my first writing was completely predicated on getting the slang of N. Y. in the period in the early '50s, down on paper somehow or another.

I can't really untangle what's class prejudice and what's sex prejudice and what's the natural desire of the ruling class to maintain its position. All those things are in there. I didn't even go to college. I left after a year, you know. The question is, is it a male dominated scene, the literary scene? Yes, and women are just beginning to get a place in it and I think your generation is the first generation of women that has had access to the information that makes you a proficient writer. Don't forget, however great your visioning and your inspiration, you need the techniques of the craft, and there's no where, really, to get them because these are not passed on in schools. They are passed on person to person, and back then the male naturally passed them on to the male, I think maybe I was one of the first women to break through that in having deep conversations with Charles Olson and Frank O'Hara. Robert Duncan and I are now conversing on those levels. I'm learning a lot from him these days.

I can't say a lot of really great women writers were ignored in my time, but I can say a lot of potentially great women writers wound up dead or crazy. I think of the women on the Beat scene with me in the early '50s, where are they now? I know Barbara Moraff is a potter and does some writing in Vermont, and that's about all I know. I know some of them ODed and some of them got nuts, and one woman that I was running around the Village with in '53 was killed by her parents putting her in a shock treatment place in Pennsylvania, that promised your loved one back to you in three weeks cured. What the parents really wanted was the illegitimate child she had had so they could raise it without making the same mistakes they'd made with her. This was the kind of general atmosphere we were up against. I don't want to rant on about individual cases, but the threat of incarceration or early death in one form or another was very real. A friend and a writer in my crowd were threatened with jail because the parent of one of them discovered that a homosexual affair between the two women was in progress. We were all under threat of being dragged into court for that. This was daily life. We wrote the way Virginia Woolf describes Jane Austen hiding her papers under the tablecloth. We really wanted to stay inconspicuous. Most of us. I was a brash little brat. Probably why I'm still alive!

I think the poet is the last person who is still speaking the truth when no one else dares to. I think the poet is the first person to begin the shaping and visioning of the new forms and the new consciousness when no one else has begun to sense it; I think these are two of the most essential human functions. Pound once said, "Artists are the antennae of the race." Whether or not we have an audience, this strong visioning and shaping of a master poem informs the conscience of generations to come. And we see very dramatically in our time how without even reaching that high plane, like Dante or Shakespeare, the work of Allen and Kerouac in the '50s and so on has informed the '70s.

Poets speak truth. A poet that is a liar is very spottable, and you leave very fast. Poetry is not a place where you can bluff. You speak directly to the hearts of people. People are hungry for that directness. It's like days of dying in the desert yearning for a glass of water, for any speech that's speech of the heart. And there's way too much speech of the brain, and there's way too much information about what's going on and not anything of the gut and not anything of the heart happening. So whatever else we do, the first thing is we reactivate the feeling, we reactivate the possibility of living a life of emotion and of the flesh, as well as of the life of the brain.

CHAPTER 11

Chanson D'Outre Tombe

Philip Whalen, San Francisco, 1972. PHOTO BY GERARD MALANGA.

CHANSON D'OUTRE TOMBE

They said we was nowhere
Actually we are beautifully embalmed
      in Pennsylvania
They said we wanted too much.
Gave too little, a swift hand-job
            no vaseline.
We were geniuses with all kinds
            embarrassing limitations
O if only we would realize our potential
O if only that awful self-indulgence
& that shoddy politics of irresponsibility
O if only we would grow up, shut up, die
& so we did & do & chant beyond
            the cut-rate grave digged by
                  indignant reviewers
O if we would only lay down & stay
            THERE — In California. Pennsylvania
Whence we keep leaking out nasty radioactive
      waste like old plutonium factory
wrecking your white expensive world.

                        PHILIP WHALEN
            TASSAJARA   27 III 79

Allen Ginsberg, Charles Plymell and Philip Whalen in front of City Lights Bookstore, San Francisco, CA, 1963. FROM ALLEN GINSBERG'S COLLECTION

Gregory Corso. COURTESY OF THE *UNSPEAKABLE VISIONS OF THE INDIVIDUAL.* PHOTO BY CHRIS CHALLIS.

CHAPTER 12

Gregory Corso

Gregory Corso, with Lawrence Ferlinghetti, Allen Ginsberg, Michael McClure, Shig Murao, Peter Orlovsky, Miriam Patchen, Kenneth Rexroth and Gary Snyder, spent the blizzardy week of March 18, 1974 in Grand Forks, North Dakota, participants in the Fifth Annual University of North Dakota Writers Conference: City Lights in North Dakota. "Conference," in retrospect, does not seem the most appropriate noun to describe what actually happened; it was a week-long festive reunion of the Beats: poetry readings, long open microphone rap sessions with large audiences, mantras, a large exhibit of Kenneth Patchen's art. Unlike a Ginsberg reading at Jersey City State College not too long ago where, according to Jane Kramer, the teacher introducing Ginsberg snatched back the microphone to proclaim, "This evening does not receive the endorsement of the

English Department," the City Lights "Conference" was sponsored by the UND English Department. Various members of the Department interviewed each of the poets, often under less than ideal circumstances, so crowded was the week with activities, so responsive and enthusiastic the largely student audiences.

The interview that follows took place at Robert King's home, the afternoon of March 22, 1974. John Little, who heads the committee responsible for the Conference, also participated in the conversation, as did Doug Rankin, a UND student.

James McKenzie

ROBERT KING: *In the introduction to* Gasoline *you said in your 17th year that people handed you books of illumination out of adjoining cells. Did that really happen? What were they?*

GREGORY CORSO: They were really dumb-ass books to begin with. There was Louis Beretti, first of all. Henderson Clarke wrote all these books about Little Italy, gangster books. That was what convicts read. All right. Now the smart man was the man who handed me *Les Miserables*. And you know who did that? Me. When I went to the prison library, I looked at that fat book and I knew what miserable meant. I was 16½. When I said they passed me books of illumination, I meant they handed me something else, not the books. Yeah, there was a guy who had a beautiful standard dictionary. He loved me, man. And he had this old standard dictionary and I studied every fucking word in that book. 1905. This big, it was. All the archaic, all the obsolete words. That's illumination, I guess."

RK: *OK, OK. Following that up, there's a lot of talk now about primitive poets as models. And now we've got Rothenberg putting out anthologies, and this kind of thing. So you must have been into that early?*

GC: No. No, but I think I am called an original and also very much a primitive type, too, in poetry. How it came to me, though, was high class. You see. Wow. I mean the first feeling I had when I wrote my first poem was like music coming through a crack in the wall, and I felt good writing it.

RK: So you're not consciously trying to recapture primitive forms or feelings?

GC: I'll tell you, I know the sestina, I know the sonnets, I know the old sources of the information that I lay out. Go back to your sources, I tell people, but not as much as my friends do about the earth, or growing food, but the head. I say check yourself out, how far back you can go that way to your sources. And this I might have gotten from the Tibetans, because they say if you're conscious on your death bed, try to think back to your mother's cunt because you came in as you go out. It's good exercise for poets. I had to go back through history to get back as far as I could go to the sources, cave paintings as I say, and all that.

RK: You talk a lot about Gilgamesh, The Book of the Dead, these kinds of things.

GC: Right. That's all relay. It passes memory. See, if you forget the past, it's gone. And who was it, Santayana who said if you don't understand your mistakes you're going to have to repeat them. A karma shot, right? I don't think anything was a mistake. I'll hold to *Gilgamesh*, I'll hold to the Bible, I'll hold to all those goodies, they're all relays.

RK: Did you ever think about going to the university and majoring in comparative literature?

GC: Well, I went to Harvard, now. It was funny, on the banks of the Charles, drinking beer, talking about Hegel, Kierkegaard, it was nice—MacLeish's class. He'd sit there like the White Father, you know, people laughing, reading their poems, criticizing each other. I just went to one because he invited me up there, and immediately I saw Keats' death mask on the wall, and immediately I said, "Ah, that's Keats." Burroughs is beautiful, teaching at CCNY. He's really got the kids going: Do you sincerely want to be a writer; that's what he's teaching. The word "sincere" is too much. As long as human beings sing, it's beautiful. In other words, man, if they want to let themselves go, that's beautiful. And they don't know what a nice teacher they have in Burroughs. What a shot that is. And that's what works.

Gregory Corso, Paris, Circa 1957.

RK: *What about poets you read early, early influences?*

GC: The one who really turned me on very much was Shelley, not too much his poetry, but his life. I said, "Ah, a poet then could really live a good life on this planet." That fucker was beautiful, a sharp man. But dumb in a way, he went to free Ireland. You know how he did it? In a rowboat, half-way sinking in a rowboat.

RK: *More his life than his poetry?*

GC: The poet and poetry are inseparable. You got to dig the poet. Otherwise the poetry sucks. If I dug the poet, then automatically the poetry worked for me. Edgar Allen Poe the same way. Then there are some poets, I just don't buy their books, I don't dig it. Pound makes it, Auden made it for me. I mean, Auden is good. I dig Auden, you see. A lot don't. Listen,

Allen wanted to sing mantras to him, and Auden said, "No, I get embarrassed by somebody singing to me. I don't want it." So Allen said, "That dumb fuck, he died and didn't realize who I was, man; I was singing to him."

RK: *Auden's life doesn't seem particularly exciting; he's certainly no Shelley.*

GC: Naw, he didn't dig Shelley, but he did dig *The Tempest*. That's Shakespeare's best shot. That's the time of the "dopey fuck" remark. Auden was reading *The Tempest* to me and it sounded beautiful. I was just a kid. Walking down the street, afterwards, feeling good, I was crossing the street when this fucking taxi driver says, "Get out of the way, you dopey fuck." Here I am alive with poetry, right? I go home, look in the mirror: am I a dopey fuck? No way!

RK: *You talk about a new consciousness in* Elegiac Feelings American. *What do you mean by that, or what do you see as a new consciousness?*

GC: That's what's happening, and very fast. It took awhile for this body to make it, but the head's going beautiful. Now I took the daddies and I said that truth was the 70s hit. But truth is the pole vault that stops you. You say, "Well I believe in this" and then you stop with it. So it's almost as bad as the word "faith" because people believe in things they don't understand by their faith. I'd rather have a little bit of knowledge than a whole lot of faith. So humor then comes after it. Humor is the butcher that gets rid of the shit. I love Americans for that, man; if they can laugh at something, it's finished.

RK: *Does America, as a country, spiritual entity, whatever, ask something different from its poets than other countries ask? There's Whitman, and then there's Crane, maybe there's the 50s . . . but I don't see guys wandering around worried about being a French poet.*

GC: Do you know how Hart Crane got fucked up? Hart Crane took the two great American poets, Edgar Allen Poe and Walt Whitman. Now, Edgar Allen Poe is in, Whitman is out. So poor Hart Crane was like an accordian, in and out, in and out. He didn't last too long, but he knew his shot. He knew who his two daddies were.

RK: *Do you feel some kind of stress to express America?*

GC: Oh yeah, I love America, I love America. And I know why. You take a mystical number, say like Columbus coming over in the Santa Maria. That may be the second coming, but it'd be the geographical number rather than a baby being born out there.

RK: *You say you love America and you do, but you're ambivalent about it; like you're afraid to go into an American Express office, or in a Poem, you're afraid to go into an American Express office.*

GC: It was a drag all the time, man, I love them but I had to wait in line for the mail, first of all, right. And you've got these old ladies from Duluth going "Ugh" to me. It was a drag going to the American Express.

RK: *But you mean more than that; I mean you're not really talking about some hassle with the American Express. You're talking about some other America, or maybe the existing America.*

GC: I'm talking about the America whose applecart I upset, man. It's gone. The old cornball America you know, where people are all regimented and all that shit. I mean, look at you with your hair and all that.

RK: *And in that Kerouac poem, you talk a lot about the fact that there are two Americas. He keeps looking for one and there's one there but that's not the one he was looking for.*

GC: Right. It was never there, you see. Whitman was at a time that was virginal and now we've got the birth.

RK: *There's a feeling around, some of it unjustified, and some of it comes out of your comments and other people's comments that books are a drag, and even the past is a drag, and everything should be spontaneous, that therefore there's no craft in your poetry. What would you say about the craft of poetry as you practice it?*

Gregory Corso and Allen Ginsberg, Grand Forks, ND, March 1974. PHOTO BY DENNIS SORENSON.

GC: As I practice it, I say I build a brick musehouse. The craft is there, man. See, words have only been written down in the last 400 years. It was always sung before that. And it's gotten back to the cycle where it's sung again with Dylan. Ok. Now. But I still say "You can just sit there, Gregory, and make the music on the page, too. Don't get up there and twang away." I use the expression "brightness falls from the air. Many a queen has died young and fair." That's beautiful music.

JOHN LITTLE: *Do you have a built in sense of form?*

GC: Yeah, I know I do. Oh sure. The "bing bang bong boom" hit it, right, with the *Bomb* poem. I mean that was real music coming out on its own, and I don't have to knock myself out too fast with it, you know.

RK: *But you don't worry around about syllables or stress or . . . ?*

GC: I like to rhyme when I want to rhyme. When I don't want to rhyme I don't rhyme. It's all music.

JL: *How did you get that sense of form? You never did cultivate it, never did study the sonnet?*

GC: That's the whole shot; if I did I wouldn't have had it. I know the sonnet . . . I can do the sonnet, the sestina.

JL: *It was there.*

GC: Yeah, because it's obvious to be there, it's one of the simplest things. Just do what you want to do, right. And poetry, top shot, poesy. I mean, that's the top profession, man. I walk down the street in New York, you know, I feel great sometimes. I look at those fuckers making millions with their Cadillacs and their businesses. But you, Corso, your fucking profession's beautiful.

RK: *Do you live in New York most of the time now?*

GC: Yeah, that's the city I'm most comfortable in.

RK: *Do you run into New York poets? By that I mean, you know, the people who call themselves the New York poets.*

GC: I don't meet many people. I used to know Frank O'Hara; now he was good. Now I don't bother much; sometimes I go to OTB and play the horses.

RK: *Do you think your poetry has changed since 1955?*

GC: You can see that's a progression there. The next book I know is going to be a top shot for me. Yeah, real smart little numbers. Those were all like just exploding out of me. This time I'm going to really look at them and say, "Ok, Corso." If I was building cars or was a carpenter I would talk that way—I'd say I built something nice—so I'll do it with poetry.

RK: *You seem to me sometimes to have two basic kinds of things that you do, which is not to suggest limits but identify a couple of things. One is a real conversational kind of thing: "32nd Birthday," for example; the other verges on incantation, "Requiem for the Indian," "Coit Tower," "Spontaneous Requiem for the American Indian." Do you try to write any one kind of poetry now?*

GC: I don't want to write elegies anymore. I don't want to get stuck, I don't want to write elegies for people, you know. And so I think that's done. Going to museums and zoos, I wrote a lot about. I felt for the animals in the zoo, and I felt the learning from seeing the great paintings, and all that. Now a very different shot in my poetry, very different number. I'd rather now live the life than writing it out on the page. But when it does come out, very rare now, seldom, it grows, like I say, a brick musehouse.

RK: *You think you're writing less now than you were?*

GC: I'm writing songs, now; I always have written songs; and to me they're love poems. People say there aren't very many love poems written today, right? I don't have to call my poems love poems, but they *are* love poems. I'm going to call these songs, though, this next book; that's the shot, man, so that the *word* has still got the music in it rather than twanging with the guitar up there, right?

RK: *Do you do more readings now than you did?*

Lawrence Ferlinghetti, Peter Orlovsky and Gregory Corso, Grand Forks, ND, March 1974. PHOTO BY DENNIS SORENSON.

GC: No. I haven't read for a long time.

RK: Do you have a small circle of friends in New York, or a wide circle of friends, or are you a loner?

GC: Yeah, I guess more of a loner than anything else. See, when I took drugs, that eliminated a lot of friends because you're always hitting them up for money and all that. They don't like that. So it's good; I got rid of them. Mainly, I sleep with my cats and the female. I love female. I've been with this one female now for a year. I like living with female. I keep close to her and all that; I don't bother much with the outside.

RK: In Elegiac Feelings, *"Geometric Poem" is an interesting thing. It's hand written, it's got little drawings on it.*

GC: Yeah, but it's wrong. You see, the Italian edition was great because it's big. That's when I learned Egyptian. But the way New Directions did it, it's very small, you need a magnifying glass. New Directions books are a particular size. So I said to him, "Don't publish the poem, I think that would just screw it up; just leave that one out." But then I realized, if you're talking about elegaic feelings, American, Gregory, and you want to go back to your sources, and the Egyptians are undoubtedly the sources, with the elegies, right? With the death shot.

RK: *Do you have a good relationship with New Directions?*

GC: Yeah.

RK: *Why did you leave Ferlinghetti?*

GC: Oh, I didn't leave Ferlinghetti, Ferlinghetti left me. You see, I wrote a poem called "power"—that's in my *Happy Birthday of Death*. My "Marriage" is in there, and some of the real goodies in that book. But Ferlinghetti thought it was fascistic; he didn't understand I was changing the word, "power." I said, "Why can't a poet handle this word, break the meaning of it?" So he wouldn't publish it. Now, I got very insulted that he sent it to some San Francisco publisher who also refused. So I said, "Well, bullshit, give me my book back," and wrote to New Directions and said, "Hey, you who publish Pound and Rimbaud, do you like long poems?" because these were long single word poems: "Army," "Power," "Police," "Marriage," —and Laughlin wrote back, "Of course," and took the book. And Larry, years later then suddenly realized, and said, "Gregory, yeah." This is a straight story, it's not downing Larry. I got to dig Larry very well, man, on this trip. I guess the one guy I didn't get too close to was Snyder, you know, because he left too soon; I don't know him too well. I dig the man a lot. I wasn't trying to sabotage anything; I think that Allen thought that I was trying to sabotage his feeling about how to survive on this planet, right? And I could get no way edgewise to say it's also a mental evolve though, too, folks, also the head—take care of it.

JL: *Has your relationship changed much with Snyder?*

GC: I don't know him that well. I knew that man very early in the game, but as I say not that well.

JL: Has it changed with the other poets here?

GC: Well, it's gotten nice with Ferlinghetti, and Allen's my old friend. He lives in New York; I see him all the time.

JL: They seem to be putting up with you at times.

GC: I don't think Ferlinghetti though. Larry was mostly the one who did not admonish me.

JL: Gregory, you said earlier that the Beats have hurt themselves but they never hurt anybody else. Gary Snyder says a different sort of thing. He said that the Beats were aware that they had to take some responsibility for the kind of things that had happened to people who had misused drugs. I was wondering if they don't have some of the same concern for you.

GC: Allen has a tendency, and he might be right—a tendency to care too much for me, to come on like a daddy, you know, and tell me, "Well, Gregory, take care of yourself and all this bit." And I had to finally straighten him out and say, "Look, Allen, we're peers, man. And if I live my way—you sit and meditate, that's good. I'm not telling you that I dig it, but you do. But I live my way." It's the only way, man, otherwise, you know, we'd break intercourse.

JL: So you don't think that they feel protective toward you, that they see in you a projection of things that they once recommended that maybe they no longer do?

GC: I think they really want to do sincerely good; I think they're telling people right and maybe some way in life how to take care of yourself. I think that's good, but that's not my hit. Mine is the mental shot; I say, "Great, if you know the info, if you've got the knowledge, get your sources . . . I love it. Whether you drink, or smoke or what your farm is like and all that, I'm not interested."

RK: Do you make a living off poetry?

GC: No.

RK: How do you live?

GC: Oh, maybe that I do because I can sell my manuscripts, and I get good money for them. Also readings; and so sporadically I do make monies. I never had to steal or anything when I used to buy dope, for instance. I never had to steal for it. But they're books, notebooks, that I write in.

JL: Who do you sell them to and how much do they pay you?

GC: Oh, I give them to Gotham Book Mart in New York, which sells them to Columbia or to the University of Texas at Austin. They get half the monies and I get a half, rather than me dealing direct with these universities. I get what, about $200 a book when I need money. It's terrible, years ago the poor poets, man, they did nothing. They'd just throw them away or lose them or some shit, right? When I needed money for dope, you see, I would never recopy out the poems. I'd just sell the book. So a lot of my poems, you know, are in the universities and have never been published . . . from 1965 to now. But the goodies I remember in my head. *Elegiac Feelings* came out only because of the death of Kerouac. The other poems, the elegies on Kennedy and the American Indian were done beforehand. That's the only reason why I put it together. I said, all right then, here's a book, there's a reason for it.

RK: Have you ever written a poem to Neal Cassady?

GC: No. No. Only to Jack.

RK: Did you know Neal?

GC: Yeah, I knew Neal. But only to Jack, yeah. Yeah. I loved him.

RK: But Neal was another death. You know, they kind of all came in a very short period of time.

GC: Yeah, but they both died pretty close. You know how Neal died? He was a railroad man, worked on the railroad. In Mexico, after a wedding, he took off his clothes and walked the railroad tracks and

163

somehow, the drinking and the cold air killed him—exposure. And then Jack went soon afterwards.

RK: *You really seem attached to poetry. Several of the other writers this week have ecological concerns, or political, or scientific, but it looks like you're naked with your poetry.*

GC: The poet and poetry is inseparable.

RK: *Doesn't it get kind of cold with nothing but your poetry on?*

GC: Oh, I've got more than that, too, you know. What is poetry but embracing the whole thing. Like I can take the megagalaxy in my head.

JL: *Like in "Bomb?"*

GC: I can take the "Bomb," or I can take blue balloons. But it's not political at all. It's a death shot. You see, because people were worrying about dying by the Bomb in the Fifties. So I said, what about falling off the roof, what about heart attack. And I used the double old-age: old age I picked as being the heaviest—"old age, old age." One line that I've written in that poem that's not in the poem, and it should be in there is "Christ with the whip," like "St. George with a lance." I read it yesterday. I don't augment or take away, but it could be a smart idea if I did add that Christ with the whip number.

RK: *Who are "old poet men" today?*

GC: Geez, there ain't any. Really, they're gone. Auden, I'd say, was the last one probably to go.

RK: *What do you think about Robert Lowell or his poetry?*

GC: I like his "Tudor Ford," a pun, right? That kind of thing. Or the "boy with curlicues of marijuana in his hair." He's sharp. He didn't dig me too well. He dug Ginsberg because they could rap about poesy and the craft of it. When he woke up that *I* was in prison as a kid . . . he was there for CO, right . . . and I was there for something else, ripping off Household Finance.

JL: Tell us about the circumstances of your arrest and what it was for.

GC: Well, 1945, the war was over. The Army-Navy stores were selling these walkie-talkies. And I was 16 years old, right? I said "Shit, man, it would be great to get three walkie-talkies" and two other guys, one guy'd be in the car saying no cops are coming along, right? We got away with 21 thou. Now I didn't know how to spend money in those days, and those guys didn't. That's how I got caught. They opened up a big hall on 99th Street, you know, Irish neighborhood. And the police asked where they got all the money. Like a dope, I gave my name to those two guys and they mentioned it. I went down to Florida and I bought a zoot suit, leaving big tips. I mean, how dopey, man alive. That's how I got to prison for three years, because the judge said I was very dangerous, that I was putting crime on a scientific basis. Those motherfuckers Household Finance, they're the ones who give you the money and take interest on it, right? I think I was a blessed man, I didn't know that. I'd have ripped off anybody, I would have done it. But I made a good shot with Household Finance.

JL: Did you pick up the term "Daddy" when you were in prison? Isn't it a homosexual term? What do you mean by "daddies?"

GC: I mean sharp people. I had no homosexual experience in prison. There was nothing like that. I was dug, though. But since I was Italian and the Mafiosi were running the shot, and I was the youngest (I entered the youngest and I left the youngest, entered 16½ and left 20), I was like a little mascot. That's where I learned to be funny in life. Because I made them laugh, I was protected. Humor was a necessary survival condition when I was in prison. Man, their hearts were broken when I left prison. They dug me so fucking much . . . I brought life to them. There were guys doing 30–40 years. They told me, "Don't take your shoes off, Corso," in other words, "you're walking right out." And the other daddy—I didn't call them daddies then—but that other daddy said to me, "Don't *you* serve time, let time serve you." That's when I got the books, that's when the books came. Then when I left, the one man who did talk to

**Kenneth Rexroth, Allen Ginsberg, Lawrence Ferlinghetti, Peter Orlovsky,
and Gregory Corso, Grand Forks, ND, March 1974.** PHOTO BY DENNIS SORENSON.

me says, "When you're talking to six people, make sure you see seven," in
other words dig yourself. Prison food was really awful, but I had good food,
because the Mafia guys got the food from the outside. They cooked steaks
and everything, and I was always invited to eat. I learned to ski in prison.
Winter time comes in Plattsburgh, snow piles up. You get your skis from
Sears, Roebuck. They had a ski lift going. The first time I put on a pair
of . . . everybody was lining up to go to their cells . . . I went down
beautifully, man, held myself right, and psshhh, stopped like that, took the
fuckers off, got right in line to go back in. Yeah, I learned to ski in prison. I
always wanted to do a play, you know, and start the play off in prison with
somebody coming down on skis.

     JL: *How come Kerouac never did deal much with homosexuality
and gaiety in his books?*

GC: Well, Jack was a beautiful, beautiful man. His sex life would have gone both ways in anything like that, you know. But then again it was more towards the female than it was anything else. But he loved his fellow man, like, he loved Neal, he loved Allen, he loved Bill Burroughs, and especially Lucien Carr. Oh wow, did you ever read Kerouac's *Vanity of Duluoz*, where his friend Lucien killed this guy who was following him in Columbia. Lucien was a very handsome young man, and this big red-haired fag was chasing Lucien all over. And Lucien finally just got tired of it, stabbed the man. The man yells out, "So this is how it happened." Not "This is how it *happens*," but "this is how it *happened*." Lucien goes with the bloody knife, up to Kerouac, who was his friend. And Jack says, "Oh-h-h, Go-o-o-d, Lucien, Lucien." Poor Jack, man. All right, you know what he did? He helped his friend out. Dropped the knife down the sewer drain somewhere. Burroughs had the other hit, killing the wife, you know . . . drunken, she puts the glass on the head . . . William Tell shot, cheow. That's the weight that these people have. Burroughs told me, "Gregory, there's no such thing as an accident." So how was I going to take that?

RK: *That makes Norman Mailer stabbing his wife in the arm with the scissors seem fairly small. Mailer's done a couple of things that tended to support, at least in the public eye, some things you were doing in the 50s, "The White Negro" essay, for example.*

GC: Well, of course, he wanted to join the bandwagon, you see. These guys who are Army writers knew where the goodies were.

RK: *Do you see him much anymore? Any? At all?*

GC: Every time I see him he wants to wrestle with me, hand wrestle. What a drag. I'll tell you, Kerouac, the football player, didn't play that shot with me. He was a strong, beautiful man; he didn't have to show his strength. He took a Columbia University football offer and then decided he wanted to write. He meets Ginsberg and Burroughs there, right, and said, "Fuck it all." No way he's going to play football. They were just all meeting in this house, rapping all the time. Beautiful.

JL: *Hey, I asked you a question awhile ago, and I wasn't really happy with the answer you gave me. Kerouac wrote a kind of autobiographical fiction. He wrote it just like it happened . . .*

GC: Right, right, no fiction—and some of it was so beautiful.

JL: *O.K., then if he's writing what happened, why does he never mention gaiety, homosexuality? You've got Burroughs, Ginsberg . . .*

GC: Because they never had it with Jack. Don't you understand?

JL: *But they had it with other people and Jack knew about it.*

GC: Yeah, yeah, Jack knew about it, and Ginsberg loved Jack Kerouac.

JL: *He had to have been thinking about it. Did he censor himself?*

GC: No. Because Jack never had homosexual affairs.

JL: *Why didn't he mention that he didn't?*

GC: Why do you have to mention what you don't have?

JL: *Carlo had it. He talked about Carlo, he described Carlo.*

GC: That's Ginsberg. Well, Allen wasn't a rampaging faggot, you know. I told you, when I first met him he was balling that chick, Dusty Mullins.

RK: *He was really with her?*

GC: Yeah. Oh, he loved Dusty. He also loved a very fine woman, another one—what was her name—in San Francisco? Allen, funny, I guess you'll have to ask him that number—the sex shot. I don't think it's any of your affair about another person's sex life, unless you want to ask them. Don't ask me.

JL: *I was asking you about Kerouac's fiction technique.*

GC: His fiction technique was very straight, it wasn't fiction. And that's what I say is so good about it.

RK: Your name, at least in the 50s, was really connected with Ginsberg, more than any of the others we've had here this last week.

GC: We were the two poets. They're novelists, you know. And Allen and I were poets. When Allen and I read poetry early in those days, he would read "Howl," very serious; and I was, like I said, giving the humor number. That's what saved it. It would have been too heavy otherwise. Gregory came over with his "Marriage" or something like that, and everybody was happy and laughing. So it worked, it was a nice balance. We were the poets, Allen and myself.

RK: So really you complimented each other.

GC: Oh, sure, sure, sure.

RK: Ginsberg's really published a lot, has all these political connections, movement connections—he may be the most famous Beat. So you could have been in a position to say, "Gee, I wonder if I should do more things like Allen."

GC: Right, and I did not. I stayed out of it in the 60s and for good reasons, too. I figured that was the route they'd taken, let them go on with it because something's going to have to happen after that; and conserve some of the energy, Gregory. Let Allen take care of it nice; and he did. You know, this man's got all his strength and his energy. You dig? I don't have to be throwing myself out like that. That's when Allen got to understand me. He was burnt up in the beginning, saying "Gregory, where are you, man, like, help us along." I said, "No, this is where you've got to understand Gregory. This is what I do now. If I'm going to go towards dope, if I'm going to make babies like I did and all that, that's my shot."

JL: Tell us about meeting Ginsberg.

GC: Oh, that's nice. But nothing was ever planned, you dig. Nothing was planned. I met this man in a dyke bar, the Pony Stabe in Greenwich Village; it was beautiful. 1950, I was about six months out of prison. I'm there with my prison poems and he just digs my face, you see, cause he's a homosexual, right. He didn't know who I was or my poems.

Sitting down, he likes me and I says, "Well, look at these poems, you;" and he says, "You got to meet a Chinaman." Now "Chinaman" was an expression meaning a second rate poet, who was Mark Van Doren. He says, "You got to meet this poet." I says, "Oh yeah? Well, O.K., great," you know. Mark Van Doren tells me that I wrote too much about my mother. That was the critique laid on me by Mark Van Doren. John Holmes, who wrote Go, said I write too much green armpit imagery. I'm getting all these fuckers laying flak on me. All right. So finally I get Ginsberg, and I said, "Look, one thing I want to know is, I live across the street in this hotel room and I see this chick through the window balling every night, shitting, taking a bath, and I jerk off to her. I would like to go up there tonight and knock on her door and say hello to her." He says, "Oh, I'm the man you see that balls her." You dig? That's how I met Ginsberg and he brought me up there, man. It wasn't through reading the poems in a magazine somewhere and saying, "Hey, let's get together." He was the one I was jerking off to, watching him fuck her.

JL: So we know Ginsberg liked your face. What did you like about Ginsberg? Just the fact that he was an act going on across the street?

GC: Aw, come on. Man, he so loved me. He introduced me to Kerouac and Burroughs. He dug me a lot.

JL: I'm asking what you felt towards him.

GC: I felt that the man dug me. Don't you understand? It was beautiful. I'm right out of prison, all right? I had those years with me. He came out of Columbia University still writing little William Carlos Williams-like poems.

RK: Prison Poems were even before Vestal Lady?

GC: Yeah, they're gone. They were lost in Florida. They were lost in a suitcase at Hollywood, Florida. A fucking suitcase in the Greyhound Bus Terminal. Gone. And Hope, my girlfriend; Hope, my first girlfriend, she went to all the Greyhound presidents to get the things back. Papers in a suitcase. But I remembered two poems from them, and they're in Vestal Lady. "Sea Chanty." That's my first poem. See, and I remember, I don't lose nothing, man.

RK: *All right.*

GC: My mother hates the sea,
    my sea especially,
    I warned her not to;
    it was all I could do.
    Two years later
    the sea ate her.

    Upon the shore I found a strange
    yet beautiful food;
    I asked the sea if I could eat it,
    and the sea said that I could.
    —Oh, sea, what fish is this
    so tender and so sweet?—
    —Thy mother's feet—was its answer.

Now that's a heavy because I never saw my mother. I heard that she went back to Italy, so she took the ocean, right? So that was my 16-year old poem of someone going across the sea—but whatever goes there comes back to the shore.

RK: *You never knew your mother?*

GC: No, no. I guess I must have been about six months old when she cut out. See, I had a double whammy laid on me. When she left, they gave me to another mother, all right? Now, I thought she was my mother, and then they took me away from her. So that's like a double whammy. That was before I was two years old. So my first memory is with the second one, and you know what it is? It's a beautiful one. In the bathtub—I remember the black hair on her cunt and the water. Now that's a good shot for a two-year old because what you got is a contemporary form of birth and that old primal shot—water.

DR: *How different is it now? You said that you sort of comple-mented Ginsberg in the old days. You were the humor and he was serious, reading "Howl." Nowadays you're still doing the same thing; you're still the humor, and yet they don't seem to tolerate you. What's happened?*

GC: But I do write serious shots, man. But then again, I'm going to have to hold respect to Ginsberg; a little bit to Ferlinghetti, but I would hold it most to Allen.

RK: *When did Peter come into all this?*

GC: Ah. Peter—ambulance driver. He was helping people who were crashing and all that, and Allen just loved him, man; here was this guy helping people all the time. He was a beautiful man.

RK: *When did he meet him?*

GC: 1954. They've been together ever since, and they will be till they go to the happy hunting grounds. They're two good people, man. Peter's beautiful, right? Remember him today? Even though he bugs about no smoking and all that shit.

RK: *He's very pure, I mean very solidly "him."*

GC: Yeah, yeah, yeah.

RK: *I don't know a lot yet about how you write a poem. There's a couple of things crossed out in "Geometric Form" cause that's in your handwriting. So I don't know if you scratch out a lot, if you think a lot. . . .*

GC: Where's *Elegiac Feelings?* I'll show you something in it. That's a good question, that goes back to craft. See that 1940 there? (NOTE: Pg. 47, *Elegiac Feelings American*) I'm into the poem of Egypt when suddenly I'm bugged about President Johnson and the bombings, "the blast and the smithered," the bombs falling from the 1940s. "On the dead body of the true President," right? When Kennedy was killed? You need a magnifying glass to read it, but it's got nothing to do with the Egyptian poem. Spontaneous poetry is also spontaneous change when you're working at it. But dig my glyphs. That's the first literal translation, man. That was good, my first transliteral glyph.

RK: *Is this from somewhere else that you wrote these things down?*

GC: No, I studied for six months in Paris, I learned to do the hieroglyphs and that's a correct literal translation. Some of these things I created, though; see, this I created.

RK: *That's a hippopotamus with an alligator in his mouth.* (NOTE: Pg. 45, Elegiac Feelings American)

GC: But dig my little bunny angel. She's dropping the geometry down on Egypt. Right? And then they did their triangles, right? (NOTE: Pg. 44)

> You O rainbow Egyp-clay
> seated upon skyey dangles
> sprinkling globes and triangles
> down upon the day

I had a ball with that.

RK: *How did you learn hieroglyphics? Did you know somebody?*

GC: Oh, six months in Paris, a M'sieur LaFrance at the Hotel Stella where Rimbaud lived. I'd get my Arab dope and I had this book from Cambridge University on hieroglyphics, and I just stayed in the room for six months all winter like that until spring. That was 1965. See, that's when I got divorced, left my wife and daughter. So I said, "Fuck it, Gregory, go off somewhere." So I went off and played around a little bit. Yeah. You know that's one that so many people like that's drawn is "The Tree." There you go. (NOTE: Pg. 39) Dig that. Now, the sun—Van Gogh did a beautiful thing of it. He did the tree and did the sun very big. You know that painting? It's beautiful. There's the sower in the wheatfield. Now this one here I learned from prison. (NOTE: Pg. 38) This guy's cleaning up things. See him? All right. Now, if that ain't Egyptian . . . but this was where I first used the great word "scrybound." You know what "scry" means?

RK: *To discern, to foretell the future . . .*

GC: Right. That is what they call the guy with the crystal ball. It's "scrying;" they usually call him a swami, right? It's scry. This is where I use my music (NOTE: Pg. 38)

> Scrybound o'er pre-Egypt's
> geometrical pool
> In mine velvet robe's varium vair
> —angel of darkest school
>
> I'll descry Wlamtrice wold brool
> its issuant gazebeasts
> and furoak oakfur meloday
> —this tenth of Atum's cursing feast

RK: *There are some things there that aren't English, Gregory.*

GC: It *is* English. They're old daddy words, my friend. I like to know my own language, you know. But this would be a hard poem, let's say, to read. Look at that one. (NOTE: Pg. 49) Here's "poet on the architect Nekhebu's knee." But you see, in the Italian edition, he's red. And there's the architect, and here's where I put myself in a shirt and tie.

RK: *I was going to ask about this picture of you on this cover. You've got a tweed coat, a tie, no hair hanging down.*

GC: Oh. The Olivetti man took that picture, the man who did the Italian edition.

RK: *Were you being an angel then, or something?*

GC: I was a wild fucker, then. Are you kidding? What about the one in *Long Live Man* now, that's a nice picture of me. I was sitting next to Allen. I wished they would have kept us together there, but they took Allen out and left my picture there. That's a dreamy fucker. That was in Tangier. Then I called the book, *Long Live Man*. I did that because of *Happy Birthday of Death*, and I said, "Oh God, Gregory, get off the death thing already. Say *Long Live Man*." I was going to do *Gregorian Rants*, but I said "I don't have to play, to entertain these people by calling my book *Gregorian Rants*."

RK: *That would be almost like Pope's "Dulness," which he refused to have his book called. You don't seem to be worrying about publishing very much. Who was it, Duncan, I think, who said he wasn't going to publish anything for 15 years because he didn't want what people were expecting or anything to have any influence on him.*

GC: Keats had that problem. See, Shelley would get along with Leigh Hunt, man, and Byron, and they'd have great raps. And Shelley was the best in it; but Keats would not join in because he didn't want to be influenced by them. And Shelley understood that—he dug Keats, you know. Shelley was a sharp daddy; oh, he's beautiful. I mean Byron couldn't stand up to him, none of them could stand up to him, when he was going good. Those meetings in the house of Leigh Hunt must have been fantastic. There are some of them written down by Mary Godwin, his wife. See, what they put down Shelley for is that he married his cousin, Harriet, she was pregnant when she threw herself in a river because he suddenly gave up on her and went towards Mary, who wrote *Frankenstein*. And so therefore, they said, there's the flaw in Shelley. No way. Harriet should have been cooler or something.

RK: *One of the flaws they say is in Shelley is the line, "I fall upon the thorns of Life, I bleed," exclamation point.*

GC: Yeah, that's a lovely line.

RK: *Now, you use exclamation points.*

GC: Right, right. I love them. That poem, "Ode to the West Wind" is one of the greatest poems ever written. You know why? It's a lyric. He smartly injected himself into it right towards the end. He said, "Make me thy lyre, even as the forest is:" right? He was always giving it to the wind but then he puts himself into it beautifully.

RK: *Where'd you get this gesture of parting your hair with one finger? It really shows disdain, like on the stage at any rate, this last week. It's really been kind of a "screw the people that are trying to talk ecology."*

GC: No, no, that's an assumption.

JL: *It is arrogant, and it's also elegant and feminine.*

GC: All right. All right. And I'll take the feminine part too.

RK: *You really surprised me the other day when you were reading. You said a line was too corny, like you really have an inner sense. Everybody says, "Gee, 'I fall upon thorns of Life, I bleed.' That's corny, that's sentiment, that's romantic." You're romantic, and all of a sudden you're a romantic saying, "Gee, that's too corny."*

GC: Yeah, of course. I'm poor simple human bones.

RK: *Are you hung up on being a hairy bag of water?*

GC: Ah, that's a good one. That's what I yell on people a lot.

RK: *You worried about it in the interview with Bruce Cook.*

GC: When did that happen? Oh. Oh, he lied.

RK: *Well, I want to hear about Bruce Cook.*

GC: Mr. Cook was a liar. I'll tell you about him. See, when I was living in New York City, he said I was sleeping in a sleeping bag. Bullshit! I was with Belle. Now I didn't know she was a DuPont lady, you dig. I mean, wow, what a house we had. She was an Aries, like me. On the floors there were big fucking rams.

RK: *He said you could just leave any day, man.*

GC: Yeah, of course. But there was the most elegant fucking house, man. Her father knocked out these lions, there were all these lions on the floor, rugs and everything, man. Shit, that dummy wanted to create something; he said, "Well, Gregory, that little beatnik, with his sleeping bag." I never slept in a sleeping bag . . . beautiful fucking bed there, man.

RK: *Have you read that book?*

GC: Yeah, I thought it sucked because he lied.

JL: *What lies?*

Gregory Corso and Allen Ginsberg, Grand Forks, ND, March 1974. PHOTO BY
DENNIS SORENSON.

GC: Well, the visit to the house. The only time he met me was at
the house with me and Belle. We served him nice drinks in the garden and
everything. Shit. He didn't mention that. He had me sleeping in a sleeping
bag. Bullshit. Do you think it's an insult that I call human beings hairy
bags of water?

RK: *I don't think so from where it comes from; I mean we're a sack
of guts. That's what people are.*

GC: That's what I mean, right. That's what they are. You see, and
it's a chemical hit. That's going to save them. Their bodies are all perfect,
beautiful. I love fucking and all that. You are a hairy bag of water, aren't
you?

RK: *You talk a lot about death.*

GC: Oh, I took death when I was a happy kid, man. Man, I took death in 1957, my death shot. I was a happy guy. I said, "Now tackle it, Corso; take the biggies." I'm no morbid soul.

RK: *Are you not worried about death now?*

GC: Oh, hell, no. I passed that shot. I told you in that poem on the airplane, I scared the guy more than the plane. And when he thanked me for it, I said, "Look, I passed that death fear shot a long time ago." You know how I passed it? In 1960 in Luxembourg Gardens in Paris, Sunday afternoon, people with their perambulators and children, old people sitting on the park benches, children pulling their boats in the pond there, lovers kissing on the grass. I said, "This is heaven, Gregory." Suddenly behind a tree I saw a guy with an axe, and I said, "Boy, he could make a shambles of this heaven—chop, chop, chop." Now who put that man behind the tree? I did; he wasn't there. But he *is* there in life, isn't he? That fucker is there with your bombs or whatever you call it. I called that heaven, the way things were going there. I saw the shambles of it, chop, chop, chop. It don't mean nothing to me, that chop, chop, chop—no more. And what about you—what about you people? Now would you get scared if you felt your heart was feeling pattering and suddenly you turned pale? And you might just have a heart attack and drop dead here? I think I'd go to a movie theater. I would. If I felt that was happening I'd run into a movie house.

RK: *Why a movie house?*

GC: I don't know . . . I thought I'd just get my mind off it or something. Can I ask you a question, John? Are you a happy man?

JL: *Right now, yeah.*

GC: I want to build up to something. Do you feel there are any mysteries? Something you don't understand?

JL: *I don't worry about them, wonder about them.*

GC: All right. Do you have any enemies?

JL: *I don't worry much about it if I do.*

GC: I don't have any; I make them all into friends, you know. All right. Do you love me?

JL: *I believe I do, and I think I loved you on first sight. You know, you got off that goddamn airplane with your fucking gold earrings, your long hair, your purple shirt, and you ran around hugging people and frightening old ladies. Let me ask my question; I'm going to ask you one. I want you to give us a chronological and exact history of your use of drugs, related to what you were writing at the time, when you first began using them, when you finished, and the effect that they had.*

GC: O.K. I took drugs after the poetry was written. I took drugs very late. I started in 1963; I was 33 years old.

JL: *Never in prison, never before prison?*

GC: No. I smoked pot in 1950 when I came out of prison. That's a joint every now and then. But I saw people shooting up. I never took the heavies then. In 1956 especially in Mexico, the marijuana was real good. But in 1963—heroin; that was the weight. I took it to experiment with my head and I forgot one thing. You said the arrogance of this gesture—I forgot that. Boy, if you get stuck on some fuck like that, then you got to give in. And that was very rough for a guy like me. I had to go beg for that fucker. So I said then it's nobody's business, Gregory—that's my medicine in the medicine cabinet, my chemistry. But I dropped it, I don't have to take drugs now.

JL: *Well, do you take methadone?*

GC: No.

JL: *How long have you been off methadone?*

GC: Methadone I've been off now two days. When I was in New

York recently I was taking drugs again, heroin. Now, if I just stop and don't take methadone I would have to go a few days real cold turkey, and I don't dig it. But if you just take a little bit of methadone, ten milligrams, not the hundred milligrams they give these guys, you can gradually be off it again, you dig? And that's why I go into drinking. A person takes drugs doesn't drink. I drink, right? And I've been feeling pretty good. I got great recuperative powers.

JL: Can you write when you take drugs?

GC: No, no.

JL: Are you going to quit? Are you going to get off drugs in order to do this big number you got planned?

GC: It's already done, this next book.

JL: You were on drugs when you did it?

GC: Ahhh, no. It's an alien substance in you. It knocked out the spirit of me. I didn't bother writing. What I dug doing with it was fucking because it erects your dick a long time. It takes a long time for you to come. So poetry was out of it. And when the poetry came, and I say it's a rare little number, this little brick musehouse that I've been doing, when it came it was intermittent. It was . . . well, I said, "Corso, is this a drag now to get the money to buy the dope and I'm being a pain in the ass among my friends by getting the money—so cool it." See, I'm no liar.

JL: O.K. How is your taking drugs and what you experienced when you take drugs—how much of that goes into your poetry?

GC: I don't take drugs to write about drugs. It's been done, right?

RK: What about Lawrence Lipton's Holy Barbarians? Did you ever feel a sense of responsibility or connection with those Venice West people?

GC: As far as responsibility, I have none. Not me, no way. That's an early book, isn't it? He was talking about people like me, right?

RK: *I think he was talking about, you know, like you get a movement and you get five poets or three poets to do something and there's an intellectual and emotional validity and spiritual validity, even. And all of a sudden there's a thousand people doing some of the things those people did, but not the other half.*

GC: I don't know about the other half. He saw me and Allen Ginsberg; we all came from the East to San Francisco, and this man, who just used to write about communist literature (all that shit!) was very, very impressed by us. It was early in the game. I don't know how it fits, or what.

JL: *Hey, do you care very much about ecology?*

GC: Should I? I don't know . . . I mean I don't *not* care, you dig what I mean? My daughter cares.

RK: *How old is she?*

GC: Ten years old. Yeah, she really cares. I stopped her from killing also. When she was a kid, she was about to step on a bug. I said, "No way." She never then killed anything. But I caught her, man, when she was about to fink on me. She was going to go tell her mommie in the other room that I was lighting up a cigarette and I said, "What? No way you tell on your father." "But I don't care. That's wrong, daddy, what you're doing is wrong." And she tells me to get fake teeth also.

RK: *Where is she now?*

GC: New York City. She just can't stand graffiti, she's so protected. She's an angel. When she sees graffiti, it really upsets her. So I said to the mother, "Well, man, I gotta be around her a little to wake this kid up fast, man. I don't want it to give her a jolt, when she gets this one shot, you know, what life is. You could easily let it grow in her, man."

RK: *What does her mother say?*

GC: Well, her mother's beginning to check me out and realize that I'm right. She's a little over-protective with the kid.

JL: You ever think about your three-year old who's going to read your poems someday?

GC: Yeah. Well, she's the angel—blonde hair and blue eyes. Her family made the atom bomb, and I wrote the *Bomb* poem. See the combine? The DuPont people were the first ones to make the atom bomb. The mother is DuPont and the daddy is the one who wrote the *Bomb* poem. So my daughter goes around and can say, "Well, O.K. If they made the bomb, look what my daddy did."

RK: The two consciousnesses . . . .

GC: Right. And that was no choice. It just happened. And Belle, beautiful. Belle is beauty, right? And she is very beautiful. Boy, she's strong and tough. Those New Mexican people, I'm telling you, man alive.

RK: Those who?

GC: People in New Mexico like they were mentioning up on the stage today.

RK: How does that tie up with New Mexico?

GC: Oh, female. Oh, because they live there, my daughter and Belle.

JL: The three-year old.

GC: Three-year old, right. But you know it's good that I have two daughters rather than, I feel, a guy because what a weight to lay on a boy, right—me? The son always tries to knock out the daddy.

RK: The girls can incorporate it more.

GC: Oh, yeah, I heard yesterday that the Women's Lib in town got to dig me. They were pissed off with me in the beginning. Reason they got to dig me was that I did say to them very straight: "Poets have been taking the whole shot all the time, you can't make a dichotomy. You can't just take half of it, you got to take the whole number. That'll save it, that'll do it."

RK: *What happened between like when you were 10 and 17? Where were you?*

GC: Ten to 17; that's good, a decade shot. One to 10, I had eight mothers, because I didn't have my mother; they sent me to all these orphanages and foster homes. Ten to 17 were really funny years cause 16½—prison, 13—bad boys' home; so from 10 to 17—institutional; out on the streets when I was 20 years old. I slept on the rooftops and in the subways of New York, man. I had no home. From 11 years old to 16½.

RK: *Do you speak Italian?*

GC: I could understand my father talk it; my grandmother, I used to understand her.

RK: *Do you know other languages?*

GC: Ancient Egyptian. Not spoken much today.

RK: *Ancient Egyptian. You'll never get into the Peace Corps, I tell you. You must look up a lot of etymology in dictionaries, like where it refers you to another word to another word to another word?*

GC: Oh, I used to. See, I know words—beautiful words from the past that people don't know, and it really saves the words. For instance, "scry" we got before, we understand what "scry" is. A pentacle-maker —you know who he is?

RK: *No.*

GC: Karcist. K-A-R-C-I-S-T. O.K., that's one for you. Now, the wind, that goes through the trees. You know what it is? Murmur, right? It's an onomatopoeic shot. You know what it really is? B-R-O-O-L.

RK: *In Old English?*

GC: Yeah. Thomas Carlyle, really. Poets can create onomatopoeia if they want, like "the duck quacked." I mean, my great little drawing of a duck, and out of the mouth comes "onomatopeia;" I don't go "quack" with the duck. I could sell that little cartoon to *The New Yorker*, I bet. I mean, it's a great one, right, a duck going "onomatopoeia." And I just love "duck,"—I love the word, "duck;" they're funny, ducks, man.

RK: *Did you read Philip Lamantia? Because you've got some images which really get into surrealism.*

GC: Yeah, yeah, him early, and Andre Breton; I dug him when I was 14 years old. Philip, now, you're talking about the guy who I dig a lot.

RK: *A lot of your images are really surrealistic: "a wrinkled angel weeping axle grease" or something like that, which is getting close to surrealism.*

GC: "Wrinkled angels," yet. I have to go back and read my poetry and learn. I love putting words together like "wheels of rainlight," "treelight."

RK: *You put words together. Like Kerouac.*

GC: Oh, yeah, that's compound, that is like chemistry. You put iron and another element together and you get a third. So that gives the birth, right? And when you put the heavies like "sexdeath" together, what do you get? You put two together, you do get a third. One and one does make three. Now, where four comes from always grabs me; really suspicious about four. I was playing around with geometry, but that's a big daddy, the number four. *Uno, uno,* and the baby out is the third, right? Who's that fourth fucker?

RK: *That's the guy with the axe.*

GC: (Laughing) The guy with the axe.

CHAPTER 13

A Version of the Apocalypse

Jack Kerouac was working on *The Town and the City* in the fall of 1947, and Allen Ginsberg was completing a long love poem to Neal Cassady. Another piece Ginsberg wrote at that time is a prose sketch of Times Square, which Kerouac adapted in *The Town and the City*. Much of "A Version of the Apocalypse" appears as a conversation between Peter Martin and Leon Levinsky [Ginsberg].

—Eds.

The storm just began. That's what Huncke said to a character we were standing with. I turned in awe to hear him say that, because I picked up on Huncke's tearful allusion to the crisis. But this character was not so frantic as we were. He stared at the tragic monkey mincing in the magic cage of glass where the weary madame in the mad bandanna poised her paralysed hands. The character nodded, but not at Huncke, and not at me, but at the deck of daemons. I did not say to myself, "This big horse is worried that his fortune is a nickel, while he was neither, at a time like this." Maybe it was J. King's shriek that I remembered, "These are not times in which one can afford to give up one's proctologist." Perhaps because the monkey was merely sad, and I was, truly, morbid. Sad, I mean, because I remember, "Triste comme la mort des singes," which I thought beautiful for years. And after all this time J.K. is in the hospital having an operation for some kind of ambiguous hemorrhoid. Yet this monkey's eyes are beads, though obviously they had once been closed in graceful sorrow. The character nibbles his nails. His fingers are peeling, of course, but so are everybody else's, in case anybody else had noticed. Or hasn't, for that matter. Anyway, he may ignore the situation, but before long his skin will turn to snow, I hope it melts on 42nd Street: perhaps a little yellow puddle in the gutter across from Pokerino. I might as well put this down once for all, that Huncke and, maybe, myself, and several mutual acquaintances all think that everybody is radioactive and nobody knows it yet. I keep running across snide little references to "explosions" in *The New Yorker*. Somebody somewhere is hip. They are probably very intelligent people anyway. Speaking of such things, there is a rudely Kafkian fable by some hysterical chick in *Kenyon Review* that talks about the Great Cold Wave or something on an H.G. Wells kick. Anyway there was some point made of how nobody could get up a fire in the imitation fireplace because all the furniture was plastic. People are beginning to notice things, but they haven't really begun gossiping about it yet. There are exceptions. Huncke told me that everyone he meets around the Square is guiltily concealing some kind of unclassifiable skin mortification. Myself, I have the peeling skin on my heels, too. Also I have the enamel particles that work out to the surface of the skin; and the little white hairs that appear out of the eyes and nose and mouth and copulate like corkscrews in the middle of the air. As well, those little retracting fungoid protuberances from the sphincter. Last month I also had a succession of throat infections followed by swollen glands. Yet I'm not unreasonable. I need more sleep, I need to keep regular hours. I saw a doctor today about my glands, and that is what he told me. Of course he evaded the question of the peeling skin, so naturally I didn't dare go so far as to mention the enamel. As for the hairs, I saw no reason to embarrass either myself or the doctor. He was practically crawling with himself anyway.

Philip Whalen and Allen Ginsberg, WNET rehearsal, November 17, 1971.

Everything is strange; I don't like to jest poorly (as I did about the corkscrews even though I was serious), but I like to think, in my own poetic way, that mother nature's going through a change of life. I am flippant, and that's foolish, but how can I write these things as other than amusements? It would not be funny, it would be embarrassing, if I assumed a confidential, Alyosha-like style, and really explained what I mean and how literally I mean it. It's beginning to drag me—all this is too theoretical, it doesn't make. Why bother? It's been a hard winter. That's what I mean.

All this snow . . . and cold. It was in the papers before, and we saw it. Huncke and I mentioned it. I'm not very perceptive about the matter, I

Hal Chase, Jack Kerouac, Allen Ginsberg, William S. Burroughs, Riverside Drive, NY, 1944. FROM ALLEN GINSBERG'S COLLECTION

just keep my mouth shut and my ears open, and I pick up on a lot. Like Huncke's remark, "The storm just began." I was wondering what the character would do. He didn't do anything at all, he was involved with the plastic gypsy. I would wonder why he had any interest in the machine; he looked too beat to care anything about poetry. He was on Benny and I suppose he was just feeling placeless and starry eyed and didn't know what else to do besides wander around like a zombie and stare at what was in front of him at the moment. Or maybe the vibration of a superstitious fancy of the moment; possibly he was a little afraid of the monkey.

Anything but radioactivity. I didn't like him, he wasn't a mad child wandering around in the Forest of Arden; he was a big sloppy horse, dirty featured, all incomprehensible. Maybe that's why I can't stand him, even if Huncke formally introduced us. Perhaps I am at fault. But he was so beat-looking and dumb. That as Huncke might point out to me, if I made an issue of it, it's part of a crassly competitive outlook. Situations are situations, but I would hate to be humiliated into admitting that I am a snob on account of that geek.

Huncke and I began to circulate. Pokerino used to be the All American Bus Terminal. I have a vague recollection of it as such a short time ago, but I never cut in there very much then, except to look for Huncke who spent a good deal of his time there, trying to steal suitcases. I don't think he was very successful, I think he almost took a fall there . . . number of times. He himself is a doomed man, in that way, and many others. I think I'd rather leave him a figment. Now, that is, I suppose it's irrelevant. Somehow everything seems that way, unless I think about it long enough. This is, just now, which shows you just how much in touch this business of mine is. Usually I get hung up one way or another, so that it doesn't matter what routine it is I'm putting down, I wind-up thinking about it, anyway. This last hassle, for instance, began when I began to figure up a pious little angle on the score, that it's a good thing that The Terminal turned into Pokerino before Huncke got busted there. However as I say, it means no difference, it so happens that he was in jail when it all happened. I meant to write the fact, also, that I have to make certain excuses about Pokerino. I wasn't in town when it happened myself. When I came back, there it was. . . . But people are always either afraid or snotty, and that won't do. I mean that I am serious. I am afraid, I am telling you this way, but it so happens that I am afraid of the real thing. As Huncke said, they are all trying to hide the plague, they think that they are personally unclean. But it's not that, it's not that at all; if they only knew, think what a load off their minds it would be. They are afraid of knowing, as if it were an unconscious kick they were on. I say, let's face it, let's gossip, let's show our peeling skins, let's carry mad little Japanese boxes around with us to collect our enamel in; or let's show a black feather on which we'll gather our dandruff serpents. Conditions have disintegrated, we must make every man and every woman understand this even if it means showing each other our fungoids. We must put an end to all of this shameful crap.

I hope you are hip that I am playing a game again. I didn't want to. I suppose that it doesn't matter one way or the other, what we think. Because I suppose it makes no difference, whatever is going to happen is going to happen. Just the same I always come back to wanting to see everybody put his mind at rest. It may be just so they won't get on my nerves so much, but it's more than that; everybody *is* worried, their psyches are continually picking up on embarrassing little routines from some fairly-well-frantic corners. Partly, I think, their character-armors are inexplicably breaking down, and these squares, some of them have never picked up on the theory before. It's a complete surprise, they suddenly are all there, set down in a physical world, completely come down, without any past, with nothing but an eternal literal Present surrounding them; they have no personalities, they discover, to carry them through. Their souls pop out in the air like flying discs. And disappear, again, of course, before anybody gets too seriously hung up. But once they dig their stiffening vanity, and their awkward pride they never forget. They remember seeing through their lies for a few seconds, they never forget. It's cruel; it's like death; everything suddenly seems real; think of the bottom of the sea. It's a mystical fright. Call it a shame, if you will, but it's your disgrace, and maybe it's your death. That's the weird answer. And I wouldn't be too surprised to see some kind of total extinction, either, I don't know. But now the subject is on it. All the characters that were asked to leave Brickfords and Horn and Hardart were falling into Pokerino; junkies from Dixon's on 8th Ave., also. Spades of all kinds; adorable sharpies and strange gargoyles, and also some pretty mad looking spade chicks were cutting in and falling into combinations around the Jukebox. Teaheads from everywhere, hustlers with pimples, queens with pompadours, lushes with green faces, fat dicks with clubs, cherubs with sycophants, wolves with adenoids, faces with blotches, noses with holes, eyebrows with spangles, old men with the horrors, bums with the stumbles and sometimes squares with curiosity or just passing through to catch a bus; and not only these few but the unprotected, the unloved, the unkempt, the inept and sick. A sensitive lyric poet who is one of my oldest friends paid a visit himself, on my recommendation, and he told me that immediately upon entering it seemed to him as if everybody was walking around under the floor. He said that he had to withdraw, so inexorable was the depression that settled upon him, almost at once. And he is not a vain man. Myself I am considered affected by the atmosphere—the wild, tremendous Jukebox, the weird overbrilliant lighting, the hundreds of slot machines that line the walls, the beat, absolutely beat, characters but the plain fact is that it is not a matter of aesthetic taste. For Hipster or Square, aesthete or philistine, or anything, so to speak, mankind is as one in the Pokerino. That is pedantic, or poetic, or sociological, as it sounds. Nevertheless one who shares each private disease must forgive all public guilt, and teach each conscience as his own. It is a result of everything that is happening right now. The time of the grand molecular come-down is coming. Pokerino is a radioactive Rose. © Allen Ginsberg

William S. Burroughs, London, 1972. PHOTO BY GERARD MALANGA.

CHAPTER 14

William Burroughs and Gerard Malanga Talk

This conversation between William Burroughs and Gerard Malanga took place in Burroughs' New York City loft on Sunday evening, July 21, 1974.

GERARD MALANGA: *I was most intrigued with the group photo of you with Kerouac, Ginsberg and Hal Chase taken in 1944. I was struck by the youthful, tightly-knit intensity that this photo evokes. Can you tell me something about how you felt being involved with these young people at the time?*

WILLIAM BURROUGHS: It's a long time ago. I remember that it was a posed deliberate 1920s photo.

GM: *You were a little older than the rest of the people in the photo.*

WB: Yes, not all that much older. I was about ten years older.

GM: *And you weren't writing at the time.*

WB: Not at all. No, that picture was taken—when is it dated?

GM: *1944.*

WB: Yeah, well my first book was written in 1952. It was published in 1953 . . . it was written in 1950–51.

GM: *Did you perceive yourself as being a writer at that time?*

WB: No, not at all.

GM: *What were your interests?*

WB: Oh, uh, nothing special. I really didn't see myself at all as a writer; it was Jack Kerouac who was *really* instrumental in interesting me in writing. He incidentally, of course, is responsible for the title *Naked Lunch*. He kept telling me I should be a writer and I said I don't know about the literary. So I really didn't start writing until quite late.

GM: *Did Allen also inspire you in some way or suggest anything about writing?*

WB: Uh, not as much as Jack did because, of course, Jack and I wound up in the same categories; I guess you can call Jack a novelist and I guess I certainly call myself a novelist.

GM: *Well at any time during the time that you were writing were you aware of being part of a scene?*

WB: Not really, because you see I started to write in Mexico and uh then I didn't come back to New York. I was briefly in New York in 1953 for about three months; but while the whole scene was going on—the readings and the Black Cat and all that—I was in Europe so I wasn't really part of the scene.

GM: Did you perceive or envision some type of a scene or movement in terms of Kerouac and Ginsberg who were hanging around you at the time in 1944?

WB: No, I did not. Not at that time. You see actually, of course, the movement of the scene was years later and I didn't perceive it then.

GM: What I meant—not necessarily the Beat Scene, but a scene in general. I came across a piece of writing in a book by Creeley—the title of the book is Pieces. Creeley writes in this book, "Allen's saying as we fly out of NYC—the look of the city underneath us like a cellular growth, 'cancer'—so that senses of men on the earth as an investment of it radiates a world cancer—Burroughs' 'law' finally quite clear." What is this law that Allen is referring to in his conversation with Creeley and on what level does it relate to a cancer?

WB: Well, of course, a cancer is a proliferation. You have proliferation of people; proliferation of population; proliferation of image; uh, proliferation of governmental departments. But I'm not quite sure of his reference there. He's speaking of New York City?

GM: Yes, he's speaking of New York City. Creeley reinterprets what Allen is saying to him. "Burroughs' 'law' [is] finally quite clear." I was just curious as to what that law was.

WB: The law is simply proliferation.

GM: What would your feelings or ideas of overpopulation be in terms of world economy?

WB: Well, I would say . . . excuse me a minute . . . get some cigarettes (gets up and walks to the far end of the loft and returns a minute later, picking up the thread of the conversation) . . . that I consider overpopulation to be one of the basic problems amidst so many other problems, insoluble now—inflation, for one. I know that Buckminster Fuller is behind this, but I just can't see how you can get away from it. There's just too many people and the more people you get, the more

William S. Burroughs, NYC, 1975. PHOTO BY GERARD MALANGA.

people you have; the more people who are able to say that apartments are high, the higher the prices are going to go.

GM: *I just finished reading the novel* Make Room! Make Room! *by Harry Harrison and it was made into a movie a couple years ago, called* Soylent Green.

WB: I heard about it; I didn't see the movie.

GM: *The movie is actually more interesting than the book.*

WB: Yes, I know this.

GM: *In the book the year is 2000. The city is New York. The population is forty million and certain groups of people are still trying to push the abortion bill through legislature to make it legal and there are these squatters' laws—if you have an empty room in your apartment there's automatic squatters' laws that say that a family can move in on you. There are no cars, no gasoline, no topsoil, no forests. Everything's been extinct for the last twenty years. It's very frightening.*

WB: And what is supporting this vast population?

GM: *New York City turns into a welfare state. I suppose it's the unwritten law of the rich get richer and the poor get poorer.*

WB: They're bound to. It takes more and more to buy less and less. And that, of course, benefits the very rich.

GM: *You mean once the momentum has started, which it already has, do you think it's impossible to reverse it?*

WB: No, it's bound to reverse itself one way or another. Uh, take these factors: overpopulation, natural resources, capital investment. Now, you can draw a graph that will show population will have to go down eventually because there isn't going to be any way to support these people as natural resources are exhausted.

GM: *Do you think maybe this book is too much of a fictionalized version of the future?*

WB: I don't think that under those circumstances or even under present circumstances that New York could even support a population of forty million. They would all be starving to death.

GM: *Well, that's what happens! Everyone's being supported by rations of water and artificial food and soybean derivatives.*

WB: Well, it's very hard to say what's going to happen. These practices are self-limiting.

GM: *What frightens you the most?*

WB: That's a very difficult question. Could you answer it?

GM: *The way we die?*

WB: No.

GM: *Could you answer it?*

WB: I was trying to think—um—it's been . . . someone asked me that before and I was not able to give a very definite answer. Some people do have very definite answers. They've got some kind of phobia, like Poe, of course, being buried alive.

GM: *What are your ties with the different cities that you've lived in and how have they effected your work?*

WB: The different cities I've lived in . . . well, Mexico City is one. Tangiers is another; London, Paris and New York. Those are the places that I've lived in for any length of time and the influence in my work I think is very clear that uh whole sections of *Naked Lunch* certainly come from Tangiers. There's a whole section on Mexico. South America I never lived in but travelled there for about six months and that's another thing of influence. Another influence is Scandinavia. Also uh Madrid. I was only there for about a month and a half or something like that. The whole concept of Freeland was born there. Copenhagen. Sweden. I was only in Sweden for about two days.

GM: *Do you think it's part of your nature to move around a lot?*

WB: I don't move around all that much. Uh, there's . . . when I was in Mexico City I did very little traveling in Mexico and the same way in Tangiers. I was there for about five years; but I didn't travel extensively.

GM: *What does living in New York City have that no other city you've lived in has to offer?*

WB: One very important thing. Every other city I can think of is going down, getting worse and this is not true of New York. New York is a much pleasanter place to live now that it was when I was last here for any length of time which was in 1965. London has been just steadily down. I just got to the point where I couldn't stand it. Higher and higher prices. More and more money to buy less and less. Duller and duller. I think that is certainly unique about New York, as the cycles go up and down; but as I say I found since I came back this time a very very pleasant place to live in comparison to its reputation for being a rude city. It's one of the most polite cities I've ever lived in. Yet, on the whole, right now, I find it a pleasant place to live. I'm very well satisfied with my decision to return here.

GM: *Do you find the books you write or do you invent them?*

WB: Both. Both, um, usually or often there's some basis in facts and fictualized that many of the phrases in *Naked Lunch* are direct quotes that I heard someone say at some time or another. Many of the characters have real faces. A great many of my characters, sets and situations I get in dreams. I'd say a good 50%.

GM: *Do you have a certain technique for notating dreams?*

WB: Well, yeah. I keep a pencil and paper by my bed. Because if you don't write them down in many cases you'll forget them. There's some basic difference between the actual memory traces of a dream and the actual event. Now I've had this happen: I'd wake up and I'm too lazy maybe to get up and I'll go over it ten times in my mind and say *well sure I'll certainly remember that*. Gone. So memory-traces are lighter for dreams than they are for so-called events. Yes, I keep a regular dream diary, because I write down any dreams that I have in the course of a night. I just make a few brief notes; that's all that's necessary. If you even have two words they can bring it back. Then I'll expand them into dream-scenes. If they're particularly interesting or important to one that might be useable in a fictional context I'll make a longer typewritten account.

GM: *Do you tend to edit your dreams in the sense that some dreams are less interesting than others so that you won't be notating all your dreams?*

WB: That's right. Yeah. Some dreams just don't seem to be very interesting and I won't bother with them. But I get long sequential narrative dreams and some of these have gone almost verbatim into my work.

Brian Gysin and William S. Burroughs, London, 1972. PHOTO BY GERARD MALANGA.

GM: *Narrative in the sense that there's dialogue in the dream.*

WB: Just like a movie. There's a whole dialogue—a story—and as

I say some of this I've been able to use almost verbatim but usually I haven't . . . I'll change to some extent when I expand upon it—amplify . . .

GM: *Do you work on a number of books at the same time?*

WB: Well, in a sense, all my books are one book; it's just a continual book. And whenever I say I publish a book—the book is 200 pages—I'll usually have 600 in which what I derived will overflow into the next book. Often I find that what I've decided to put in is not as good as what has been left out.

GM: *What do you do with the pieces you leave out if they're better than the ones you keep in?*

WB: Oh, I use them in a subsequent book.

GM: *So, it balances out.*

WB: Balances out, yes.

GM: *How long does it generally take you to finish a book?*

WB: Approximately two years.

GM: *Do you talk to other writers about your work?*

WB: I don't really know too many other writers.

GM: *How many hours in a day do you spend writing?*

WB: Lately I haven't done much writing. I gave a course at CCNY. I came over here in February and that took up all my time. And then I've been moving in to this loft here. This kind of interrupted my work schedule. I haven't really gotten back into it yet except, you see, the lectures that I gave at CCNY will be made into a book. I've been going over transcripts trying to get those into some sort of order.

GM: *Do you have a publisher that's going to bring it out?*

WB: I already have a French publisher. I'm having difficulty getting an American publisher. The transcripts are in a terrible mess.

GM: *Will you be teaching again in the Fall?*

WB: I hope not. I found it a terrible strain. An awful lot of work. And something I'd hesitate to do again if I had any viable alternative. In other words I wouldn't do it if I could avoid it financially. I have an offer from Buffalo which I may or may not accept. It's a very good offer financially. Much better than the CCNY. If you're going to give a reading that's another matter. You get up there and it's a one-shot thing; but if you got to get up there twice a week sometimes you don't feel like it at all. It's like suppose you have to give a reading twice a week for four months. I wouldn't say I didn't enjoy aspects of it—it did help me clarify my thoughts on a whole lot of subjects and I think it was a valuable experience. But it is just something I would think twice about undertaking it again.

GM: *But now you have the possibility of a book coming out of the whole teaching thing.*

WB: That's right. Actually if I had to teach again it'll be much easier, because I've got a whole course. Here I kept thinking—Oh my God! what am I going to say in the next lecture. Because I've never done it before and it took me about six hours to prepare a lecture. Two a week. It just didn't leave me time for anything else.

GM: *How do you prepare a lecture?*

WB: Well, you just sit down and type it out. I just sit down and type it out. I have found that's how long it takes. 10-pages is about an hour with questions.

GM: *And what was your approach in class? Did you read from notes you took?*

WB: I read from the notes. I had the lecture typed out and in many cases also rehearsed; which is to say I read it into a tape recorder. Now I've found that with readings, if you don't rehearse the reading there will be certain words you'll stumble over. So, if you rehearse it then you'll find why am I stumbling here. Well, it may be that a certain combination of words is difficult to say. You change them or you make a note there or you say them over into the tape recorder until you get them right. I was just rehearsing this afternoon. I have to give a talk in Albuquerque. No, I mean in, well, Santa Fe. I guess it is. And I got my lecture together in one hour and read it into the tape recorder.

GM: *But do you feel giving a lecture or a talk or giving a reading of prose is different from giving a poetry reading? Maybe you wouldn't need to rehearse if you were giving a poetry reading.*

WB: I don't know; I've never given a poetry reading. All my readings have been in prose and you certainly do need to rehearse for those just like an actor gives a performance and so does a lecturer.

GM: *Do you have a favorite contemporary writer whose works you go back to from time to time?*

WB: Well, yes. There's Genet, Beckett. Those are the only two I can think of immediately.

GM: *Are you aware of anyone in particular who's been most influenced by you?*

WB: Been most influenced by me? No, I wouldn't say so.

GM: *Are you very self-critical or critical of others?*

WB: Well, I think I'm certainly very self-critical. I'm critical of my work. And I do a great deal of editing. Sinclair Lewis said if you have just written something you think is absolutely great and you can't wait to publish it or show it to someone, throw it away. And I've found that to be very accurate. Tear it into small pieces and throw it into someone else's garbage can. It's terrible!

GM: *Whom do you learn a lot from: men or women?*

WB: Men.

GM: *Why is that?*

WB: I don't see many women, actually.

GM: *In a relationship do you tend to be more aggressive?*

WB: I never thought of myself as being particularly aggressive. No, but then, of course, I'm not in a business where aggression is mandatory.

GM: *What's better than sex?*

WB: That's the most difficult question of all. There's a lot of things involved. You see we have been conditioned on this planet to think that sex is displeasure, or pleasure, or pain. Or that sex is the greatest pleasure. We know also that there are pleasures that undercut sex like junk which, of course, is completely anti-sexual. What would be your answer to that question?

GM: *You could always channel that sexual energy into your writing.*

WB: Well, the answer might be what sex essentially is. And that's something I don't think anyone knows much about: what is sex? Why is it pleasurable? Do you have any answers to that?

GM: *Pleasure can cause pain in certain instances. Or pleasure can lead to pain.*

WB: Well, the theory, of course, that sex is simply a relief from a certain tension.

GM: *Which is probably beneficial.*

WB: Well, undoubtedly. Like the pleasure of thirst when you're really thirsty.

GM: *Maybe people who tend to shy away from having sex are the ones who are more susceptible to disease. Or cancer or various ailments.*

WB: Well, you know about the works of Wilhelm Reich. He says that cancer is essentially a disease of sexual suppression. That all cancer patients are equal to people who are sexually suppressed. Well, I think there is quite a lot of evidence of that.

GM: *Have you ever had a strong relationship with a man that wasn't sexual?*

WB: Yes, many. Depends on what you mean by strong. I've had all sorts of relationships. Business relationships to a wide extent. Intellectual relationships. I've had quite a relationship with Paul Bowles, Brion Gysin, both of which were completely non-sexual and, of course, I've had long business relationships with publishers and agents which are also social relationships. Friendship relationships with people like Terry Southern who is a very good friend of mine. Dick Seaver who is my publisher and also a very good personal friend.

GM: *Did you get to know Paul Bowles while you were in Tangiers?*

WB: Oh, yes. I'd known Paul for years.

GM: *Before you went to Tangiers?*

WB: No. I didn't know him before Tangiers. I met him in Tangiers and we became very good friends and I saw quite a lot of him there. And Maurice Girodias, my first publisher and I also had a long friendly relationship. With Maurice, not altogether compatible—capable of business disagreements. But on the whole it's been a most cordial relationship. Most cordial.

GM: *How did the relationship progress with Paul Bowles in Tangiers? What were your interests or what did you do together?*

WB: Talked. He has a vast library of Moroccan music and Indian music. Talked. Listened to music. He's extremely knowledgeable about Morocco and particularly about Moroccan music. We always had a lot to discuss. You've been to Tangiers?

GM: *Yes, but for a very short period. I was there in '65 with Warhol.*

WB: Yep. Oh, with Andy Warhol!

GM: *Do you attract comments from people on the street? Do people recognize you?*

WB: Much more here than they do in London. I had quite a few very pleasant encounters with people on the street.

GM: *Do you find your work makes relationships with people more difficult?*

WB: No . . . no . . . In what way do you mean?

GM: *Well, in terms of schedules . . .*

WB: Oh that, yes . . . yes, of course, I do spend a great deal of time alone. I'm not very gregarious. I don't like parties or sort of miscellaneous gatherings with no particular purpose. I see people on business which is often also a matter of friendship like, say, with Dick Seaver or somebody like that. I have a lot . . . not a lot, but a few close personal friends that I see regularly. The point is I don't see a lot of people. I don't move around a lot.

GM: *You have a book coming out soon with Dick Seaver?*

WB: I have a film treatment of Dutch Schultz which should be out in September. That'll be the next book.

GM: *Wasn't that published in London awhile ago?*

WB: It's a completely different version. This is a shooting script that I wrote which is 195 pages—an expansion of the book that came out in London. And we're publishing it with a lot of stills—pictures of all the people in it, like Dutch Schultz and Legs Diamond and all the characters from the newspaper files.

GM: *Do people tend to love you for who you are or what you do?*

WB: Well *that* is a very difficult question. Say with a stranger

—someone I don't know. Often they have a picture—an image—that they have projected on me which may have nothing at all to do with me at all.

GM: *Do you think that has a lot to do with the media imposing the image on you? On your own writing?*

WB: Well, whether the media people will tend to have—whether it's the media or their impression of me they've gathered from my writing anyone I think *will* tend to have a certain image imposed on them which may not have anything to do with what is actually there. I also feel that for a writer to be a novelist doesn't have by nature of his profession a clear-cut image of himself or a clear-cut image in general. And if he cultivates his image too much his work will suffer. For example, take a perfect case in point is Hemingway. His determination to act out what I might call the least interesting aspects of his own work—the big game hunter and all that. And to do everything that his characters could do and do it well. Always shooting and fishing and all that. I feel that his work suffered from that. So, finally you get . . . there's nothing there but the image: Poppa Hemingway.

GM: *Maybe those are the only characters he could actually relate to in his writing. Maybe some of the other characters he found less interesting in actuality.*

WB: Yes, but you can trace a steady deterioration of his work with emphasis on his own image.

GM: *In terms of those characters like the machismo images.*

WB: Yes. The image of Poppa Hemingway which took over more and more and then I think it was disastrous to his work; that's what finally killed him: his own image.

GM: *Because the image was disillusion.*

WB: As I said the image related to the least interesting aspects of his work. Now I found some of his earlier work, like *The Snows of Kilimanjaro*—I think is a great short story. When we get things like *Green Hills of Africa, Across the River and into the Trees*, his image has taken over there. And finally there's nothing in there, in the work but Poppa

Alene Lee and William S. Burroughs, NYC, Winter 1953. PHOTO BY ALLEN GINSBERG

Hemingway. The image. The whole matter of image I think is a very dangerous thing for a writer: too much image.

GM: *But no one escapes the media.*

WB: No one escapes the media; no, I wouldn't say that. I think someone has escaped the media for awhile. There's Beckett. No one's been able to pin an image on him.

GM: *In other words you're saying that in order to have an image pinned on you, you have to be in the news or written about.*

WB: I think there's probably more to it than that. Whether that is part of it, certainly; but I think that you have to go along with it at some point.

GM: Well, *let's say that a certain author or poet assumes an image of himself because he perceives himself as an archetype of a writer or poet in the past. So, he pursues and cultivates that image of himself in the media—by manipulating the media. Just as the media can manipulate the image of someone, so that person can also manipulate the media to his advantage. I was thinking that maybe Hemingway sort of plugged into a specific archetype of himself.*

WB: Yes. I think that this is something that is very dangerous for a writer, very dangerous for his work.

GM: *Do you think that such writers pursue this idea of image or archetype through the media crave for attention that they feel they might otherwise not receive?*

WB: Well, they may or may not be, but if they get, as it were, stuck with one image, of course, they are, if it's in a sense like an actor who gets stuck with one part.

GM: *Typecasting.*

WB: Typecasting, yes.

GM: *What would the remedy for someone who gets typecast be?*

WB: Well, they have to either break out of it or accept it. Now, look at Graham Greene. Look at the typecast as the bad Catholic, the old whiskey priest and you get further and further into it.

GM: *You think it's because it's an easy thing to do, an easy way of expression in terms of writing . . .*

WB: It's also, of course, an easy thing to do financially. If you have a certain product, like a painter will have a certain product—that is, something he does well and the people in the art galleries don't want him to change that product 'cause that's what they're selling. And writers can get into exactly the same bind where they are producing a certain product.

GM: *Do you think that one solution of breaking away from being typecast is to disappear for awhile and then come back at a later date with something new to present?*

WB: Uh, yes. Many writers do that. If they're in a position to do it financially; that is to not write anything for six, seven, eight years.

GM: *Well, what I meant was that they would be personally inaccessible, but still continue to write and then maybe come back as a different person. It's allowing for change in yourself as a person and as a writer.*

WB: Beckett, for example, has always been extremely inaccessible. He doesn't give any interviews. He will not allow his voice to be tape-recorded.

GM: *Does he allow himself to be photographed?*

WB: On occasion.

GM: *Did you have similar problems with being typecast or being an archetype for a certain lifestyle or certain types of associations with drugs?*

WB: I wouldn't say so. I've had a certain problem with attempt at typecasting; but, no. I wouldn't say that's been a problem. Because I don't feel that I have a definite image.

GM: *Do you have a desire for a certain type of image of yourself?*

WB: No.

GM: *Are you temperamental?*

WB: Temperamental? What does that mean exactly?

GM: *Unpredictable.*

WB: In what circumstances? I don't know. You know, when I think of temperamental I think of actors and actresses throwing tantrums which are actually very predictable. Nothing more predictable than a temper tantrum. In other words if you said that someone is temperamental I would say that they are trying to be unpredictable and not succeeding. In that sense, no.

GM: *I would like to get back for a moment on what we were talking about in terms of typecast and image in regards to yourself. It seems that through the course of your writing you tend to lean towards gangsters, drug addiction, certain types of crises that seem to have a connection with one another and I was just thinking that just your name in itself—WILLIAM BURROUGHS—would become a typecast brand name. All of a sudden people would identify your name with junkie or homosexuality or gangsterism.*

WB: Yes. I think that any writer is to some extent naturally typecast by his choice of subject matter. Like Genet is typecast as the saintly convict. Uh, yes, there's no avoiding that. And Graham Greene, of course, it's the old whiskey priest. Uh, of course, I'm no longer a drug addict.

GM: *Is there something you'd like to write about that you haven't written about? Something that is a complete change in terms of characters or subject matter?*

WB: Yes. I've been thinking a lot about that lately, of writing something completely different; but haven't really. I've made a number of attempts that haven't really worked out. I've been thinking of writing a completely straightforward novel with a beginning, a middle and an end.

GM: *In a sense then you'd be attracted towards a challenge in terms of change.*

WB: Yes, very much so. But as of late I haven't been able to make a complete change of subject; a new subject that I can write on. I even thought of writing a best-seller.

GM: *What's your definition of a best-seller? What's the formula for a best-seller?*

WB: Oh, the formula. The formula for a best-seller is very simple.

There are two basic formulas. One is something that people know something about and would like to know more about. The *inside* of Hollywood, the *inside* of advertising, whatever. If they don't know anything about it, no. The other, of course, is the menace, challenge, disposed, and the way this challenge is met, trying to resolve, like *Jaws*. A friend of mine who had to change his name to Ted Morgan, wrote an article on *Jaws*, called "The Birth of a Best-Seller." That is the formula of a best-seller. It's a very good book. It's worth reading. It's entertainment, to be sure; but it's expertly written about the challenge posed by a shark. The way in which this challenge is met and the final resolution of the challenge when the shark is finally killed. The challenge can be an epidemic; it can be a war; it can be almost anything.

GM: *It's interesting because Maurice Girodias just brought out a book called* President Kissinger, *which he's having a great deal of trouble with.*

WB: I hear he's getting thrown out of the country.

GM: *Yes, and I think what you said about the first point would relate to what people who already know something about Kissinger would like to know more about him.*

WB: It has to be something that people know *something* about. They want to know more about it. If they don't know anything about it, you don't have a best-seller, you've got nothing.

GM: *What do you think would be a theme that you feel people know about a little bit but would like to know more about that you might think about writing?*

WB: I haven't been able to think about it. Everyone I think of doesn't work.

GM: *Is that because maybe you don't know too much about it or don't know anything about it at all?*

WB: No. You see as Morgan said in his article, best-sellers are written up to the level of a person's ability. If you try to write down, to artificially create a best-seller, it doesn't work. So most of the subjects that I thought of in that connection didn't work. In other words, I had perhaps chosen a subject people knew practically nothing about and didn't want to know more about, like bacteriological warfare. They don't want to know about it.

GM: *Do you think that people don't want to know about things they're afraid of?*

WB: Of course not. Not if they're really afraid. It's like a horror movie. It can't be really horrible if you want to go see it.

GM: *To change the subject, when do you fall in love and how do you know it?*

WB: I don't know exactly what *falling in love* for me is. Hum, oh yes, the whole idea of love, of course, came in the Middle Ages: the concept of romantic love. Now remember, the Arabs don't even have a word for love—that is, a word for love apart from physical attraction or sex. And this separation of the two is a western concept, a Christian concept, as I say came in the Middle Ages—you know, romantic love, the knight and his lady and all that. So, as to what falling in love means I'm just a little bit uncertain. Love; well, it means simply physical attraction and liking a person at the same time.

GM: *Do you believe in a power greater than yourself?*

WB: Well, I think the self, what you call your *self*, is like the tip of an iceberg. So much appears above water and there's so much under water. If you could contact all your own abilities—uh, your abilities are incredible! For example, everyone knows what time it is at any hour of the day or night. I can set my mind, say if I have to wake up at 6 o'clock. I just have to say I have to wake up at 6 o'clock and I'd wake up right on the dot of 6 o'clock. I think what we think of as ourselves is a very unimportant, a very small part of our actual potentials and that this is undoubtedly part of the larger potential. Um, yes. I would say that I certainly believe in powers greater than myself. I would find it difficult not to.

GM: *Do you feel that you're guided in your writing, then?* **213**

WB: In my writing and in everything.

GM: *How have you changed in the last five years?*

WB: Well, I would say instead of becoming more sure of myself I have become less sure of myself. I'm more aware of the limitations of the self—the ego—and gain more realization how unimportant what you think of as your self actually is. And how small a part of what you really are and what you think of as your self actually is.

GM: *In general, what are the people you know most interested in?*

WB: Well, of course, there's a whole matter of business relationships. And people who are interested in writing, publishing. I have a number of friends who are painters and I've learned something about painting and the problems involved in painting from them. I'm interested in a number of scientific subjects although I don't have any actual friends who are scientists. I'm extremely interested in the whole area of Extrasensory Perception. Here are books on the subject; *Psychic Discoveries Behind the Iron Curtain. Journeys Out of the Body* by Monroe.

GM: *Is ESP something that has helped you in your writing?*

WB: Yes, I think all writers are actually dealing in this area. If you're not to some extent telepathic, then you can't be a writer, at least not a novelist where you have to be able to get into someone else's mind and *see* experience and what that person feels. And I feel that telepathy far from being something that few people have—it's something everyone has and everyone uses all the time. And a business man is in the area of ESP.

GM: *Has your interest in ESP helped you tap sources that you might otherwise not have been aware of before?*

WB: Why, certainly.

GM: *Has ESP made you a better writer?*

WB: Well, as I said I don't think anyone can be a writer who is not telepathic. I mean that in a very precise way; but as I say I see telepathy as something that just happens all the time. I've seen, when I was in Texas, a horse trader just see this figure taking place in his mind, *this horse is worth so much*. The other guy knows this is the figure he will not go above, etcetera, as you go in such a mundane transaction as a sale of a horse, there's a great deal of telepathy involved. The same thing, of course, applies in business, applies in all walks of life.

GM: *Would you ever like to apply your knowledge of telepathy in areas other than writing? Let's say, the stock market.*

WB: A deep misuse of these powers is always going to fuck you up. Gambling. And, uh, I used to do some gambling—horse races. I've had dreams and intuitions, and something always went wrong. That is, I had the number but I didn't have the horse or I had the horse and didn't have the number. I think this is a misuse of telepathy. If you're trying to take something from this level and bring it down to this level, you're gonna get fucked every time. The classical story about that was *La Dame Pique*—a Russian story about someone who was getting telepathic tips on gambling and, of course, finally got fucked.

GM: *So you think that using telepathy for gambling purposes is a disrespect of one's power?*

WB: All gamblers use telepathy, all gambling works on telepathy; but it's a very tricky area. And gambling is something I absolutely don't want to know about anymore or let's say the use of telepathic powers or Extrasensory Perception in those areas, 'cause I know sooner or later you're going to get the shaft and you'll well deserve it.

GM: *I think someone like Edgar Cayce realized that, because he refused to have his powers exploited on a media level. He felt that his powers were God-given and if he was to allow these powers to be exploited by the media they would disappear, or they wouldn't be beneficial to mankind.*

WB: In regards to the stock market you're going up against very old pros. It's all a matter of gold, price of gold. Someone was telling me you should buy gold. No. I don't want to touch it.

GM: *What would be a safe bet?*

Allen Ginsberg and William S. Burroughs, August 1, 1982, Boulder, CO.
PHOTO BY ARTHUR WINFIELD KNIGHT.

WB: There are no safe bets, because the whole monetary machine is manipulated by big money. Okay, people are telling me gold is going up to $200 an ounce. I said it's not going to do it and I was right. But, you see, if anyone's got $40,000,000, they can manipulate the price of gold, right, okay. It's $144 an ounce. All they gotta do is dump $40,000,000 worth of gold on the market and it goes down to $120. You think that's the bottom. You can't be sure. When they reach their bottom then they buy to force it up again. It's a question of the amount of money they have. But it's nothing for amateurs to fuck around with. Like in Switzerland, they have supermarket gold buyers. You can buy a bar of gold on your way out of the supermarket. Not me. I won't touch it, because you're getting into someone else's game.

GM: *What would you invest in if you had the opportunity to invest in something you already know about?*

WB: Now look, ten years ago I knew what to invest in and didn't have any money. Real Estate. If I had $100,000 then, I would have $1,000,000 now. I didn't have it. Now, Real Estate is leveling off because of the high interest rates and mortgages. You can't be sure that there'll be anything to invest in now.

GM: *Yes; but this is a bad time for people to sell who have land. A lot of people are still selling, like this year it wouldn't be a good time to sell, so some people are holding onto what they would normally sell at another time; but still some are selling off land. So, it might be a good time to buy land only if you have a large capital to work with.*

WB: Might be.

GM: *Because it might get higher next year.*

WB: Might be. If you're operating on small capital there aren't any good investments. Particularly not now.

GM: *Do you think with the buying and selling of land there would be an opportunity at some point in the future that would make it a good investment or do you think good investments run out?*

WB: I don't think that there are any good investments involving a small income, with a small amount of money. The prices are completely manipulated by people who have large amounts of money.

GM: *Do you own any land?*

WB: Don't own a thing.

GM: *Are you interested in buying land if the price is right at some later date?*

WB: I would be very interested in having a country place, yes. Very interested, indeed.

GM: *Are you very optimistic?*

WB: That's a meaningless word—optimism. Optimism is a hope, and that is uh, that is meaningless. I mean it's a question of what is actually happening. For example, the captain says the ship is sinking. Is he being pessimistic? The captain says the ship will weather this storm. Is he being optimistic? That depends on whether the ship sinks or not, alright. Optimism is actually a word that doesn't have any meaning.

GM: *But I never associated the two words, optimism and hope. Maybe they mean the same thing; but I always perceived being optimistic as assuming the role of a warrior in any type of situation that demanded it.*

WB: Yep, in other words someone is optimistic; that means he thinks the price of land or gold or cigarettes are going up. He may or may not be right.

GM: *But that's the idea of being optimistic without being hopeful —of just plunging into the situation headfirst.*

WB: Yes.

GM: *Are you surprised by your life?*

WB: Yes, sometimes. If you weren't surprised by your life you wouldn't be alive. If your life didn't contain any elements of surprise and recognition, you wouldn't be alive at all. Someone who is completely unsurprised by his life—that is, he considers his life completely predictable, is not alive. *Life is surprise!*

GM: *In the course of your career as a writer which decade have you found to be the most dramatic: the Fifties, the Sixties, or the Seventies?*

WB: Well, I would say that to me the Fifties were the most dramatic. Because I'd been working at a great intensity at that time and it was in 1959 that *Naked Lunch* was published in Paris. Someone named Sinclair Beiles came over from Maurice Girodias and said, "I want to publish your book." He said, "I want to publish it in a few weeks." So I had this vast stack of manuscript, maybe 1000 pages. I got it together in two weeks. The manuscript was, of course, later *Naked Lunch*. And a month later the book was out. It was certainly the most dramatic period of my life.

The moment when someone said we're going to publish *Naked Lunch* and a month later the book was actually published.

GM: *Would you say that, since the publication of* Naked Lunch *the amount of time spent in getting your work published has been less of a dramatic venture for you?*

WB: Much less of a dramatic venture, yes. The first time is always the most dramatic and after that it becomes, as you know, well I've got this book on the rails and that book on the rails and talk to the publisher and the agent and business and so on.

GM: *Do you see some situations in black and white and others in color? We could include dreams as part of that context.*

WB: Ah, yes. There are black and white dreams and there are color dreams and I have a lot of color dreams. Some dreams in black and white.

GM: *Do you have image-dreams where there are no words involved and upon waking you notate the images in terms of words?*

WB: Oh, no. Usually dreams are mixed. They are both words and images; they're movies. I will sometimes wake up with just words. Generally speaking, my dreams are like a film, let us say, or words and dialogue. Do you dream much?

GM: *Yes. I keep a notebook by my bed. My problem is that sometimes the dream is so overwhelming it's difficult to write out. I find it very easy to notate images if the dream appears to have a sequential flow, although all dreams actually are very non-sequential. Two nights ago I had a dream of two potato roots growing out from either side of my cock and they were just about to bud. And that was the image that stayed with me upon waking. I did have the sense that sequences of images were lost upon waking—images that preceded and followed the image of the potato roots; but upon waking they faded—went out of focus. I was then confronted with how I would reconstruct the dream—notate the image in terms of language.*

WB: That's a Mayan image, plants growing out of your cock.   **219**

GM: *By coincidence my last name means potato root in Spanish. I wonder if that has anything to do with the image in the dream. Do you know what this dream signifies?*

WB: Well, I don't know what it signifies; but I know that this is an image in Mayan mythology and in South American mythology of plants growing out of the cock. Well, it probably signifies the idea of the maize god and the plant as the seed. The equivalence of the seed being semen.

GM: *Would it have something to do with frustration?*

WB: Not necessarily at all. I don't know what dreams have to do with . . . I don't agree with Freud's dream interpretation at all. I couldn't give an interpretation.

GM: *What's your greatest strength and weakness?*

WB: My greatest strength is to have a great capacity to confront anything about myself no matter how unpleasant. My greatest weakness is that I don't. I know that's enigmatic.

GM: *So, in other words it would depend on the mood you're in or the situation.*

WB: That was for naught. There are so many misconceptions about strength and weakness. The only real strength, of course, is confrontation of yourself. The only real weakness is being unable to confront yourself.

GM: *Are you bothered by interruptions?*

WB: Sometimes, but not all the time.

GM: *What do you do to relax?*

WB: That is one reason why I would like to have a country place. The best relaxation, of course, is physical exercise, which I don't get too much opportunities for. Of course, I do use dumbbells and that sort of thing.

Allen Ginsberg and Peter Orlovsky, East 10th St., NYC, June 18, 1966. FROM
ALLEN GINSBERG'S COLLECTION

GM: *Do you find it hard to exercise living in the area that you're in right now?*

WB: No, but I would like to be able to get out and take long walks and cut wood and do that sort of thing. Physical exercise is the best relaxation you can have.

GM: *Is beauty only skin deep?*

WB: Well, well, well; what do you mean by that? (giggle)

GM: *Well, in regards to what is apparent; what appears to you on the surface and do you stop there, or do you go further into it in detail—whatever it is that seems to appear beautiful.*

WB: If you have a relative, comparative universe, then beauty only exists in relation to ugliness. What do you mean by beauty? You mean something is beautiful in relation to something that is ugly? The two concepts then become completely interrelated. Which is true of all other concepts. What does weakness mean? Weakness only has meaning with relation to strength, right? Weakness means that someone is stronger than you are.

GM: *A weakness can also be an advantage.*

WB: Perfect example.

GM: *Do you have a lot of secrets?*

WB: I would say that I have no secrets. In the film *The Seventh Seal* the man asked Death, "What are your secrets?" Death replied, "I have no secrets." No writer has any secrets. It's all in his work.

GM: *In an article by your son that appeared in* Esquire *you were quoted as saying "All past is fiction." Maybe you could explain this further.*

WB: Sure. We think of the past as being something that has just happened, right? Therefore, it is fact; but it is nothing that could be further from the truth. Right. This conversation is being recorded. Now suppose ten years from now you tamper with the recordings and change them around; after I was dead. Who could say that wasn't the actual recording? The past is something that can be changed, altered at your discretion.

GM: *The past can be changed in the present for the future.*

WB: Yeah. (Burroughs points to the two Sonycorders facing each other that are taping this interview.) The only evidence that this conversation ever took place here is the recordings, and if those recordings were altered, then that would be the only record. The past only exists in some record of it, right? There are no facts. We don't know how much of history is completely fiction.

GM: *Can you give me an example?*

WB: Yes. There was a young man named Peter Weber. He died in Paris, I believe, in 1956. His papers fell into my hands, quite by chance. I attempted to reconstruct the circumstances of his death. I talked to his girlfriend. I talked to all sorts of people. Everywhere I got a different story. He had died in this hotel. He had died in that hotel. He had died of an OD of Heroin. He had died of a withdrawal from Heroin. He had died of a brain tumor. Everybody was either lying, covering up something, it was a regular rash moment story, or they were simply confused. This investigation was undertaken two years after his death. What accuracy do we have in, let's say, something that was fifty years ago or one hundred years ago?

GM: *Wouldn't you notice all or some of the contradictions would connect in some way to reveal the truth; where a lot of contradictions would negate themselves?*

WB: They did not, they did not. What he died of, where he died, I still don't know. And I talked to all sorts of people connected with him.

GM: *Is there going to be a book of his poems published at some point?*

WB: I don't think so. It was just a handful of poems that came into my possession. I got them from his girlfriend. But that's something—two years after someone's death. Now imagine the inaccuracy of something that was one hundred years ago! The past is largely a fabrication by the living. And history is simply a bundle of fabrication. You see, there's no record this conversation ever took place or what was said, except what is on these machines. If these machines—the recordings were lost, or they got near a magnet or something, and were wiped out, there would be no recordings whatever. So what was the actual facts? What was actually said here? There are no actual facts.

GM: *Would you care to say anything else?*

WB: I'm trying to think . . . "as always the scroll of my authority presents to me efficiency and dirth." That's from Edward Arlington Robinson. A very good poet, incidentally. I always end up very dissatisfied with an interview. I feel that everything that should have been said hasn't been said, somehow. I think of things later that should have been said. When I answer the questions, so many questions are unanswerable actually.

CHAPTER 15

William Burroughs Letter to Jack Kerouac

May 21, 1955
Tangier

Dear Jack, (Kerouac)

Allen is all right and probably in Mexico City by now, en route to Frisco. Thank God he is O.K. I don't know what I would do without him.

As always you go direct to basics of situation: "If I love Allen why don't I return and live with him?" You are right. I will unless he can arrange to come here very soon. One basic fact I learned on this trip is how much I need the few friends I have. So far as companionship goes, I can't live off the country. There are only a few people in the world I want to see.

As you know I picked up on Yoga many years ago. Tibetan Buddhism and Zen you should look into. Also Tao. Skip Confucius. He is sententious old bore. Most of his sayings are about on the "Confucius say" level. My present orientation is diametrically opposed, therefore perhaps progression from Buddhism. I say we are here in *human form* to learn by the *human* hieroglyphs of love and suffering. There is no intensity of love or feeling that does not involve the risk of crippling hurt. It is a duty to take this risk, to love and feel without defense or reserve. I speak only for myself. Your needs may be different. However, I am dubious of the wisdom of sidestepping sex. Of course women have poison juices I always say.

What are you writing? I have been working on a novel. Enclose a dream routine derived from your dream of the iron racks and the tremendous, overcrowded cities of the future. This is definitely hope and along the lines of faith I have come by in last few months, a conversion like. I *know* that the forces of spontaneous, emergent Life are stronger than the forces of evil, repression and death, and that the forces of death will destroy themselves.

What is new with Lucien? I may see you in New York fairly soon. Enclose routine about purple assed baboons. And Tangier miscellanea.

Love,
Bill (Burroughs)

* *

I plan to organize forays into the mountains of The Riff to hunt the purple assed baboons that abound there, to hunt the baboons with spears from motorcycles. Baboon sticks.

The Huntesmen have gathered for the hunt in The Swarm Bar, a hangout for elegant pansies. The Huntesmen strut about with imbecile narcissism in black leather jackets and studded belts. They all wear enormous falsie baskets. Every now and then one of them throws a fag to the floor and pisses on him.

The Huntesmen are drinking Victory Punch concocted of paregoric, Spanish fly, heavy black rum, molasses, Napoleon Brandy and canned heat. The punch is served from an enormous, hollow, golden baboon, crouched in snarling terror, snapping at a spear in his side. You twist the baboon's balls and the punch runs out his cock. From time to time hot hors d'oeuvres pop out the baboon's ass with a loud farting noise. When this happens the Huntesmen roar with bestial laughter and the fags shriek and twitch.

The Master of the Hunt is Captain Everhard, who was drummed out of the Queen's 69th for palming a jock strap in a game of strip poker.

Apocryphal scene: Motorcycles careening, jumping, overturning. Spitting, shrieking, shitting baboons fighting hand to hand with the Huntesmen. Riderless cycles scrabbling about in the dust like crippled insects, attacking baboon and Huntesman.

Tangier conversation:

Two fags pass woman with her nose eaten away: "My dear these people lose their noses through sheer carelessness. I mean one shot of some *marvellous* new medicine . . ."

"My dear I can tell you where to buy the most marvellous cakes. A very attractive boy who, by the way, is available cooks them *right there* in hot grease . . ."

****

DREAM OF THE CITY

This is one of worst habits I ever kicked. I sit for an hour in a chair unable to get up and fix myself a cup of tea. I need Allen here to take care of me. Early this morning, shivering in a light junk sick fever, half-awake, had vivid dream fantasy. The hypersensitivity of junk sickness is reflected in dreams during withdrawal—that is, if you can sleep.

In the dream I go to an elaborate house on a high cliff over the sea. An iron door opens in limestone cliff, and you get to the house in swift silent elevator.

I have come to see a sexless character who wears men's clothes, but may be man or woman. Nobody knows for sure. A gangster of the future with official recognition and arbitrary powers.

He walks towards me as if about to shake hands. He does not offer his hand. "Hello," he says. "Hello . . . there." The room is surrounded on three sides by a plastic transparent shell. "You will want to see the view," he says. A plastic panel slides back. I step out on a limestone terrace. Cut from solid rock of the cliff. No rail or wall. A heavy mist, but from time to time I can see the waves breaking on the rocks a thousand feet below. See the waves but I don't hear them, like a silent film. Two body guards are standing a few feet behind me.

"It gives the sensation of flying," I say.

"Sometimes."

"Well, feller say only angels have wings," I say recklessly. I turn around. I say "Excuse me." The body guards don't move. They are standing with their backs to him. He is arranging flowers in an obscene, alabaster bowl. The guards cannot see him and he says nothing, makes no sound, but a signal has been given. The guards step aside to let me pass back into the room.

I walk up to the table where he is arranging flowers. "I want to know where Jim is," I say.

"Mmmm. Yes. I suppose you do."

"Will you tell me?"

"Maybe Jim doesn't want to see you."

"If he doesn't I want to hear it from him."

"I never give anything for nothing. I want your room in The Chimu. I want you out of there by nine tomorrow morning."

"All right."

"Go to sixty at 4th street, coordinate 20, level 16, YH room 72."

The city is a vast network of levels like the Racks connected by gangways, and cars that run on wires and single tracks. You put a coin in a vacant car and it will take you anywhere on its track or wire. Everyone carries an instrument called a coordinator to orient himself.

The City is in the U.S. The forces of evil and repression have run their course here. They are suffocating in their armor or exploding from inner pressure. New forms of life are germinating in the vast, rusty metal racks of the ruined City.

It takes me twelve hours to find the address. A padded hammer hangs from a copper chain on the door. I knock. A man comes to the door. Bald. Looks like old actor on the skids. Effeminate but not queer. A dumpy middle-aged woman is sitting in a purple velvet brocaded chair leftover from 1910. She looks good natured. I say I want to see Jim.

"And *who* might you be?" the man asks.

"I'm Bill."

He laughs: "He's Bill, Gertie." He turns to me. "Someone was just here asking for Bill."

"How long ago?"

"Just five minutes," the woman says.

"Can I stay five minutes?" I ask. "I mean if someone was here five minutes ago asking for *Bill*, and now I am here asking for *Jim* . . . Well."

"You don't have to *slug* me with it," the man says. "But I never heard of Bill or Jim."

"Oh let him stay," the woman says.

Five minutes later there is a knock. The man opens the door.

"Hello," he says. "You wouldn't be Jim by any chance?"

"Yes, I'm Jim. I'm looking for Polly."

"Polly doesn't live here anymore." The man sings it. Jim sees me.

"Hello, Bill," he says. He smiles and cancels all reproaches I had stored up.

"Let's go, Jim," I say, standing up. "Thanks for your trouble," I say, turning to the man and woman.

"Any time, old thing," the man says. He is about to say something more.

"That's O.K., boys," the woman cuts in. We walk out together.

"I need a drink," Jim says. We find a bar and sit down in a booth. There is no one else in the place. Jim is incredibly beautiful, but the kind of face that shows every day that much older. There are circles under his eyes like bruises. He drinks five double Scotches. He is sweet and gentle when drunk. I help him out of the bar. We go to my room and sleep there. Next morning I throw the few things I have, mostly photos and manuscripts, into a plastic bag and we leave.

Jim has a place on a roof. You unlock a metal door and climb four flights of rusty, precarious stairs. One room with a mattress, a table and a chair. Metal walls. A toilet in one corner, a gas stove in another. A tap dripping into a sink.

Jim is trembling convulsively. "I'm scared, Bill," he says over and over. I hold him, and stroke his head, and undress him. We sleep together until twelve that night. We wake up and dress and Jim makes coffee. We take turns drinking from a tin can. We start out looking for Polly. Jim gives me an extra key to his place before we leave the room. The City is honeycombed with nightclubs and bars. Many of them move location every night. The nightclubs are underground, hanging from cables, and built on perilous balconies a thousand feet over the rubbish and rusty metal of the City. We make the rounds. We find Polly in Cliff's place. The room shifts from time to time with a creak of metal. It is built in a rusty tower that sways in the wind.

"This place is too good to last, kids," Cliff says, laughing.

Polly is a dark Jewish girl. She looks like that picture of Allen on the beach when he was three years old. Jim is talking to some people at the bar. I put the key in her hand and press it there. She kisses me lightly on the lips and then on the ear, murmuring "Billy Boy."

I find a car and ride down to the waterfront. I see a light. A man is standing in a doorway.

"You open?" I ask.

"Why not?"

I go in. The place is empty. I sit at a table. He brings me a soft drink without asking what I want, and sits down at the table opposite me. A gentle, thuggish face. Broken nose, battered but calm and kind. A lithe, youthful body.

"Where you live at?" he asks me.

"No place now."

"Want to shack up here?"

"Why not?"

I finish my drink and he leads the way to a round metal door that opens soundlessly on oiled bearings. He motions me to go in. His hand rests on my shoulder, slides down to my ass with a gentle forward pat.

CHAPTER 16

Lepers Cry

PETER ORLOVSKY

When I was in Banaras
India in 1961 Summer I was
so so Lazzey that it was
a bit shyly fitting for me to
go see how the poor sick
week thin no legs no hands no
fingers, only stubbs of joints
with the finger bones pokeing thru.
A bit like pigs feet in clean store
jars only these were the Lowest of
the Low of India the Leppers
or a fraction of the fractions
in this one small Lane near

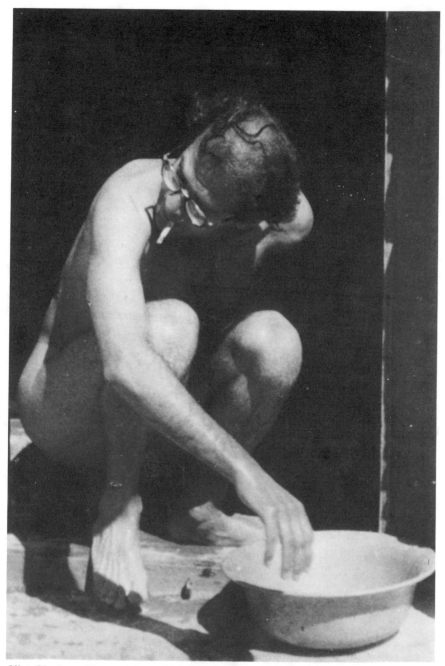

Allen Ginsberg, Kausani, Circa 1962. PHOTO BY PETER ORLOVSKY.

Dasadsumad Ghat—this, maybe
32 yr old woman rapped in pure dirt
Burlap string strip arround waist—whear
the Tips of her Toes should be were
her bone Toe stubs protruding out
still infessted with active
Leprocy growing by eating
away the flesh that surrounds
her extremities—she
could only crall on her rear
she can not walk and to
eat she has to use her rotten
sore Lepper fingers—

I gave some helpfull Indian soul
to go get her a new fresh Clean
sarrie a few ruppies
and began to help her change
her apparel when there to
Eyes on her Left
I saw a 4″ ring of open
saw infection full of magots
cralling and happiley alive—I
was so surprised I dident know
what to do for a second—then
I hide tailed it to a doctor
in his office a bit across the street

asking him what to do
No I asked him to come down and examin
this street Lepper & that I would pay
him good for his expert servace—
He said he had to stay in his office
and told me to get some
Hydrogen Peroxide—cotton and
I think some sulpher ointment
to first clean out the infection
& kill the maybe, 30 or 50 maggots
in her side above the thigh—you

know that big round mussle
that is divided into two sphears

well on her Left spear (ass)
played these maggots and as I
poured the Hydrogen Peroxide—I had to
turn her over on her side—the
maggots became more alive and
active & danced into the air
above her side more. It was
difficult to get all the maggots
out so after a few
pourings and cotton cleaning I
covered it with sulpher ointment of
I dont quite remember because its
been 10 yrs ago and I have

been so too lazzey fingers to write
This real sad tail—which is
another discusting disease in its self
and Taped it with 5″ × 5″ compress pads—
and had some one bring her some
food and a clean mat for her to
sit on—for all this took place
in the poor beggers sick alley decked
with watery shit plops and I
finally got into the swing of
cleaning with my hands—that
the first problem was to clean up
all this free Floating Shit splashings all about

and it was on the next day I saw
her again and this Time I looked
on her right side and there
was another maggot soupe dish
on her right rear side a big eaten
down to her thigh bone the
muscles getting eaten & sucked thin
jucey human sore magget puss—

have you ever smelt magot
puss on the body of a poor Human
Being—dont bother—it may make
you vommit—keep away—
Let the Prows attend the Nose.

I just diden expect to see the same
horrible infested condition on the
exact opposite side of her body—
I was now more suprissed and
taken aback—and now I Looked
into her eyes & she had very
dark olive calm eyes peasefull sweet sad
eyes that seemed to tell me
I am okay—its nice of you
to have some food brought to me
and I want to thank you
but I dont know yr Language
so I say silently with my

eyes—I gave her friends
food money for a varried diet
for a week & told them to get
her yougart & they got some
& spoon fed her—
and then I disappeared for a week
or a month and I saw her
again—in a bigger Square—up
above Dasadsumed—she—I
saw her from a distanc of about
70 feet—she was on her back—
in rigamaroartus I could Tell
by the ways her knees

& arm were sticking up into the
air—it looked like—I forgot her
name—I think I asked
or I forgot—I steared away
I could see the problem of

Burreing her or Burning at
the Funeral Pire at Manakarmake
Gat—it was—I figured
the proper Government banaras workers
would come and gather her up—
I was sad to see her end this way
I dident think she would go so soon.
what fooled me was her calm eyes

Liveing so peasefulley
above her hip woe—
her hip infection
and then I thought that maybe me
by killing the maggots
it opened the Blood Veins
or something to cause premature
death—its all so sad—and
now to this day I feel all
the more Lazzey & Dumb
and all the more domb & Lazzey
Lazzey Bastard of a selfish
Human Creap Sleep/

                    Halloween Night 1971

CHAPTER 17

Love Me for the Fool I Am

MICHAEL McCLURE

LOVE ME FOR THE FOOL
I AM .
(the laughing angel-imbecile).
The thrill
of kissing you
is seeing me
reflected in your eyes.
We try for purity
but
still
we're glorious
blobs
of meat.

I worship you
like blood
or oil or wheat.
Our love is flawed
and swallowed
by the rush of time.
A mindless innocence,
they say,
is crime.
We dance on borrowed feet.

—Michael McClure

Jane, Michael and Joanna McClure. PHOTO BY ANNIE LEIBOVITZ. COURTESY: MICHAEL McCLURE.

Carl Solomon, Boulder, CO., July 25, 1982. PHOTO BY ARTHUR WINFIELD KNIGHT.

CHAPTER 18

John Tytell Talks with Carl Solomon

"Howl," perhaps the best known poem written by an American since T.S. Eliot's "The Waste Land," is dedicated to Carl Solomon, and partly inspired by some of his more volatile actions. His presence now combines a sweetly naive idealism, an utter sincerity, an ardor for argument that is redeemed by an instinct for the absurd, and some rare flashes of the kind of quick rage one finds in Blake's portraits of children. The anger was greater when Allen Ginsberg first met Carl Solomon who was being wheeled into a ward at Columbia Psychiatric Institute after an insulin shock treatment —but Carl still had the wit to come out of his coma with a Dostoevskian repartee. Much of Carl's fury in being was dissipated during his eight years of residence at Pilgrim State Hospital on Long Island. The opening line of "Howl," "I saw the best minds of my generation destroyed by madness," evokes Carl's attempts to reach far beyond the incipient apathy of the post-war years for some otherworld of excitement, stimulation and inspiration. Genius and disease, as Edmund Wilson so aptly suggested in "The Wound and the Bow," are inextricably mixed in the modern artist as each quality illuminates the other. Of this magical reciprocity, Carl Solomon is a representative illustration.

Like Kerouac, Ginsberg and Snyder, Carl Solomon began shipping out in Merchant Marine vessels right after World War II while still a student at the City College of New York. His precocious curiosity led him to search for existentialists and surrealists in Paris, and so he learned about writers like Artaud and Michaux even before they became esoteric. Carl once sent Allen Ginsberg an unsigned telegram that simply stated: "VANISHED!" I take it as an index of an irrepressibly anarchic humor and ebullient gaiety, but also as a register of the writer sensing the totalitarian potentials of his age—one can hobo to the road or be kidnapped to the camps. For Carl Solomon epitomizes the Beat notion of the writer as *outcast* which is a magnification and a departure from the Lost Generation's idea of the writer in comfortable exile in Montparnasse. In this sense, Carl Solomon exists as one of the key progenitors of the literary underground that has so vitalized our culture with spirit in the past decade.

Called the "Lunatic Saint" by his friends, and feeling entirely obligated to fulfill the implication of that quixotic title, Carl became the world's intellectual antagonist. His two books, *Mishaps Perhaps* and *More Mishaps*, both published by City Lights, are polemical, impious and impish, controversial, outrageously funny, and a reminder of the sort of suffering our society offers to unconventional minds who would refute its dogmas and violate its taboos. Carl Solomon, who accepted, edited and prefaced William Burroughs' first book, *Junkie*, was one of the untouchables who motivated the Beat Movement; a model of a man who takes risks to define his convictions in an era of easy compliance with authority. He has been somewhat softened by the knocks of time, and now chooses to live quietly in our more rebellious age, but still is, as ever, devoted to words, books, and the lore of the writer. I recorded this interview in my apartment in Greenwich Village, New York in November of 1973.

John Tytell
February 9, 1974

242

JOHN TYTELL: *When did you first travel to Europe?*

CARL SOLOMON: I joined the Merchant Marine in 1945, just before the war with Japan ended. I went to various places, France among them, and I jumped ship in 1947 in France . . . I stayed there, went to Paris, and learned about Artaud, and Michaux, and Isou.

JT: *Isn't it curious that so many writers like Kerouac and Ginsberg were joining the Merchant Marine?*

CS: Well, there were movies in those days romanticizing it— "Action in the North Atlantic" with Humphrey Bogart—so that sort of thing was in the air then.

JT: *Before going to sea you attended City College?*

CS: I started there in 1943, when I was fifteen.

JT: *When did you leave City College?*

CS: Well, I kept on shipping out intermittently, going to school one term and to sea the next.

JT: *So you were an early dropout?*

CS: Yes, although I hadn't dropped out completely. I had neglected my studies really, and I got sort of low grades.

JT: *Were there any teachers there that you still remember?*

CS: Leffert, he was a specialist in Modern Literature—a very sharp, very classy sort of guy who seemed to love Gide.

JT: *Was there anyone else?*

CS: Then I had Abraham Edel in Philosophy who was very bright.

JT: *Was CCNY a very active place politically?*

CS: Yes. While I was there I joined the AYD (American Youth for Democracy). This was the Communist front organization of that period when they were anti-axis and for the war. The AYD group was known as the Tom Paine Club. The Communist Party went out of existence then, and they called it the CPA—Communist Political Association during the Browder period which is now regarded as a revisionist period. Browder felt there would be collaboration between capitalism and communism, and that the Party should go out of existence. So I joined the CPA which was part of the progressive movement and it was considered the left.

JT: *Is this the origin of what is now known as Progressive Labor?*

CS: No, no, no. That's Maoist and from the second wave of leftism in the late fifties or early sixties.

JT: *Do you remember whether many students were similarly involved?*

CS: Yeah. They had a very large membership. As a matter of fact, during those years the Communists dominated the CIO (Congress of Industrial Organizations), and they even elected two members to the New York City Council in those years, Ben Davis and Cacchione in Brooklyn.

JT: *Didn't you also attend Brooklyn College at one time?*

CS: Well, I broke with my CP friends that I had made at CCNY, and I moved down to the Village and became interested in avant-garde art and existentialism with a circle of people disillusioned with the left, ex-liberals and progressives I should say. I began to read *The Partisan Review*, and a flock of other little magazines like *Horizon*. I went to Brooklyn College because I had a friend going there who said that it would be better for my literary interests than CCNY which was geared for engineers and science.

JT: *In* Mishaps Perhaps, *you write that you witnessed an Artaud reading in Paris, 1947.*

CS: First of all I was looking for existentialists. So I went wandering around San Germain de Pres and came to a gallery with a crowd standing outside. I can't recall the name of the street, but I read an account about it when I returned in *Partisan Review*, how Artaud had been screaming his "Damnation of the Flesh"—I've forgotten the Rue

(Was it Rue Jacob?), but to me it's the Rue Impasse or Satan. So I stood outside, and first a young man with black hair descended from upstairs, and he was trembling, and he read what I later found out was Artaud's "Ci-Git" preceded by the "Indian Culture;" then I remember another man in a turban screaming. He had been there before the young man. Originally, I had thought the young man was Artaud, but later I learned Artaud was an older man then—he was 51. I remember one line the young man read: "Papa, Maman et pederastinne" and that tickled Kerouac in later years. The story I gave to him was that the reader was pointing at me but he was really pointing at the crowd.

JT: Did you have any further interest in Artaud?

CS: Oh yes. In 1948 I worked on a ship again since they hadn't ousted me for deserting and I went back to France. This time I got a couple of days off from my job as a dishwasher, and I made the long trip to Paris just for one day where I bought, in the same neighborhood, Artaud's book on Van Gogh, *The Man Suicided by Society.*

JT: I wanted to ask you about that. In Mishaps Perhaps *you summarize Artaud's condemnation of all psychiatry, and his argument that those who are in turn condemned by psychiatrists are gifted with a superior lucidity and insight. It occurs to me that such notions are extremely prevalent in radical psychiatry in England and America today with people like R.D. Laing, David Cooper and Thomas Szasz.*

CS: Yes, today. Artaud began to be absorbed in certain areas later on. When I first read Artaud it was still something very esoteric. Later, when the theater of the absurd became prominent, his theatrical ideas at least came through. Anyway, I got *The Man Suicided by Society*, and then moved to West Fourth Street and attended Brooklyn College. At that time I was spending a lot of time in the 42nd Street Library where I found the lettrist magazine, *La Dictature Lettrice,* and I read through that. I was twenty years old at the time, and reading Artaud's letters. Then I cooked up a thing with Leni Grubes and Ronnie Gold—who is now one of the heads of the Gay Activists—and we staged a dadaist demonstration, and threw potato salad at Markfield.

JT: Wallace Markfield?

CS: Yes, he was lecturing on Mallarme.

JT: *Isn't there a line in 'Howl' about that experience?*

CS: Yes. At that time Ronnie and I were discussing the validity of suicide, and I read *Lafcadio's Adventures*, you know, the idea of the gratuitous crime, but I backed out of all this. I did steal a sandwich at Brooklyn College and showed it to the policeman, got sent to the psychologist, and then they sent me up to the Columbia Psychiatric Institute. I was in a very negative, nihilistic mood, things seemed so sick to me, and I wanted a lobotomy, or to be suicided. I thought I was a madman.

JT: *Was this in any way a reaction to a dullness in the culture you felt at the time?*

CS: Yeah, it was a reaction. Just before that my mother and I had moved to Parkchester, which I used to refer to as a Cubist colony because of the way it was arranged, cold, abstract, futuristic, regular houses which are now very common, but that was the first of the large projects. My old neighborhood, Prospect Avenue in the South Bronx, had been an ordinary sort of Jewish neighborhood with brownstones.

JT: *Was this the Amalgamated project?*

CS: No, Metropolitan Life Insurance Company, and in the beginning they didn't let Negroes in, you know, it was a place where everybody seemed to be a stereotype. And my rebellion against that led to the avant-garde involvement which led to the insulin shock treatment up at Columbia Psychiatric.

JT: *Isn't that where you met Allen Ginsberg in a Dostoevskian encounter with you introducing yourself as Kirilov, and Allen as Myshkin?*

CS: Yes, I met Allen after coming down from the insulin ward, just emerging from a coma; comas, no less, to come out of reading and ideas! The story is in my "Afterthoughts of a Shock Patient." When I came out of the hospital, supposedly cured, Allen introduced me to Neal Cassady and that bunch, and Landesman.

JT: *Had you appeared in* Neurotica *before?*

CS: No. Before that I wasn't really interested in *Neurotica,* although I had seen it around.

JT: *What was Landesman like?*

CS: He had an art gallery in St. Louis, a patron of the arts, and as Jack Kerouac characterized him he was a playboy.

JT: *John Clellon Holmes has an interesting description of him in* Nothing More to Declare.

CS: They were close friends.

JT: *You met Allen in '49? He had been placed there because of the ride and Little Jack Melody. How many months were you together at that time?*

CS: Oh, a couple of months, and I got out before he did.

JT: *Did you have freedom to meet?*

CS: We used to meet on the ward, and write, and read things to one another. I introduced him to works of Artaud and Genet; he read Yeats to me, Melville, and spoke of his friends, Kerouac and Burroughs. But he was highly critical of me. He thought my ideas at that time would lead me to a worse insanity, and perhaps under his suggestion that's what ultimately happened when I went to Pilgrim State.

JT: *Well, that is a kind of negative influence.*

CS: I suppose it was.

JT: *In* More Mishaps, *you write that Allen was taking notes on your adventures while at Columbia Psychiatric, and some of those notes appeared in a different form in "Howl."*

CS: He sat there, and I used to come out with very surrealistic aphorisms which he would transcribe.

JT: Can you remember some instances in your life that are reflected, however prismatically, in "Howl?"

CS: The remark about the pubic beards was mine, and the harlequin talk of suicide.

JT: In your books, I thought I detected a sign of hostility as well as admiration towards Ginsberg and his literary friends?

CS: I was angry because of my second sickness. I thought that they had all rejected me because I was madder than they were. I thought that they were neurotics and I was a psychotic, an outsider.

JT: In your books you always tease your readers with differences you had with Ginsberg, such as the way you saw Whitman.

CS: We were continually fighting. I saw Whitman as a political revolutionary, and Allen saw him as a sexual revolutionary. When I first met Allen I called him a dopey daffodil because he symbolized to me what poetry was then, referring to Wordsworth, I guess, the idea of poets as sensitive souls rather than Artaud's conception of the poet as brute. But Allen turned out not to be a dopey daffodil at all, but that's the way he looked then, a neat haircut and horn rim glasses. He seemed to me to be like the conventional English major who couldn't stand up to me at all. I thought I was much greater than these types, much more unconventional. I identified with the Beat Generation in much the same way as Artaud himself identified with the Surrealists: he felt that they were his ultimate enemy.

JT: You mean as a possible close source of betrayal because they couldn't really live up to his ideals?

CS: Yeah. Like when I escaped from Pilgrim State Hospital once I went over to Allen's brother's house, and while he talked to me, his wife called the hospital.

Carl Solomon at work in a bookshop in the Port Authority Terminal, Circa 1971.

JT: How did you escape?

CS: I just walked off.

JT: What kind of treatment did you receive at Psychiatric Institute? Was it group therapy or individual analysis?

CS: Individual; they had group therapy at Pilgrim State.

JT: What kind of analyst did you have at Columbia Psychiatric —what school was he from?

CS: She—Washington School—Harry Stack Sullivan.

JT: What about Allen's analyst?

CS: I think he was Freudian. We had many fights about our analysts and their virtues. That happens in all hospitals, by the way. There was a situation out at Pilgrim State where the gentile patients wanted Jungian analysts, and the Jewish patients wanted Freudians.

JT: In Mishaps Perhaps you state that you had been conditioned in illness by classical surrealism.

CS: I meant Artaud's void. Also ideas like the derangement of the senses, and things that Ronnie Gold and I used to do. We used to hang out in gay bars then, Mary's and Main Street which were both on Eighth Street in the Village, hubs of activity then. They were crowded outside and inside, a real super-decadent atmosphere. Ned Rorem used to go there, he was always at the bar. Ronnie Gold and I used to eat benzedrine. To me decadence meant absinthe, or green drinks like pernod, or creme de menthe. My idea of decadence was something that made Jack Kerouac write to me when I was at Pilgrim State: "Lautreamont, cafe noir, sans sucre." I never actually became a junkie or anything like that, and I was probably really afraid of more serious drugs, so I sort of dabbled in safe affectations. Stanley Gould says that I talked my way into all these hospitals, that I gave them the impression of being sick without really being sick.

JT: Do you think you were helped by being in those hospitals?

CS: It was bad as far as my record goes.

JT: *I don't mean that, but your general attitudes to life and yourself?*

CS: Oh sure. At Pilgrim State, for instance, by urging wholesome things on me, a tame life, the attendant used to treat me like a soldier and say to me "front and center." The psychologists tried to steer me away from the Beat Generation.

JT: *Did you learn the lesson of psychiatry as being an adjustment, in fact an acceptance of exactly what you were rebelling against? I would equate that with aging, with abandoning or forgetting youth.*

CS: Well, I find myself in that position now.

JT: *In* Mishaps Perhaps, *you claimed that your friends in 1949 made you assume the role of a lunatic saint. Who did you mean specifically?*

CS: Oh, Leni and that bunch, like Bob Reisner who was in my class at Brooklyn College, he wrote a book on graffiti. They thought that kind of thing was great. Reisner and I used to do many funny things, like I once pretended to be W.H. Auden at some exhibition, and there I was signing Auden's name.

JT: *Somewhere in* Mishaps Perhaps *you mention that you were betrayed by Wilhelm Reich. I couldn't understand what you meant by that?*

CS: I have this anger at anybody who has done anything against me or criticized me in any way. So now up in the Bronx I'm just the poor innocent who has returned completely healthy after being driven mad by the captious criticism of all the intellectuals in the Village with their Reich and all the rest of it. And also I go back to the days when I was in high school at James Monroe, where I was into Whitman who seemed to me to be the greatest poet, and all these others were into more sophisticated things like Eliot—but that wasn't so bad—the worst was that some of them were into Reich. These same people were criticizing me as being overly

251

naive about sexual matters, but to me they were trying to shock me, while generally mocking me.

JT: *How did* Junkie, *Burroughs' first novel, get to you?*

CS: My uncle, A.A. Wyn, was the publisher of Ace Books. He gave me a job, and I was trying to make a big impression, and Allen thought it was a great idea to bring out these writers, and if we could make Genet and these others well known to the American public we would be accomplishing something. I don't see what we've accomplished, but we were trying to do that anyway, to change the consciousness. It was largely an educational mission.

JT: *And Wyn was interested in this project?*

CS: Yes. I don't think he was primarily interested in the commercial end, I think he saw their possibilities as writers.

JT: *Did Allen give you the manuscript of* Junkie?

CS: We got it chapter by chapter from Burroughs in Mexico City. He would send them to Allen who brought them to me at Ace.

JT: *That's about Burroughs' earliest writing, although I've read in the correspondence up at Columbia University that he and Kerouac collaborated on a detective book right after World War II.*

CS: He sent me another book, *Queer.*

JT: *Why didn't that get published?*

CS: My uncle and I didn't feel it was up to *Junkie.* That's never been published, but it probably should have been, especially for anybody interested in Burroughs' work. I once made him very angry because when he sent up *Queer,* I suggested that we should change the title to *Fag,* and Burroughs wrote back to Allen saying that he would cut my balls off because he made a distinction between the words, a fag being someone effeminate and a queer is a masculine type of homosexual.

JT: *I have the hunch that parts of* Queer *may have found a way into*

Naked Lunch. *Did you have any correspondence with Burroughs in later years?*

CS: Yes, in Pilgrim State. He once sent me a cryptic note saying I should become a waiter. I didn't know whether he meant that I should wait until I was cured, or whether I should work in restaurants.

JT: *He was opposed to psychoanalysis. He profoundly distrusts it.*

CS: He probably did.

JT: *In your preface to* Junkie *you call Burroughs "a curious adventurer."*

CS: Because of things like his trip to the Amazon.

JT: *As well as mental trips inside the mind. By the way, have you read his more recent work,* The Wild Boys, *for instance?*

CS: I glanced at *The Exterminator*; I've been selling it. I'm a little wary of Burroughs now because he's into a kind of general espousal of youth revolt, and it's necessary for me in my present state to keep a very straight, pro-social, even patriotic outlook. During the Vietnam thing I participated in no protests; I voted for Procaccino, and I was on the verge of voting for Nixon, but I ended up voting for McGovern. But at the same time I'm doing crazy things like reading Marx.

JT: *In* Mishaps Perhaps *you discuss—not in connection with Burroughs but with Surrealism—the impulse to make the ugly beautiful which is just the approach I am taking in my own attempts to describe Burroughs' fiction. You also deal with diabolism.*

CS: All this is secondary, later than "The Report from the Asylum" which I still consider the clearest statement of my ideas—after that I was just trying to relate to my legend. That's where the diabolist stuff occurs.

JT: *Then you have no chronology in your book because the "Report" is near the end?*

CS: Yeah, there aren't any dates. At the time I wrote "Report from the Asylum" I was very careful, and I used to edit closely, but I reached a phase where the whole thing got out of my control, sometimes agreeing to things I disliked out of weariness or confusion. Of course legally, I lost my rights in 1956 when I was committed to Pilgrim State.

JT: *Getting back to your work as an editor at Ace, I understand that you were also at one time considering publishing Kerouac?*

CS: We had paid him an advance of $500, and I had visions of myself as being his Maxwell Perkins and him being my Wolfe because his first novel resembled Wolfe.

JT: *I read a letter you wrote to Kerouac at Columbia University Special Collections in which you said that the Wolfean aspect of* The Town and the City *was a charade that bespoke a repressed surrealism and a repressed homosexuality.*

CS: I must have been very erudite in those days.

JT: *What happened with the contract because Kerouac never published with Ace Books?*

CS: Well, we rejected *On the Road*—he sent us this long scroll. My uncle said it looked like he took it from his trunk.

JT: *The teletype roll. Did he get that from Lucien Carr at United Press?*

CS: I don't know where he got it, but we were used to these neat manuscripts, and I thought, "Gee, I can't read this."

JT: *You didn't accept it as a surrealist antic, then?*

CS: Because at that time I probably wasn't into that. I went through many phases while I was an editor: a Buddhist phase, then I read this book, *Philosophy of a Lunatic*, ultimately.

JT: *Who wrote that?*

CS: John Custance. Nobody has ever heard of the book but me. I bought it in the Gotham Book Mart while working for Ace Books. To me it seemed the ultimate mind-blowing thing, going beyond Zen which was a great step toward the elimination of myself. It was an existentialist version of Armageddon, the forces of God against the forces of the devil.

JT: *What was Kerouac's attitude to publishers in general?*

CS: Bad! He thought of them as skinflints, and he used the term "Broadway Sams"—he meant Jewish liberal intellectuals. He was snide about anybody who worked in offices.

JT: *Was there any problem with getting Kerouac to make revisions?*

CS: Yes. He got very angry when I wrote him suggestions.

JT: *Did Kerouac send you anything after* On the Road?

CS: Then I flipped and was sent to Pilgrim State. But the house continued to deal with him, and they accepted things, and then later reversed themselves.

JT: *Did Kerouac try to interest you in publishing Cassady?*

CS: He had mentioned that Neal Cassady wrote, but he wasn't trying to get us to accept anything. That later became *The First Third.*

JT: *Did you ever meet Neal Cassady?*

CS: Oh yeah. When I came out of Columbia Psychiatric Allen wanted me to throw a New Year's party. So I got a cold water flat on 17th Street and threw a party at which Neal Cassady was one of the star performers. He played one of those sweet potato things that make music, you know, and we were wearing those funny noses with the bebop eyeglasses.

JT: *I've heard that Cassady had magnetic sexual appeal?*

255

CS: Not to me.

JT: *What was his appeal, then?*

CS: He was always bouncing around—sort of kinetic energy more than anything else.

JT: *What about his speech? His rambling monologues?*

CS: He did one funny routine at the New Year's party, an Amos and Andy routine.

JT: *He was influenced by radio?*

CS: He knew a lot about popular culture. He was very American where a lot of us were rather frenchified.

JT: *What kind of jobs have you worked in your life? In* Mishaps Perhaps *you have this anecdote about selling ice cream in front of the United Nations.*

CS: That was after *Howl* had just come out, and I was considered to have gone mad again. I was working for Eskimo Ace. I've worked on ships as a messman, in the steward's department, as an editor, with books in bookstores, when I was sixteen on a farm in Smyrna, New York, where I shoveled manure and worked a horse drawn plow trying to make even furrows, and earlier, when I was fourteen I bundled the Sunday Times. I also worked for Nugent National Stores in the garment district, and delivered womens wear. When I met Allen we all worked in market research. I was married then, and my wife and I coded for N.O.R.C. John Holmes also worked there.

JT: *Let's talk about your own writing. One of the qualities I love in it is your humor which is so often a function of epigram, puns and word play, like calling Poe's "The Raven" "the ravin." Or saying that if you lose contact with the zeitgeist, never fear, you may reach the poltergeist.*

CS: The use of puns is not entirely natural to me. That was the Michaux influence.

JT: *Can you find ways to sustain that humor in your own life?*

CS: I've tried, but it's dropped off. Now my jokes are very bad. I've exhausted my humor, and can't work my brain to that extent because I have to be responsible for my own functioning.

JT: Do you feel that you were part of a movement?

CS: As a matter of fact, I hadn't felt that. I had just been through with a movement, and I had an aversion to movements—after all I had just finished with the Communists. I was living on 113th Street, and I knew this guy Don Cook, and he first mentioned the idea of a movement in reference to the Beats, and I was shocked—here I was trapped by something I had been trying to get away from!

Bob Kaufman and Jack Micheline, Washington Square Park, North Beach, San Francisco, May 29, 1974. PHOTO BY ED BURYN.

CHAPTER 19

Laughter Sounds Orange At Night

E
I
L
E
E
N

K
A
U
F
M
A
N

Mark Green had been clueing me that there was really nothing going on in North Beach at the moment, but when Jack Kerouac, Allen Ginsberg, Bob Kaufman and Neal Cassady came back, there really would be something happening.

The third week in May, Mark seemed unduly excited. He whispered to me, "That one there—in the red beret—that's Bob Kaufman."

I looked over. I saw a small, lithe brown man/boy in sandals . . . wearing a red corduroy jacket, some nondescript pants and striped t-shirt. A wine colored beret was cocked at a precarious angle on a mop of black curly hair . . . and he was spouting poetry. A policeman came in and told Bob to cool it. He stopped—only until the cop left. Then once more, he began. This time, he jumped up on the nearest table in the Bagel Shop. "Hipsters, Flipsters and Finger-poppin' daddies, knock me your lobes." He was quoting one of his idols, Lord Buckley.

Next, he began to shout some of his own poetry. Everyone was laughing, listening to this poet. When he left the Bagel Shop, everyone within hearing seemed to leave with him. We all wandered over across the street to what was then Miss Smith's Tea Room. And Bob proceeded to hold court at a large round table like a latterday Francois Villon.

Flashing black eyes dancing as he spoke, gesticulating as a European does. I couldn't believe this. It all seemed to me like a scene from one of my favorite operas that I had sung the year before.

Rudolfo from "La Boheme" must have appeared like this bard . . . even down to the black goatee. And watching Bob hold court in the Tea Room at the huge table filled with artist friends and admirers, generally leaving the bill for the enthralled tourist . . . it seemed very much that scene from Boheme wherein Musetta joins Marcello, Mimi, Rudolfo and their artist friends, leaving her wealthy escort to pay their outrageous bill.

I think I began to play Mimi subconsciously—in the hope that this dynamic Rudolfo would notice me. No luck that evening, but a few nights later, still recuperating from my first head spinning peyote trip, instead of going off to Sacramento to write copy—I remained in the pad which my friend with the MGA and I maintained for weekends. We sublet it to Joe Overstreet, a painter, during the week.

There were four rooms with a long hall connecting them. One in back—a store room—a small kitchen, a bathroom, a tiny living room, and the bedroom which Joe used.

Lucky for me that I kept the apartment and used it. For it was on this night that Skippy, Bob Kaufman's old lady, chanced to throw him out.

I was still asleep beside Mark Green when I heard the voice I recognized from the Bagel Shop.

"Let me in. I need a cuppa' coffee . . . you know?"

That voice was hoarse and low. If you ever heard it, you could never mistake it for another. After ten minutes of Bob's pleading, Joe Overstreet came in and said, "For God's sake, somebody, get Bob Kaufman a cup of coffee so we can all get some sleep."

I got up, curious to see the small brown bard again. I went to the window. Mark was visibly annoyed. I padded over and opened the door. "Just a minute, o.k.?"

Suddenly I was looking into the deepest brown eyes I have ever seen—a well I was to explore for many years. I asked him in. Bob never stopped his monolog.

"Hey, man . . . my old lady, she threw me out . . . and I need a cuppa' coffee . . . Can you give me a cup, huh? I don't even have a dime . . ." and on . . . and on, while I slipped on my poncho over black leotards and t-shirt.

We walked down Kearny, crossing Broadway, over to the original old Hot Dog Palace on Columbus, where El Cid now sprawls on the triangle. Bob sat on a stool near the door. It was such a tiny place that anywhere you sat, it was near the door.

I paid for three cups of coffee for Bob while I drank hot chocolate. All the time we were there, he was charming everyone within earshot with his poetry, his quotations of great poetry of the ages, and his extraordinary insights. I was so completely overwhelmed by this young poet that I lost all sense of time, forgot my surroundings . . . everything banal.

Bob was teaching. Money was not important . . . a fact that I was fast coming to believe . . . Living was. Awareness is all. High on Life.

Time drifted by in the Hot Dog Palace. Bob was rapping on every subject known to Man . . . giving us all a show . . . expounding on history, literature, politics, painting, music . . . He kept repeating after every heavy subject that his old lady had thrown him out . . . truly confused that such a thing could be.

We finally left the stand. We walked in the damp San Francisco fog up the Kearny Steps. It might have been the Steppes of Central Asia. It might have been Hawaii. I was neither hot nor cold. I could only hear that hoarse, low voice.

When we got to the flat, I asked Mark for the key to his apartment on Telegraph Hill. I didn't want to disturb Joe further. We three walked to Mark's pad below Coit Tower.

Bob kept up a running conversation, and Mark went to the kitchen to look for food and tea. We just couldn't talk to each other enough. There were so many things we had to find out about each other all at once. Bob had seen a poem of mine which Mark had pinned on the Bagel Shop wall, without my knowledge.

Then Bob quoted one of his own poems to me. "An African Dream."

> In black core of Night, it explodes
> Silvery thunder, rolling back my brain,

Bursting copper screens, memory worlds
Deep in star-fed beds of time,
Seducing my soul to diamond fires of night.
Faint outline, a ship—momentary fright,
Lifted on waves of color,
Sunk in pits of light,
Drummed back through time,
Hummed back through mind,
Drumming, cracking the night,
Strange forest songs, skin sounds
Crashing through—no longer strange,
Incestuous yellow flowers tearing
Magic from the earth,
Moon-dipped rituals, led
By a scarlet god.
Carressed by ebony maidens

With daylight eyes,
Purple garments,
Noses that twitch,
Singing young girl songs
Of an ancient love
In dark, sunless places
Where memories are sealed,
Burned in eyes of tigers.

Suddenly wise, I fight the dream.
Green screams enfold my night.

I was overwhelmed. Here was a real poet. He reminded me of Coleridge, my childhood favorite. Bob was not one of those schlock artists who write just to be doing something. This man was real, a genuine poet with that calling.

I thrilled every time I looked into his dark, serious eyes. It wasn't hypnotism, because I was fully conscious. But the dynamic glance and depth of this poet's eyes was too much to bear for seven hours. This is how long we talked. We had to get through to each other immediately. I knew that I had suddenly fallen in love with a poet. I had been entranced—from the moment Bob began to talk . . . running down the hill, hand in hand, to the Hot Dog Palace.

Left to right: Phil Whalen, Bob Brannaman, Anne Buchannan, Allen Ginsberg, Bob Kaufman, Lawrence Ferlinghetti, Allan Russo, Charles Plymell—in front of City Lights Bookstore, San Francisco, 1963.

We left Mark at his pad (I can't really say that I considered his feelings. I was too mad about Bob Kaufman). My Rudolfo and I wandered back to my flat hand in hand. Joe slept on—unaware of the changes I was experiencing. We sat down on a mattress in the back room and talked softly.

"You are my woman, you know," said Bob. I just gazed at him with newly opened eyes, now wide in disbelief.

He whispered, "You don't believe me now . . . but you'll see."

His arm was around my shoulders. I was standing next to him. I swayed a little then, and he caught me in his arms, broke my balance, and together—we fell laughing onto the bare mattress. He was laughing at me, and I was laughing because, well, I was a little scared and kind of high from our meeting and subsequent conversation.

Suddenly, I sat up straight and leaned over Bob, letting my hair fall into his face. He took hold of my long, loose hair with one hand and

263

pulled me down to him. Then he kissed me. Except for holding hands or casually putting his arm about my shoulders, that was the first actual physical contact with him.

I shivered, and he pulled my hair a little harder and, consequently, me closer. How did I feel? Like sunsets and dawns and balmy midnights and ocean voyages. My pulse was dancing a wild Gypsy rhythm, and I felt alive! We searched each others' mouths for a time. Then, as if we had found an answer there . . . without a word, we broke apart . . . and each began to undress the other.

It was a simple task for me, because Bob wore only trousers, t-shirt and sandals. I was eager to feel his strong brown body. It seemed a long time until I was in his arms and stroking that sensual body. This man—with the body of Michelangelo's David—wanted me—and yes, oh yes, I certainly wanted him—for as long as he would have me.

When you find your soul mate, there can be no question, no hesitation, no games. You have been lovers before in many other lives, so you are attuned to each other immediately.

Why else is there love at first sight? Hollywood is often chided for its use of music coming out of nowhere in a big love scene. Believe me, there is music then—music from the spheres.

Without the slightest formal introduction on my part to Eastern eroticism, Bob and I became Tantric lovers spontaneously that morning. That was my second psychedelic trip in two weeks in North Beach.

It is true that your soul leaves your body during a very passionate love embrace. It happened to me just that way. And I suspect that Bob experienced a bit of magic too . . . as he held me throughout the entire tidal wave.

When I caught my breath, I looked at him and smiled. I noticed that he was lying beside me drenched and spent. He said it again. "You see? You are my woman. You have absolutely no choice in the matter."

For the first time, I began to think. How can you ponder what is happening in a vortex . . . at the eye of the hurricane . . . in a whirlpool? You can only swing with it and hope you don't go under permanently. Was I going under? Up to this point, I hadn't even cared.

But now, I leaned on one elbow and looked down into Bob's smiling eyes. I said it as well as I could. "It's just all too overwhelming for me, Bob Kaufman. Go away please and leave me for a few hours . . . till maybe 6 tonight, ok? I really have to think about everything that's happened last night and this morning."

Bob's smile faded.

"But hold me now. We can talk later," I added.

He brightened and seemed to understand. He turned on his side, folded me back into his arms, and went to sleep. I may have slept, but I heard him when he got up to dress. I opened my eyes and said sleepily . . . "See you around 6 tonight . . . on Grant."

Bob said, "Then you'll be my old lady. You have no . . ."

I put my fingers over his mouth lightly. "Tell you then. I really have to be alone all day to think it out. Bye."

Bob kissed me lightly on the mouth and vanished. He was gone as suddenly as he had arrived.

I danced the rest of the day through in a hazy kind of mist. I wasn't high on peyote any longer. I was high on Bob Kaufman. Maybe contact high—maybe more, since he had all kinds of dope available to him . . . and he has never been known to turn down any of it!

I dressed slowly, brushing my hair overtime, taking a little more care with the black eyeliner . . . too excited to eat anything, I threw on my poncho and ran out the front door. We didn't have a clock in the pad, and I wasn't going to be late for this important decision.

I ran down Green Street, turned the corner at Grant. Walking down past the Bagel Shop, I saw Bob on the opposite side of the street. He stared at me intently and clenched his teeth, as he has a way of doing when asking a silent question. I just nodded. He came bounding across the street. I said, "You're right. *I'm your woman.*" And he hugged me tightly in answer.

We started to the Bagel Shop. Bob read a few victory poems there, drank a few beers and laughed a lot. He told everyone, "Meet Eileen, my old lady."

That very night, I got my first taste of life with a poet. And that taste has since stayed in my mouth. I could never love a lesser man than an artist.

Bob began to hold court in the Coffee Gallery about 7:30 in the evenings, and for several hours while the locals and the tourists brought him beer, wine, champagne—anything, he, in turn, would speak spontaneously on any subject, quote great poetry by Lorca, T. S. Elliot, e e cummings, or himself. I would just sit adoringly at his side.

I wish that I had been able to tape every conversation, every fragment, because each time Bob speaks it is a gem in a crown of oratory. His wit . . . Cities should be built on one side of the Street . . . His one-liners . . . Laughter sounds orange at Night . . . and his prophecies

—all are astounding. Bob's entire monologue is like a long vine of poetry which continually erupts into flowers.

In the late 50s the Coffee Gallery was arranged differently. After the management took over from Miss Smith, the Gallery became the "other" place in the 1300 block on Grant.

There was no partition for the entertainment section, and jazz was played throughout the place any time the musicians fell by. Spontaneity was the key word in our life style in North Beach. This is what made it "the scene," for one never knew in advance just who might show to read a poem, dance, play some jazz, or put on a complete play.

The tourists were delighted to buy a pitcher of beer, bottle of champagne, or anything we wanted—just to be a part of the Life emanating from our table. The Life was, for the most part, Bob, and his hilarious monologues, sparkling wit and funky comments. Even the "Mr. Jones" who didn't know what was happening in the late 50s knew that *something* groovy was going on, and he would *buy* his way into it, by God, if he couldn't get in any other way! That's where we accumulated our camp followers, hangers-on and groupies.

Some nights Bob would really get it on. In the early evening he would be writing on note paper, napkins, finally toilet paper, just to get his speeding thoughts down. I began to keep these valuable fragments for him so that he could finish the poems when he got home.

In the early morning, Bob would wander out and take one of his dawn-morning walks—harking back to walks with his great-grandmother. Sometimes I would go with him. Other days I would sleep in. Bob and I would begin our Grant Avenue odyssey around three or four each afternoon. And whatever happened would happen. We would run down the hill, laughing, and brighten the lives of tourists, adding to the disorder of the day. We proceeded to urge on any musical activity in Washington Square. (New Yorkers, please note: We have our own in North Beach.) Bob might recite a poem or write a new one in the Bagel Shop . . . or we might drink wine or smoke grass at someone's subterranean pad. We spent a lot of time on the rooftops smoking hash.

When I met Bob Kaufman, King of North Beach, my values changed overnight. I had been a greedy, mercenary career girl whose only object was to get it while you can. But the very night I met Bob, I could see these values totally changing. When Bob read "African Dream" to me, I knew I had met a genius.

And so I knew at once what my life would be: Tempestuous,

Adventurous, Passionate, but always new experiences. I reached out for Bob Kaufman, the man and his poetry. And he made my life a shambles. It was not as though I didn't ask for it. I knew at a glance and after one night that this man could create my life or destroy it. The life I had known was in ashes, and like the Phoenix, my new life had begun. It was to be everything I had seen in the flash of an African Dream . . . and more. Suddenly wise, I did not fight the Dream.

Ted Joans, October 13, 1985, NYC. PHOTO BY KIT KNIGHT.

CHAPTER   20

The Wild Spirit of Kicks

T E D   J O A N S

THE WILD SPIRIT OF KICKS

(in memory of Jack Kerouac)

JACK IN RED AND BLACK MAC
RUSHING THROUGH DERELICT STREWN
    STREETS OF NORTH AMERICA
JACK IN WELLWORN BLUE JEANS AND
    DROOPYSWEATER OF SMILES
RUNNING ACROSS THE COUNTRY LIKE A
    RAZOR BLADE GONE MAD
JACK IN FLOPPY SHIRT AND JACKET
    LOADED WITH JOKES
OLE ANGEL MIDNIGHT SINGING MEXICO
    CITY BLUES
IN THE MIDST OF BLACK HIPSTERS AND
    MUSICIANS
FOLLOWED BY A WHITE LEGION OF COOL
    KICK SEEKERS
POETRY LIVERS AND POEM GIVERS
PALE FACED CHIEFTAIN TEARING PAST

THE FUEL OF A GENERATION

AT REST   AT LAST

JK SAYS HELLO TO JC
JOHN COLTRANE, THAT IS

—TED JOANS
    OCT. 22 HARLEM 69

Arthur Winfield Knight and Ted Joans, October 13, 1985, NYC. PHOTO BY KIT KNIGHT.

CHAPTER 21

Gerald Nicosia
Talks With Ted
Joans

Ted Joans is sharp as a razor and a walking library of Afro-American cultural history. He can relate the sexual etymology of "rock-'n'-roll" as vividly as he recreates the funky, mad, and tragic lives of artists he's known on the streets of America, Europe, and Africa. The following interview was done in August, 1979, shortly after Ted Joans began his first visit to San Francisco. The day Ted arrived, August 6, 1979, the city was hit by the biggest earthquake in 68 years, registering 5.9 on the Richter scale.

Meeting for the first time one night in North Beach, we eyed each other across a Chinese restaurant dinner table of fellow writers, and at one point, where I made one of my traditionally naive remarks, he said,

"You're funny, Gerry," and after that we started to become friends. Later he asked for a couple of bottles of Bass Ale to get warmed up for our interview, and I bought us a whole sixpack. We walked up Columbus to his flophouse, where he phoned his lady while I set up my tape recorder in the bare, dingy room. Then, swigging from the bottles and shooing his querulous pussycat, we both got down on the floor to talk about the "old days"—which had begun to blur uncannily into the present moment.

Gerald Nicosia

GERALD NICOSIA: *How did you get involved with the Beat writers?*

TED JOANS: I came to New York City in 1951, after graduating from Indiana University with a degree in painting. I knew Gregory Corso around the Village—Gregory used to come to a lot of my parties. We used to have big rent parties, costume balls, and things like that. Later I met Allen and Peter, when they were living over on the East Side in a place called the Croton Apartments. In fact, one of my most popular poems was dedicated to them, a poem called "The Truth."

GN: *How did you first hear of Jack Kerouac?*

TJ: I was standing outside the old Fifth Avenue Hotel with a guy from Cuba, Chris Ruliana. They had one of the few outdoor cafes in New York at that time, but Chris and I weren't at the cafe—we'd never have been able to afford it. Chris laid a hardback copy of *On the Road* on me, and said, "I know you don't get into reading novels, but this is prose stuff."

GN: *What was your impression of reading* On the Road?

TJ: It didn't hit me with an impact because of, first, being a black cat with uncles who had, not hitchhiked, but who had hoboed across America; a lot of things that Jack was bringing to the *other* Americans, I had already heard firsthand from people who had been on the road. And then, after all, I was sort of born on the road myself because my mother and father worked on a riverboat that went up and down the Mississippi and Ohio Rivers, so I was always moving around and running into those kind of people. It was a different thing that I dug, because he was one of the few that was writing with an interest in jazz. I could see that he was picking up the language and the rhythm of jazz, that he wasn't following the European tradition.

GN: *How did you meet Kerouac?*

TJ: I met the cat in the Village at somebody's party. I wanted to talk about writing, and he says, "Aw no no no! You're just like LeRoi Jones! Let's not talk about literature. Let's have a good time, man!" Then he asked me "Have you been up to Harlem? You gotta come up and see so-and-so."

TJ: *He was talking about musicians?*

GN: Yeah, Jack knew lots of jazz musicians, people who were living in the Village at that time, like Brue Moore, a tenor saxophonist, and Don Joseph, who blew trumpet. Then there was an Italian trumpet player by the name of Tony Fruscella. These cats all lived around West Fourth Street. Sometimes they'd be with Stanley Gould, our pet junkie. The term "pet junkie" means that everybody knew about Stanley Gould's malady, and we all respected Stanley Gould, Stanley Gould respected us, and it was cool. We used to meet at the Cafe Rienzi on MacDougal Street. That was the first important coffee shop in the Village. It had opened around '53 or '54.

At that time I was living in a place I used to call in bad French *La boite de telephone*—it was like a telephone booth. It was a little room up over a staircase that was a linen closet. I slept there, had my record player and records up under the bed. You came in, you got in bed, and that was it. You couldn't stand up in it unless you were a midget. I used to paint a lot of little pictures there, lying down. One night Kerouac wanted me to come with him to visit someone, and I had to go home to get some money. So we went in, and he said, "You live in here, man?" I went up four little steps, a ladder, unlocked the door, and opened it. He said, "Goddamn it! I never saw a pad like this before!"

Then we got on the A Train, and he started singing. We were singing "Take the A Train" on the subway, and people were looking at us real strange. We'd be pointing at each other, like, "You must take the A train . . . if you want to get up to Harlem." We get off at 125th Street, and then Jack says, "Come on!" Jack knew places up there that I didn't know, because after all, he had been in New York long before I had been. He took me down to the Cecil Hotel, where Minton's Playhouse had been;

273

Minton's Playhouse was supposed to be the place where bop was born. We had a good time. He knew black chicks—I didn't know them, *he* knew them. Then we went into little greasy-spoon places, where he'd say, "Man, this place's got the best fish!" And he knew these places from experience. Like if someone would show up in some town in Europe or in Africa—I know the scene, I could take them around and do the same thing. It was really a funny bit—the white hipster showing the black one around Harlem.

GN: *Was Jack accepted up there?*

TJ: Yeah, there were no hassles in those days. The white hipsters who came up there or lived up there were knowledgeable about the folklore, and knowing the folklore of Harlem they were able to make it.

GN: *Then you weren't struck by a sense of Jack's uniqueness?*

TJ: I didn't feel that. I can't say I felt about him like I did Charlie Parker. Jack was just another cat. It was just that . . . it had a lot to do with Jack's background. He was born in the United States, but to me he was still like a French Canadian. In fact, at that time I wrote a funny little bit of doggerel: "I know a man who's neither white nor black/ And his name is Jack Kerouac."

GN: *You had actually never been to Harlem before Jack took you there?*

TJ: In 1951 I came to Harlem and walked up where the Savoy Ballroom still existed. Before I came to Harlem, I had arrived in the 34th Street bus station and walked over to the William Sloan YMCA, where I had a reservation, so that I'd definitely have a place to stay in New York. And I had a cultural shock! It was like picking up a log and seeing crawly things under it. Man, I had never seen so many homosexuals in my life! Me coming from Indiana, where nothing was that blatant, it was really a shocker! Charles Henri Ford is going to publish a part about that I've written in an autobiographical bit called *Spadework—A Book to Be Dug: the Autobiography of a Hipster.* The only homosexuals I had met in Indiana—*met?*—we knew about—we'd snigger about the woman who was a gym teacher and then the cats who were teaching English or the

274

librarian who would shake your hand and hold it for an hour, with big fishy eyes, but there was nothing like at the Sloan House! After spending two days there, I ran up to Harlem and stayed in the Harlem YMCA at 135th Street between Lennox Avenue and Seventh Avenue. I stayed in the Annex there, and was down the street from the Schoenberg Collection. I was doing sort of like Langston Hughes had done when he first came to Harlem—he stayed there. I've always written poems because I ran into Langston Hughes's poems at the age of ten.

When I ran into Kerouac, I had already moved to Greenwich Village. At that time Harlem was still the hip scene. Greenwich Village didn't have the music then, I mean as far as strong music like jazz. They had some folk places, but most of the clubs were kind of commercial —places where black women, chorus girls, were dancing, and things like that—but the live exciting jazz music was up in Harlem. Now it's the reversal, it's all down in the Village and Soho.

GN: *What year did The Open Door open?*

TJ: Well The Open Door had always been there, but they didn't have music till later. Bob Reisner was a friend of mine. Bob Reisner talked the minor mafia who ran the place into allowing him to present things there. So he had lots of wonderful people there. I never went there with Jack.

Another person I knew at that time was Charlie Parker. For a while I lived up over the Rienzi, 107 MacDougal Street; then I ended up at Number 4 Barrow Street, where I had a room smaller than the room we're sitting in now. It had one bed, a sort of imitation double bed. A friend of mine next door, Ahmed Basheer, got put out, so he started staying in my place. Bird had already been his guest in his place, so I had Charlie Parker, Ahmed Basheer and myself staying in this one bed. We used to even take turns. Bird said, "I don't come in till 3 or 4 in the morning—you cats should get up and let me sleep."

GN: *I read about that in* Bird: The Legend of Charlie Parker.

TJ: Yeah. At that time everybody was around. Steve McQueen wasn't *the* Steve McQueen then; he was around, he was still studying with Strasberg. And Harry Belafonte and Sidney Poitier had just given up their place at Sheridan Square and gone on uptown to stardom. James Dean was still around on the scene. And there was a place called the Montmartre where Charlie Parker played, and one night he came early and Moondog was still playing so he did some things with Moondog.

Now Kerouac would come in to New York, he was sort of like, "Momma let me out to play." I'm putting it like that because that's the way it was. I used to call out there [when Kerouac lived in Northport, Long Island], I couldn't even talk to him.

GN: *You mean his mother wouldn't let you talk to him? She answered the phone?*

TJ: That's right! At that time the publicity was coming out on the Beat Generation, and all sorts of people were coming out, chicks and journalists and everything else. But the thing about it is that we all had our little funny problems. That's the reason I used to have these parties—it wasn't some kind of hedonist reason. I had these parties to raise money so I could pay rent, because I was painting and nobody was buying those paintings; and not only that, some of them weren't up to the par, anyway. Shit! I mean, you can study a thing, but maybe it just doesn't come out like you think it was going to come out. I was a good person to take tours of people around through a museum and talk about paintings, but as far as painting myself . . .

GN: *There's a big gap between studying and producing.*

TJ: Right, and I was around the heavies. My second week in New York I met Jackson Pollock at the Remo. Later on I met giants like DeKooning, Rothko, Franz Kline, and countless others.

GN: *I'd like to hear about a few more of your escapades with Kerouac.*

TJ: Jack and I went to The Five Spot to hear Horace Silver. Everybody was digging Horace Silver. He's a very nice guy, all the chicks liked him because he was a very handsome man. Horace Ward Martin Tavares Silver—Afro-American poesy from up in Massachusetts or Connecticut. The Five Spot was on Cooper Square, and my studio was at 12 Cooper Square. Jack was coming in, but he didn't want to come up to my studio. I said, "All right, I'll meet you in front of Astor Liquors." He said,

"Yeah, we'll get a bottle and drink it on the way." So we bought a bottle and took our time walking to The Five Spot. If we'd've had smokes, we would've smoked before going to the place. See, if you go to a place and want to feel kind of high, drink the stuff before you get to the club, then you can nurse your drink, which fucks up the waiters. That's the way Jack and I did it.

So Jack and I are listening to Horace Silver. At intermission, Jack says, "You got one of those unforgettable faces!" I said, "Yeah? Not like Huncke?" He says, "I'll draw a picture of you while you write a poem of me, and then I'll write a poem of you, and you draw a picture of me." So on the Horace Silver advertisement from The Five Spot I did this drawing, and he did the poem, and then we exchanged. I remember one phrase from his poem: "My Dravidian keeners, my holy twot."

GN: *Was the poem a portrait of you or just a poem that came to him?*

TJ: Spontaneous, because he knew how I had the attitude about surrealism, automatic writing . . . Jack always felt that he had an attitude more allied toward blowing a jazz solo than what Breton and the surrealists were doing with automatic writing from the subconscious mind. His way was Americana more than the European thing.

When Horace Silver's group started playing again, some woman came over to the table and said, "Are you Jack Kerouac?" He says, "Ssssshhhh!" and she says, "Don't shush me! Are you Jack Kerouac? Answer me!" He says, "He'll be right back, he's going to the toilet, sit down!" So she sits down, she says, "You're Jack, aren't you?" He says, "When he comes back from the toilet, I'll tell you a secret. Be quiet, Horace Silver's playing!" This was Diane Barrymore, drunk! The last of the family—she's dead now—she didn't make it like the others. I told her, "Look, if you won't be quiet, woman, go sit somewhere else." She says, "Who are you?" and Jack says, "That's Ted Joans! You have to be careful. He'll fuck you at the drop of a hat!" I said, "Jazz is my religion." She bought us drinks, and then the two guys she was with came over and said, "Diane, it's time for us to go." She said to Jack, "I want to talk to you about your books, give me your number," and Jack wrote down my telephone number.

Another time there was a reading at the Seven Arts Coffee Gallery, which was on 9th Avenue between 43rd and 44th Streets. The guy who

Ray Bremser. DRAWING BY ROBERT LaVIGNE.

organized it was John Rapinic. I had been doing some drawings, and Allen Ginsberg said, "You should come up and read some evening." Kerouac was there, Ray Bremser, and everybody. Then Allen relinquished his spot to allow me to read. Shit, I said, "I'm just a painter who's been writing poems a long time, but I didn't write any poems to be read, I didn't ever think about that." But then Don Allen says, "I hope you write better than those crap paintings you did!" So Don Allen saying that made me angry enough to read. I read this poem, I looked right at him: "If *you* should see/ a man/ walking down a crowded street/ talking aloud/ to himself/ don't run/ in the opposite direction/ but run towards him/ for he is a poet./ You have nothing to fear/ from the poet/ but the truth"—and that was it. Gregory says, "Great! Great! Sock it to him, Ted! You're like an image of me!" Kerouac said, "Here, take a drink out of my bottle!" We couldn't applaud then, we had to snap our fingers.

GN: *I heard that Jack was shy about reading his own stuff.*

TJ: No, if he had his bottle, baby, he'd read!

GN: *But not in public? With friends?*

TJ: Yes, with friends there, that's it. If there was a poetry reading, he participated, but I never heard him read at the Gaslight on MacDougal Street. He would be there in the audience shouting all sorts of things.

GN: *Max Gordon told me that Jack really sweated through the readings at the Village Vanguard.*

TJ: But the other readings we had up at the Seven Arts Coffee Gallery or even over at the Artist's Studio on First Avenue were a different kind of thing. Poets reading to poets with a few friends of the poets around—that's all. I organized the big reading at George Preston's studio on a Sunday afternoon (he called his studio the Artist's Studio). I had everybody—Frank O'Hara, Jack Kerouac, Allen Ginsberg, Peter Orlovsky, LeRoi Jones, Diane Di Prima, Gregory Corso, Steve Tropp and Gloria, Tuli Kupferberg. Fred McDarrah took a lot of pictures there. You'll see Jack reading in George Preston's studio on the cover of *The Beat Scene.*

GN: *Was this the occasion when Jack accused Frank O'Hara of reading with too much affectation?*

TJ: That's another reading, that was the thing at the Living Theatre. See, Jack would be back there with that bottle, drinking, and shout out something, but Frank was cool—Frank, unlike his contemporaries John Ashberry, Kenneth Koch, Gerard Malanga, and a few others I put in that crowd. These are literary literary lit-er-ary Americanas who still kiss Europe's ass, and Frank knew all that, but Frank went beyond Proust and Valery and all the other people that these poets have so high respect for. Frank wrote Americana. These other cats went into a little funny dribble, a highly nouveau European intellectualism. Like this month's *American Poetry Review* [July/August 1979] has John Ashberry on the cover, and they give John about twenty sides inside. I mean [Joans whistles] . . . but I dare him to read that before any audience in the United States, or even in England. It's like someone designing the sleekest plane in the world—it's so beautiful, but it don't fly! And we're living in the age where we like to move! There's no reason for you and I to sit here, and you have a carved-out-of-black-marble cassette. You set it down and say, "Try to pick it up," and it's heavier than hell, but it don't work, it's just a sculpture of a cassette—well that's what I mean.

GN: *I'd like to get back to that scene of Jack being drunk and insulting O'Hara. A lot of people I talked to had a negative impression of Jack's drinking as a kind of withdrawal. LeRoi Jones, for one, felt that Jack was using the booze to separate himself from other people.*

TJ: He could've fooled me, then, if he was! See, Jack'd knock on my door, there he's standing with some guys, some girls, and some drinks, and good-timing. He got out of that damn house with Memere. Jack came in town to have fun. I used to read a poem called "125 Ways to Sex" and then he started beating on things, like impotent sex, important sex, and paper sex, and so-and-so sex, and dum de dum"—he'd start playing, he didn't want to get over-serious. He'd say, "Shit, it's enough to just get by." Another thing, Jack wasn't making the money like Gore Vidal and Norman Mailer.

One night we were at my studio, and Jack wanted to have a little party up there with these chicks, and Jack wanted to get some more to drink, and I said, "No, man, it's all gone, and I ain't got nothing but this rent money." He said, "Give it to me! I'll straighten it out." So he went out and got something, but he paid me back, he sent a check to the Eighth Street Book Shop with a little note saying, "I'm sorry I spent your rent money, I'll never do that again." I still have the receipt [Kerouac would give people receipts when he borrowed money]. And Jack used to write on his letters to me, on the envelope he'd write, "To His Other Hipness" and things like that. He said, "One thing about you, Ted Joans, I always liked your style because you were like me . . . living and sharing the poem of life." Poesy for me is just the poem of my life. I don't mean I'm living wild, but I use the term like people say "wild animals." The animals are not wild, they're *free*.

GN: *Yet there was a commercial side to the Beat phenomenon too. I know you weren't too happy about Fred McDarrah's description of you in* The Beat Scene, *where he stresses that poetry had become a way for you to make a living.*

TJ: Fred McDarrah's the one that started the "Rent A Beatnik" thing. Fred ran an ad in the paper just for the fun of it, "Rent A Beatnik," and then people started calling in. I was over at the *Voice* at that time, and Fred said, "Maybe you should go in and read some of your Beat poetry and bring some beatniks with you." I said, "What will I get?" He said, "You'll make at least twenty or thirty dollars." So I got a cat who called himself *the* beatnik—Dick Woods from Tupelo, Mississippi, a lanky hillbilly cat—two of Dick Wood's chicks, and myself, and we went out. They got $5 each and transportation there and back, and I made $35.

It was incredible—we got a write-up in the *New York Times, Time* magazine, and some other things. Then Paddy Chayevsky, who took the whole thing seriously, was going to do a thing called "The Angel-Headed Hipster." He wanted me to be in that, because he had seen me in a short film called "Greenwich Village on a Sunday." It was in color, I'm reading a poem called "The Sermon," which was very popular in those days—it helped sell a book of mine called *All of Ted Joans and No More*. In those days I used to read two and three coffee shops a night. "The Sermon" begins: "So you want to be hip, little girls,/ and you want to learn to swing/ you want to be able to dig and pick up on everything/ well dig me pretty babies . . . all you need now baby is you/ and people that are hip enough to dig what's happening/ so if your neighborhood ain't hip, split"—that was part of it, and I used to say, "You should have a copy of Jack 'On the

Road' Kerouac on your shelf/ and know thyself by reading Norman Mailer's 'White Negro'!

GN: *It seems that as time went on, you gained more of an appreciation of* On the Road.

TJ: Yeah, that's right. It's a very important book because a whole generation went "on the road." Even Ginsberg, who traveled down to Mexico and all of that . . . Ginsberg making that big step to India turned all the Western youth there.

GN: *What was your last contact with Kerouac?*

TJ: After *The Subterraneans* movie I didn't see Jack any more. The rumor around the Village was that he was embarrassed about what Hollywood had done to the thing. I was getting myself straight to go, I was leaving the States. Then he wrote to me in North Africa, and I sent him a long rhyming poem of mine, of me coming to Timbuktu. He dug it so much he sent it right here to this city, San Francisco, and Ferlinghetti published it in the *City Lights Journal*, No. 1. At the end, I'd get reports that what Kerouac said about the Vietnam War and demonstrators was strictly Rightist, sounds like something coming straight from Ronald Reagan, but I still felt it came from home—mom, his wife. I feel that Jack, as I say, "I know a man who's neither white nor black/ And his name is Jack Kerouac." And then when Jack died, I was in Harlem. I heard from McDarrah that the *Voice* had asked several people to write an obituary poem, and nobody would write anything, so I just wrote that simple thing. It came from my heart and what I believed: a big chieftain dressed in this red and black mac who raced across America "like a razor blade gone mad."

Oh yeah, and at the Cedar Bar one night Jack bounced into the men's room, it was full up; ladies room, shit, a few of them standing outside. This is in the back of the bar. In between both toilets is a little half-moon sink. He could've run outside and peed between the cars, but he didn't. Jack says, "Keep talking so you can block this." So the girl I was with, I put her behind Jack, and I'm talking to her, facing her and seeing Jack. Jack was peeing in the sink with his hands up in the air, pointing at things. He said, "Look, man, no hands!" Then we went and sat down, we stayed a little while and we left. The next day I bounced back in, the bartender says, "We don't want you people in here, you dirty bastards peeing in the sink! We're barring all of you out. Look at the sign." He had a sign up there: "No Beat Nicks"—like Saint Nicks!

When I made this trip, I stopped in Denver—I have poems in my book about Denver—because the only person that ever interested me in Denver was me reading his writing and him talking about Denver. I looked for his Denver. The Paris he saw was very dull—I sure wish I could've showed him another Paris. Jack was always saying, "You gotta go to San Francisco!" I told him, "If I go, they'll have their biggest earthquake," and I arrived just a few days ago, and it occurred.

INDEX

Kerouac, Jean 122
Kerouac Conference, 182, 77
Kesey, Ken, 60, 61, 63
Kherdian, David, 7
Kierkegaard, Søren, 153
King, Martin Luther, 11
King, Robert, 152-84
Kingsland, John, 105, 106
Kline, Franz, 276
Knight, Arthur Winfield, 35, 270
Knight, Glee, ix-xii
Knight, Kit, xii-xiii, 35
Koch, Kenneth, 143, 280
Korean war, 73, 86
Kupferberg, Tuli, 279

La Vigne, Robert, 66
Lady Chatterley's Lover (Lawrence), 129
Laing, R.D., 245
Lamantia, Philip, 110, 111, 126, 184
Landesman, Jay, 77, 246-47
Lautreamont, Comte de (Ducasse), 250
Lax, Bob, 112
Le Pellec, Yves, 36
Leary, Timothy, 11, 12
Lee, Alene, 208
Leventer, Maggie, 1, 6-7, 10, 12-15, 22-25
Levinsky, Leon, 185
Lewis, Sinclair, 95, 203
Lipton, Lawsrence, 180-81
Little, John, 1, 22-27, 152, 158, 162, 165-70, 175, 178-81
Living Theater, The, 140-41, 280
London, England, 198, 199, 206
Long Live Man (Corso), 174
Lorca, Federico Garcia, 265
Los Gatos, Ca., 30, 35, 37, 50, 121
Lowell, Robert, 164
LSD (lysergic acid), 12, 23, 64

Mafia, 165, 166
Mailer, Norman, 167, 280, 282
Malanga, Gerard, 193-224, 280
Malcolm X, 134
Mallarmé, Stephane, 246
Man Suicided by Society, The (Artaud), 245
Mann, Thomas, 92-93

Manson, Charles, 24
marijuana, 33, 41, 44, 47, 79, 116, 130, 164, 179, 265, 277
Markfield, Wallace, 245-46
Marlowe, Alan, 141
Marx, Karl, 10, 253
Masaryk, Jan, 74
Mayan mythology, 219-20
McCarthy, Joseph, xi, 10, 118, 131
McClain, Christopher, 59, 111
McDarrah, Fred, 279, 281, 282
McGovern, George, 253
McClure, Joanna, xii, 40-45, 239
McClure, Michael, xi, xii, 2, 3, 13, 14, 26, 42-45, 50, 51, 143, 151, 239
  poetry, 40-41, 141, 237-38
McKenzie, James, 1-27, 151-52
McQueen, Steve, 275
Measure magazine, 127
media, 207-9, 215
Melville, Herman, 59, 78, 110, 112, 136, 247
merchant marine, 242, 243
merry pranksters, 55, 64
Merton, Thomas, 112
methadone, 179-80
methedrine (speed), 59, 62
Mew, Charles, 121
Mexico, 54, 90, 116, 121, 179, 194, 282
Mexico City, 50, 198, 225, 252
Michaux, Henri, 242, 243, 256
Micheline, Jack, 126, 258
Miller, Henry, x, xiii, 75
Mishaps Perhaps (Solomon), 242, 244, 245, 250, 251, 253-54, 256
Moore, Brue, 110, 273
Moraff, Barbara, 144
More Mishaps (Solomon), 242, 247
Morgan, Ted, 212
Mountains and Rivers Without End (Snyder), 18-19, 20-21
Mullins, Dusty, 168
Murao, Shig, 14, 26, 151
Murphy, Anne, 58
Myths and Texts (Snyder), 7

Nagel, Ernest, 68
Naked Lunch (Burroughs), xiii, 194, 198, 199, 218-19, 253

289

1   7 0 2 2